MERGERS IN HIGHER EDUCATION:
LESSONS FROM THEORY AND EXPERIENCE

Around the world, organizations of all kinds are merging at a frenetic pace. In this comparative study of two mergers of Canadian institutions of higher education – that of the Ontario Institute for Studies in Education with the University of Toronto in 1996, and that of the Technical University of Nova Scotia with Dalhousie University in 1997 – Julia Eastman and Daniel Lang examine why and how universities merge and why some mergers succeed while others fail.

Drawing on extensive interviews with faculty, university and government officials, students, and experts in organizational restructuring, as well as on their own professional involvement in the two mergers, the authors look at what prompts higher education mergers, what is involved in the process, and what determines the outcomes. They link practice with organizational theory and offer observations about the roles of history, economics, institutional power, and human relations in postsecondary educational systems. Of interest to university and college officials, educators, social scientists, and policy-makers, *Mergers in Higher Education* is an indispensable resource for anyone who has a stake in the planning and negotiating of university and other public sector mergers.

JULIA EASTMAN is Coordinator of Policy Development in the Office of the President at Dalhousie University in Halifax.

DANIEL W. LANG is a professor in the Department of Theory and Policy Studies at OISE/UT.

Manisol.

MERGERS IN HIGHER EDUCATION

Lessons from Theory and Experience

JULIA EASTMAN
DANIEL LANG

UNIVERSITY OF TORONTO PRESS
Toronto Buffalo London

© University of Toronto Press Incorporated 2001
Toronto Buffalo London
Printed in Canada

ISBN 0-8020-3525-6

Printed on acid-free paper

National Library of Canada Cataloguing in Publication Data

Eastman, Julia
    Mergers in higher education : lessons from theory and
experience

    Includes bibliographical references and index.
    ISBN 0-8020-3525-6

    1. Universities and colleges – Mergers – Nova Scotia – Halifax –
Case studies.   2. Universities and colleges – Mergers – Ontario –
Toronto – Case studies.   3. Technical University of Nova Scotia –
Case studies.   4. Dalhousie University – Case studies.   5. Ontario
Institute for Studies in Education – Case studies.   6. University of
Toronto – Case studies.   I. Lang, Daniel, 1944–   II. Title.

    LA417.E28 2001   378.1   C2001-901354-X

The University of Toronto Press acknowledges the financial assistance to
its publishing program of the Canada Council for the Arts and the
Ontario Arts Council.

University of Toronto Press acknowledges the financial support for its
publishing activities of the Government of Canada through the Book
Publishing Industry Development Program (BPIDP).

For
Harry Claude MacColl Eastman
29 July 1923–20 April 1999

Contents

Figures and Tables

Preface

University mergers have been rare in Canada in recent decades. We were at the centre of two that occurred within less than a year in the mid-1990s.

Julia Eastman was executive coordinator of the 1997 amalgamation of the Technical University of Nova Scotia with Dalhousie University in Halifax. In his capacity as vice-provost and assistant vice-president for planning and budget of the University of Toronto, Daniel Lang was deeply involved in negotiating and implementing the 1996 integration of the Ontario Institute for Studies in Education with the university's Faculty of Education.

The literature provided little guidance on how to plan, negotiate, and manage the two mergers. There are a host of anecdotal accounts of higher education mergers, and a small but growing number of analytical pieces, but very few works that link theory and practice. The literature on corporate mergers is of limited relevance to the higher education sector – and, in particular, to mergers of publicly funded universities.

Our desire to learn as much as possible from the two mergers and to make the resulting insights available to others provided the impetus for this project. We began by documenting the two processes and interviewing the principal participants in each. We conducted forty-three interviews with university officials, board members, government officials, faculty members, and others involved in the mergers. To achieve greater objectivity, Julia interviewed those involved in the merger of OISE and the University of Toronto, and Dan conducted most of the interviews in Nova Scotia. We compared the two cases systematically and formulated a set of observations about the process and outcomes of higher education mergers. Aware of the danger of generalizing from two cases, we identified and discussed these observations with a number of consultants with expertise in public sector mergers and other forms of restructuring. These interviews strengthened our confidence in our preliminary findings.

We are immensely grateful to all the people we interviewed for sharing their knowledge and insights. Their generosity will make it possible for future mergers to be more fruitful and positive experiences.

No doubt, the theoretical and practical findings of this study will be modified and enlarged upon by both scholars and practitioners. In the meantime, we hope our findings will prove helpful to individuals seeking to understand mergers in higher education – in particular, to those faced with the challenge of planning, negotiating, and managing one.

Mergers are powerful, complex, and far-reaching events. We played parts in the events described in this book and were swept up in their unfolding. We have made every effort to tell the stories of the two mergers accurately, objectively, and fairly. To the extent that we have gotten either story wrong, we apologize.

Acknowledgments

This book would not have been possible without the contributions of the following members and former members of Dalhousie University, the Ontario Institute for Studies in Education (OISE), the Technical University of Nova Scotia (TUNS), and the University of Toronto, whom we interviewed:

Adam Bell, former dean, Faculty of Engineering, Dalhousie University, formerly, Technical University of Nova Scotia

David Cameron, professor of political science, Dalhousie University

Orest Cochkanoff, professor emeritus, Faculty of Engineering, Dalhousie University, formerly TUNS

Stefan Dupré, professor of political science, University of Toronto

Andrew Eisenhauer, last chairman of the board of governors, TUNS

Michael Finlayson, former vice-president (administration), University of Toronto

Jack Flemming, former chair, DalTech Board; former member of the board of governors, TUNS

Carrie Gates, systems manager, Faculty of Computer Science, Dalhousie University

Carl Hartzman, former interim dean, Faculty of Computer Science, Dalhousie University

James Heap, former chair of theory and policy studies, Ontario Institute for Studies in Education of the University of Toronto (OISE/UT); former chair, higher education group, Ontario Institute for Studies in Education (OISE)

Angela Hildyard, former associate dean, OISE/UT; last executive director, OISE

Dexter Kaulbach, former vice-president (administration), TUNS
Jane Knox, last chair of the board of governors, OISE
Arthur Kruger, former executive director, OISE
Rick Lowery, DalTech administrative officer; former director of financial
    services, TUNS
Brian Marshall, director of human resources, University of Toronto
Bryan Mason, vice-president (finance and administration), Dalhousie University
versity
Eric McKee, vice-president (student services), Dalhousie University
Anne Millar, former associate dean, OISE/UT; former associate dean,
    Faculty of Education, University of Toronto
Ian Nason, director of financial services, Dalhousie University
Sherwin Nugent, professor of engineering, Dalhousie University
Chris Oke, budget manager, Dean's Office, OISE/UT; former secretary to
    the board of governors, OISE
Robert Prichard, former president, University of Toronto
Andrew Rau-Chaplin, professor of computer science, Dalhousie University, formerly, TUNS
sity, formerly, TUNS
Edward Rhodes, former president, Technical University of Nova Scotia;
    principal, DalTech
Denis Riordan, professor of computer science, Dalhousie University, formerly TUNS
merly TUNS
Michael Roughneen, assistant vice-president (personnel services), Dalhousie
    University
Adel Sedra, provost, University of Toronto
Michael Shepherd, professor of computer science, Dalhousie University
Jacob Slonim, dean, Faculty of Computer Science, Dalhousie University
Susan Snellings, human resource manager, OISE/UT
Mary Stager, executive assistant to the dean, OISE/UT
Tom Traves, president, Dalhousie University
Barbara Watt, former executive director, community relations, TUNS
Chris Watts, professor of engineering, Dalhousie University, formerly
    TUNS

We also interviewed the following individuals outside the universities:

Susan Clark, chair, and Peter Rans, senior policy advisor, Nova Scotia
    Council on Higher Education
David Coulter, former senior policy analyst, Ontario Ministry of Education and Training
    tion and Training

Janet Halliwell, former chair, Nova Scotia Council on Higher Education
John MacEachern, former minister of education of Nova Scotia
John Murray, Genest Murray, Toronto
Charles Pascal, former deputy minister, Ontario Ministry of Education and Training
John Stubbs, mediator of OISE/UT integration discussions
Royden Trainor, former senior policy advisor to the Minister of Education of Nova Scotia

We are immensely grateful to the following for sharing with us their expertise and experience in change management and public sector mergers:

Rainer Beltzner, KPMG, Toronto
Murray Glow, KPMG (formerly, ARA Consulting Group), Toronto
George Hamilton, Ernst & Young, Toronto
Bob Kanygin, planning and quality management, Queen Elizabeth II Health Sciences Centre, Halifax
Rachel Martin, Coopers Lybrand, Halifax
Martin McGrath, Accentive, Toronto
Frank Schwartz, KPMG (formerly, ARA Consulting Group), Halifax
Valerie Wheeler, KPMG (formerly, ARA Consulting Group), Toronto

We also extend thanks to Sandra MacDonald and Heather Holdway for their invaluable assistance in the preparation of the manuscript.

Abbreviations

Dal	Dalhousie University
DalTech	The name of the college within Dalhousie University that succeeded the Technical University of Nova Scotia immediately following the universities' 1997 merger
DER	Department of Educational Research, Ontario College of Education
FEUT	The Faculty of Education of the University of Toronto
NSCHE	The Nova Scotia Council on Higher Education
NSTC	The Nova Scotia Technical College, renamed the Technical University of Nova Scotia in 1980
OCE	Ontario College of Education
OISE	The Ontario Institute for Studies in Education
OISE/UT	The faculty of the University of Toronto formed by the merger of the Ontario Institute for Studies in Education with the Faculty of Education of the University of Toronto upon the 1996 merger of the institute and the university
Tech	The Nova Scotia Technical College, renamed the Technical University of Nova Scotia in 1980
TUNS	The Technical University of Nova Scotia
U of T	The University of Toronto

PART ONE

Higher Education Mergers: What They Are and Why They Happen

ONE

Introduction

Mergers have become ubiquitous. At the start of the twenty-first century, the volume and scale of corporate mergers are unprecedented. Their global dollar value increased more than five-fold between 1995 and 2000 (Breidenbach, 2000) to a record $1.14 trillion in the first quarter of 2000 (Segil, 2000). Drug companies, car manufacturers, financial institutions, media empires, telecommunication companies, agro-businesses, resource firms – all appear to be combining in the largest and most dramatic wave of mergers ever witnessed.

Although corporate merger activity captures the most attention, the phenomenon of merger is not restricted to that sector. In the 1980s and 1990s, major reforms in public sector management took place throughout Western democracies. In Australia, Canada, and the United Kingdom, government departments and portfolios were consolidated and their numbers reduced (Aucoin and Bakvis, 1993). Municipalities were merged, often against the wishes of local governments. Hospitals, too, merged in the interest of efficiency and economies of scale. In the higher education sector, the subject of this book, smaller universities merged themselves into comprehensive ones – some voluntarily, others by government design.

Merger is a flexible instrument that is available to many organizations to achieve various ends. The forces that drive mergers – and the ends to which they are pursued – change over time. According to McCann and Gilkey, the principle motive of the first major wave of corporate mergers, which began in the late 1800s, the principle motive was horizontal integration: firms bought others in their industries in order to add capacity with which to serve rapidly expanding markets. The second wave – the purchase of firms involved in another stage of the same production process – was driven mainly by the desire of corporations to achieve economies of scale through vertical integration. Until the Second World War, most corporate mergers thus involved firms in the same industries or production processes. Beginning in the 1960s, however, there was a trend toward conglomeration, driven by a desire to circumvent regulatory constraints, stabilize financial performance, and build earnings through merger and acquisition activity itself. Aggressive companies sprouted into conglomerates. The results of many of these mergers were disappointing; many conglomerates were dismantled and the prevailing rationale for merger changed once again. Faced with rapid globalization and rampant technological change, companies merged increasingly often with others in the same or related businesses in order to achieve global scale and reach, thereby enhancing control and counteracting uncertainty ('How to Make Mergers Work,' 1999). By the end of the twentieth century, a wave of mergers radically redefining entire industries was well underway (McCann and Gilkey, 1988).

There have been fewer studies about public sector mergers; even so, evidence abounds that their causes and purposes are equally diverse. To cite but one example: teaching hospital mergers occurred in the 1990s for different reasons in the United States (in which most hospital care is privately funded) than in Canada (in which hospitals are publicly funded). In the United States, such mergers were driven mainly by the need faced by hospitals to build market share (Topping et al., 1999). In contrast, most teaching hospital mergers in Canada were instigated by governments in response to factors such as technological change, declining medical school enrolments, and the need for sufficient critical mass to support specialized services (Denis, Lamothe & Langley, 1999). In the public sector as in the private one, mergers are driven and shaped by the political, economic, and technological contexts in which they take place.

This is no less true in higher education. The environment for higher education is changing rapidly today as a result of globalization, new information technologies, increased market competition, and other powerful forces. How universities and colleges will react to these changes cannot be predicted, but it is probable that mergers will be one route they take. It is therefore vitally important to understand what drives higher education mergers, what forms they can take, what objectives they can achieve, and how they can best be planned and managed. This book, rooted in existing theory and in case and professional experience, addresses these pressing issues.

Mergers in Higher Education

Throughout most of the history of higher education, the natural disposition of colleges and universities has been to 'go it alone' wherever possible. As institutions, colleges and universities are often cranky and eccentric in their individuality, jealous of their autonomy, and aloof in their relationships with other institutions and social estates. In spite of this history of zealous independence, universities and other institutions of higher education were not immune from the merger virus of the late twentieth century. Higher education mergers were relatively rare in Canada, but occurred in waves in a number of other jurisdictions.

In publicly funded, centralized higher education systems, mergers took place mainly through the actions or inducements of governments. Beginning in the 1960s, the Australian and British governments used mergers to create colleges of advanced education (CAEs) and polytechnics, respectively. In the 1970s and early 1980s, governments in Australia, the Netherlands, and Britain brought about further higher education mergers with the goal of rationalizing teacher education. In the mid-1980s, government-induced mergers transformed the Dutch non-university sector. Australia's binary (university/college) system was transformed by means of mergers into the Unified National System a few years later (Goedegebuure, 1992).

The first of these waves of government-initiated mergers was the product of direct government intervention, but by the 1980s the Australian and Dutch governments had adopted a more subtle approach. They simply declared that institutions would have to be of a certain size (in terms of enrolment) to be eligible for particular types of funding. (For example, the Australian government declared that institutions must have at least 2,000 full-time equivalent students in order to receive federal funding; 5,000 to be funded for a broad range of teaching and specialized research; and 8,000 to be funded for comprehensive involvement in teaching and research.) As a result, institutions sought out and merged with partners large enough to enable them to exceed these minimums. Governments provided powerful inducements; institutions then rationalized themselves. There is no exact count, but by the 1990s there had been at least five hundred mergers in the public higher education sector in developed nations (Goedegebuure, 1992; Martin and Samels, 1994).

Governments' motives in promoting higher education mergers were several. As with the early waves of corporate mergers, many mergers were directed at building capacity, improving efficiency, and achieving economies of scale. But higher education merger has managerial as well as economic dimensions. It reduces the number of separate organizations for which executive responsibility must be taken; in other words, it sharpens the peak of the organizational pyramid. In the public sector, governments and the intermediary 'buffer' agencies that act on behalf of governments often find consolidation attractive for this reason, even if it does not reduce costs. Consolidation makes systems of higher education look less complex. Policies can be simpler and politically more comprehensible and credible. 'Visible equity' is more easily achieved. Special interests are pushed downward to the merged institutions.

Privately funded universities and colleges, and institutions in less-centralized public systems, merged for their own particular reasons. As the title of the American book *Colleges and Corporate Change: Merger, Bankruptcy and Closure*, published in 1980, suggests, merger was at that time one of a number of options for private American colleges in financial distress. A merger made it possible for the trustees of a failing college to fulfil their fiduciary responsibilities, and provide some degree of continuity of education and employment to students, faculty, and staff (O'Neill and Barnett, 1980).

Of course, 'bankruptcy/bailout' was not the only form of higher education merger in the United States. According to Harman, many mergers in American higher education since the early 1970s have fallen into four other categories: mergers of small women's colleges into larger coeducational institutions; consolidation of public institutions into state systems; court-mandated mergers for racial desegregation purposes; and mergers of institutions with complementary missions and strengths (Harman, 1988, 6). The latter type of merger became increasingly common in both Europe and North America as the twentieth century neared its close (Martin and Samels, 1994).

This brief survey of postwar trends in higher education merger attests that for universities and colleges, as for corporations and hospitals, mergers are means to many possible ends – ends shaped by the systems in which the institutions are embedded.

The Cases

The two Canadian higher education mergers at the centre of this book – the 1996 merger of the Ontario Institute for Studies in Education (OISE) with the University of Toronto (U of T) in Toronto, Ontario, and the 1997 merger of the Technical University of Nova Scotia (TUNS) with Dalhousie University in Halifax, Nova Scotia – resembled the Australian and Dutch mergers of the 1980s insofar as they were encouraged, rather than imposed by governments. The governments in question were provincial rather than national, Canada being a federation in which education is a provincial responsibility. Government support for the mergers was not a function of public policy to encourage higher education mergers at large, as was the case in Australia and the Netherlands. The Australian and Dutch governments had set out to transform their higher education systems through mergers; the governments of Ontario and Nova Scotia were encouraging only these particular ones. That said, there are indications that the Ontario government regarded the OISE/U of T merger as a possible model for future university/university and university/college mergers.

The two mergers are of academic interest in part because the systems in which they took place were in transition. In 1991, Stuart Bosworth described 'the history of the expansion of universities in the United Kingdom [as] a history of producer-dominated [as opposed to consumer-dominated] institutions in a dependent relationship to government with government being by far the major provider of funds for higher education.' The same could have been said of the postwar expansion of higher education in Canada.

In the early postwar period, the shift from élite to mass higher education was a clear social and economic priority. Funding for colleges and universities was relatively plentiful. Universities could afford to protect their autonomy and individuality. Governments could afford diversity in higher education and were willing to tolerate duplication in the interest of accessibility. But by the late 1980s, circumstances had changed substantially. Canada, like many Western countries, was beset by poor economic performance and high unemployment. Its federal and provincial governments were struggling with high deficits and debts. The widespread conviction in the postwar years that education was vital to economic growth had given way to substantial dissatisfaction on the part of governments and the public with universities' contributions to collective and individual prosperity. A feeling that universities were not responding to the needs of students and society – that they weren't 'doing their part' – led to calls for more 'accountability.'

All the while, public funding for universities was being reduced as provincial governments struggled to reduce their expenditures. As funding shifted, first, from covering average costs to covering only marginal costs and, then, to not recognizing growth at all except at the expense of quality, colleges and universities were forced by economic necessity to seek other means of delivering programs. Institutional identity became more difficult to defend. Some colleges and universities, especially smaller and more specialized ones, reached the limits of internal economies of scale, and came under pressure to seek partners – usually larger or more diverse ones – to renew the potential of economies of scale.

Reduced public funding also forced institutions to generate additional revenues from tuition fees and other sources. In other words, it required them to be more businesslike and sensitive to the markets for their educational, research, and related services. Higher education was becoming a less public good; the university system was being defined and shaped more by market forces than by overt policy. One result was to make marginal institutions even more vulnerable.

Higher education in Canada was in transition at the time of the mergers at the centre of this book. It follows that those mergers had features both of mergers in a state-dominated environment and of mergers in the American-style, market-driven environment. In both mergers, governments played an important and traditional role; that said, other factors were involved, including institutional considerations of capacity and image in relation to changing markets for education and research.

Several paradigms, presented in Chapter 2, have been developed to explain higher education merger. Common to most of them is the assumption that mergers in higher education are prompted by changes in the external environment, whether those changes take the form of escalating demands for education and research, diminishing resources, changing markets, threats to the continuous supply of critical resources, obstacles to organic growth, or changing ecological niches. Merger is a means of responding to environmental threats and opportunities.

The global environment for higher education is changing dramatically today. The advent of the 'knowledge economy' and the revolution in information technology that made this new economy possible are changing higher education and research in profound ways. More than ever before, governments and corporations are looking to university research as the fuel for innovation and growth. Funding for education and research increasingly comes with strings attached, and this results in more competition between universities for students, grants, contracts, and donations. Besides competition within the higher education sector, universities are beginning to face competition from the corporate sector and, in particular, the 'infotainment' industry. The emergence of technology-based education delivery systems is opening up new markets for higher education – markets that are very attractive to newly aligned corporate players in the information industry. Corporations and networks of universities are forming global partnerships aimed at amassing electronic content and staking out powerful market positions (Association of Commonwealth Universities, 2000).

If theoretical assumptions about the role of the environment in stimulating mergers are valid – and if the examples of the private and health care sectors are any guide – the pace of higher education merger activity will increase. Some of the challenges and opportunities in response to which universities have traditionally merged will no doubt recur in the future – for example, the challenge of achieving greater scale, strength, and efficiency; the opportunity to acquire undervalued resources; and the challenge of maintaining quality in the face of insufficient resources. To these challenges and opportunities, new ones will be added as the global political economy, and the contexts in which higher education is provided, evolve. Merger is one means by which institutions will respond to this evolution.

It is therefore desirable for those involved in and concerned about higher education to ask these questions:

- What outcomes are achievable through mergers in higher education?
- What forces shape these outcomes?
- How can mergers be planned, negotiated, and implemented so as to optimize the prospects for achieving the desired outcomes?

The literature on higher education mergers is not yet sufficiently well developed to provide answers to these questions. Much of the literature on the subject is anecdotal in nature. Notwithstanding important contributions by Leo Goedegebuure, Grant Harman, Lynn Meek, Gail Chambers, and other authors, theories of higher education merger remain underdeveloped. Literature on the planning, negotiation, and management of higher education mergers is almost non-existent.

This book addresses itself to that gap. The events on which it is based took place in the context of the same political and economic forces that are shaping higher education in many jurisdictions today. The lessons drawn from the cases in this book are therefore likely to be useful to members of universities and other institutions contemplating merger in the years ahead. The lessons are, of course, preliminary, drawn as they are from limited literature and experience, and will no doubt be modified and expanded in light of future analysis and experience.

Above and beyond their implications for the theory and practice of higher education merger, the cases in this book are of interest for two reasons. First, they have important implications for other forms of major organizational change in higher education. To survive and prosper in today's rapidly changing environment, universities are changing in many ways, of which merger is but an extreme form. Many of the lessons drawn from the cases studied in this book – about the need to align mission, structure and resources; the 'limits to participation'; the organization of space; and other matters – also apply to other forms of restructuring.

Second, the findings may be of interest to sectors other than higher education. To succeed in turbulent environments, firms in many sectors have had to empower small groups of expert and creative individuals – groups that, not surprisingly, come to behave in ways traditionally associated with academic departments. The insights derived from this study may inform how mergers of such firms ought to be managed. For example, it is often assumed that merger is more difficult in organizations in which professionals have considerable power and autonomy than in those in which authority is centralized (see, for example, Denis, et al., 1999). In contrast, this study suggests that the allegiance of professors to their disciplines – and their tendency to be somewhat suspicious of 'the administration' – can enable academic units to merge relatively quickly and effectively. Chapter 6 suggests that this is most likely to occur where the units are of approximately equal size; where any members who are unable to reconcile themselves to the merger are allowed to make graceful exits; where there is a real opportunity for the newly merged unit to plan its future; and where there is the prospect of securing badly desired new resources through collaboration in the development of a good plan. These types of insights into the management of mergers in decentralized organizations may be of interest to readers in other sectors.

TWO

Why Mergers Happen

The Motivation to Merge

Colleges and universities are attracted to merger, and to other forms of inter-institutional cooperation, by the chance to do things that they cannot do individually, usually because of a lack of wherewithal. Throughout the research literature about mergers, the dominant theme is economy and efficiency. This is as true of involuntary mergers initiated by governments as of voluntary mergers initiated at the institutional level. Burton Clark, in his study of entrepreneurial universities (1998), described the problem well with this succinct term: 'demand overload.' Demand overload refers to a situation in which the resources that support a college or university become more and more limited while the services demanded of it increase, along with their concomitant costs. Given the rapid expansion of knowledge and the diversification of scholarship, colleges and universities are suffering from a kind of scholastic inflation that makes it more and more expensive for them to maintain the status quo.

Broadly speaking, the value of merger is basically practical and in many cases measurable, in expectations if not in outcomes. Where adequate resources – financial, physical, human – are available, merger presumably will not be undertaken. This presumption is not unreasonable: colleges and universities traditionally aim to be distinct and self-sufficient. Each college or university seeks to be complete in terms of its own goals and standards. Moreover, that is how they tend to describe and market themselves. Governments, for their part, promote diversity over homogeneity when they can afford it (Lang, 2000).

Knowledge, too, is organized in a form that coincidentally supports the tradition of institutional balance, identity, and completeness. For example, the arts and sciences and many professional programs are often described as constituting unitary and organic bodies of knowledge that cannot be diffused. According to this tradition – indeed, in some points of view a paradigm (Birnbaum, 1983; Huisman, 1998) – the college or university is like an atom: it cannot be split without utterly losing its very being. Nevertheless, colleges and universities do change, and when they do their behaviours can be explained in several ways, for example, as a function of market competition or as the workings of an institutional version of Darwinian natural selection.

Whether or not the tradition of the unitary college and university has been realized and remains tenable in fact, the tradition and image remain, and as such are disincentives to merger and indeed to any formal, structural forms of inter-institutional cooperation. The tradition suggests that colleges and universities are as inclined to compete with one another as to cooperate. Indeed, competition is the more basic impulse. In other words, the first reaction to 'demand overload' is more likely to be in the direction of intensified competition than of cooperation leading to merger. This is the first hurdle that virtually any attempt at merger must overcome.

From these observations, it follows that mergers among colleges and universities are neither spontaneous nor natural. Rather, they are the result of conscious, deliberate, and carefully considered choices. They are usually extremely difficult choices. When institutions do overcome the inertia of tradition sufficiently to consider cooperation with other institutions, they are then faced with two ineluctable questions: What form should inter-institutional cooperation take? And should that form lead ultimately to merger?

Answering those questions requires two distinct understandings. The *first* relates to the institutional political economy that inspired a consideration of merger in the first place. The *second* relates to the forms that inter-institutional cooperation may take, to the attributes – pro and con – of those forms, and to the continuum along which the several forms may be aligned and understood. Once they have been motivated to consider merger, colleges and universities then follow a number of different paradigms of institutional behaviour.

The Political Economy of Merger

For the purposes of this discussion, the political economy of the university or college is relatively simple. The model, essentially, has four or five parts:

1. *Scale*, which may be a matter of economies of scale or of the capabilities of sound management.
2. *Breadth*, which usually is construed as an array of academic disciplines and fields of study, but from the perspective of a publicly funded system of higher education may represent the array of institutions within that system.
3. *Quality*, which may be a matter of standards applied across an institution, or of standards determined externally (as would be the case whenever governments or buffer agencies apply performance indicators).
4. *Distribution*, which may relate to modes of program delivery (full-time, part-time, co-op, distance) or to the geographical location of programs and campuses.
5. *Economy and efficiency*, which in practical terms represents the expense and efficacy of delivering programs while balancing scale, breadth, quality, and distribution.

Regarding the last point, one can argue that striking the correct balance is the essence of the political economy of any college or university. One can argue further that inter-institutional cooperation in one form or another, including merger, is a means of recalibrating the balance in ways that would be either impossible or impractical for a college or university acting alone.

This description of the political economy of a college or university explains why, in public systems of higher education, governments may be interested in merger even though it is essentially an institutional phenomenon. Governments as well as individual colleges and universities seek to strike a balance among scale, breadth, quality, and distribution, and then balance all of these against economy and efficiency. However this balance is struck, we may discern two important facts. *First*, the first four attributes – scale, breadth, quality, and distribution – would be expected to correlate positively with cost, while the fifth – economy and efficiency – would correlate negatively with cost. The juxtaposition of the four attributes that correlatively positively with cost and the one attribute that does not represents the fundamental problem in the political economy of higher education, whether at the system level or the institutional level. Where this correlative 'dissonance' exists, the interest in merger as a means of striking the balance grows.

Second, an individual college or university must attempt to strike the

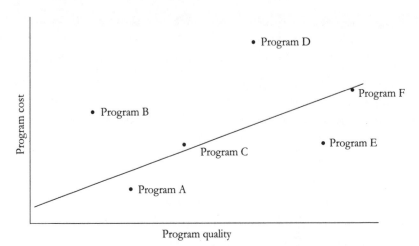

Figure 2.1   Cost/quality: Locating programs optimally

same balances among its programs. Figure 2.1 explains this political economy further, specifically with regard to the problem of balancing cost and quality. It shows two programs – Program C and Program F – that are optimally situated on a line that represents a balance between cost and quality. The line is an expression of an institution's strategy and role; as such, it can vary from institution to institution, including institutions considering merger or some other cooperative arrangement.

The fundamental problem is to determine how the remaining programs can be relocated to the line that represents the optimal balance, or if this is possible at all. It is obvious from the graph that some low-cost, low-quality programs, such as Program A, are in effect 'cash cows' that benefit programs of higher cost and higher quality, such as Programs E and F. Depending on the distances between the current locations of the programs and the line of optimal balance, a college or university might find it highly difficult if not practically impossible to move each program to an optimal position.

Understanding these attributes and relationships is central to understanding the economic anatomy of merger – that is, when it can make a difference and when it cannot. By combining resources, cooperating institutions can shift the line of optimal balance and change the relationships of different programs to that line. A successful merger depends not only on understanding this but also on a prior assessment of each prospective partner's array of programs and cost structures.

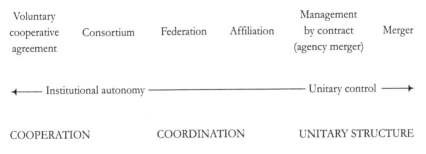

Source: Modified version of figure in Harman, in Harmon and Meeks, 1988, p. 3.

Figure 2.2 Continuum of higher education linkages

The term 'merger' is often used loosely in reference to all sorts of cooperative arrangements among colleges and universities – consortia, federations, affiliations, and so on. Be warned, however: an affiliation is not a federation, and a federation is not a consortium, and a merger isn't any of the above. Yet the fact that the various forms of inter-institutional cooperation are different and far from interchangeable does not mean that they do not occupy a common theoretical continuum or evolutionary stream.

Such a continuum was developed by Grant Harman (1988) to explain a lengthy series of mergers that were instigated as a matter of public policy by the government of Australia. In connection with Harman's study, one should note that Australia is a federal post-secondary system with only one or two colleges and universities that could be classified as private or independent. Harman's continuum is illustrated in Figure 2.2.

Harman's model does not refer to every form of inter-institutional cooperation. Two – affiliation and management by contract – are left out, but it is not difficult to locate them in his paradigm. 'Voluntary cooperation' doesn't really explain affiliation, nor does it distinguish an affiliation from a consortium or federation, both of which are also voluntary. Affiliation would probably fit between federation and merger because it allows the least autonomy (relative to consortia and federations) and is therefore closest to merger, which radically changes the autonomy of at least one of the participating institutions. Management by contract then fits between affiliation and merger, and for mainly the same reason: its effect on autonomy.

Harman's model, because it explains mergers in Australian post-secondary education – and perhaps also in the Netherlands (Goedegebuure, 1992) – does not consider in depth the institutional motives for cooperation. That it does not is neither surprising nor unexplainable. In Australia and the Netherlands, inter-institutional cooperation was driven initially by government as part of a broader scheme for rationalizing and reorganizing post-secondary education. Without government intervention and pressure, few colleges and universities in those countries at that time would have had much interest in cooperation, and even fewer would have extended cooperation to include merger. But when there are institutionally generated reasons for considering merger, the model requires elaboration. There are several models for combining colleges and universities, which are summarized in Table 2.1.

The forms that inter-institutional cooperation takes depend greatly on the structure of the public system of post-secondary education of which the institutions are a part. Every public system of post-secondary education is unique in some way; that being said, they are all basically the same in the social and economic demands they face. The systems vary in how they are structured to respond to those demands. Each has a different centre of gravity, which may rest with the institution itself at one extreme, or with the government at the other (Volkwein, 1989).

The social and economic demands on colleges and universities call for responses in terms of scale, breadth, quality, and distribution. When the need for economy and efficiency is added to those demands – especially as a result of cutbacks in public funding – the impetus toward inter-institutional cooperation becomes particularly strong. Some systems are so vast in scale and diversity that they can respond to the demands 'across the board' at relatively low marginal cost. But where a system is not large and diverse, or is saturated to the point that every institution in it is at capacity, cooperation and merger soon arise as alternative means of responding to diverse social demands. Again, following Harman's paradigm, there is a clear incompatibility and 'trade off' between cooperation and autonomy. In fact, one could just as easily describe Harman's model as a model of *autonomous* behaviour as of *cooperative* behaviour; the two work in opposite directions in an inverse relationship.

On the continuum, each institution gains or loses autonomy as it loses or gains from cooperation. Thus, any location on the continuum – for example, a consortium – is proximate and the product of optimization. The location is not and cannot be construed as ideal or perfect. Rather, it is an optimal balance of advantages and disadvantages. Presumably, the ideal would have been the prior *status quo* had it not been judged untenable. From the point of view of this model, then, merger and other forms of

TABLE 2.1
Models for combining higher education institutions, some key characteristics

CONSORTIUM
The formal organization is distinct from its constituent members.
Membership is voluntary.
Membership is institutional (as opposed to subinstitutional).
The consortium is incorporated separately from its members.
The corporation directors are appointed by the constituent members.
The CEO is appointed by the board and employed by the consortium.
The consortium is legally responsible for assets and liabilities, and has its own staff and budget.
The consortium usually provides a program or service solely to its members.
Example: Five Colleges Incorporated (U.S.)

FEDERATION
Each participant in a federation remains independent and autonomous; retains its board of directors and authority to grant degrees; controls its own assets and liabilities; and offers employment.
Only one member actually offers degrees; the others voluntarily hold in abeyance their authority to grant degrees. Students may work toward a degree at any member institution, thus broadening academic diversity at low marginal cost.
The member actually conferring degrees usually sets the academic standards – including terms of academic appointment – for the entire federation.
Member institutions can continue to provide services and offer other programs outside the federation.
Federations are organizationally and managerially complex.
Examples: University of London, University of Toronto

AFFILIATION
Design is usually bilateral – that is, involving only two institutions – but an institution may be involved in several affiliations simultaneously.
One partner in an affiliation has the authority to grant degrees, while the other does not.
Partners do not offer overlapping programs.
Affiliation is fundamentally a form of contract leading to a highly specialized division of academic labour.
Example: The Ontario Institute for Studies in Education and the University of Toronto, prior to their merger.

MANAGEMENT BY CONTRACT
This model occurs in highly centralized public systems of higher education.
The inter-institutional format is contractual.
The government formally and legally delegates managerial, fiduciary, and accountability responsibility for a smaller, specialized institution to a larger and more comprehensive 'host' institution.
Examples: Ontario (Canada) agricultural colleges managed by the University of Guelph; Los Alamos National Laboratory (New Mexico) managed by the University of California.

MERGER
Two or more institutions combine to form a single new organization with a single governing body and chief executive.
At least one institution and potentially all merging institutions relinquish autonomy and separate legal identity.
All assets, liabilities, legal obligations, and responsibilities of the merging institutions are transferred to a single successor institution.
Mergers are virtually impossible to reverse.
Examples: The Technical University of Nova Scotia and Dalhousie University; the Ontario Institute for Studies in Education and the University of Toronto.

inter-institutional cooperation are not natural behaviours. They are more the result of overcoming institutional inertia than a response to institutional momentum. Their motivating factors are mainly external.

A final important point: the model demonstrates that merger is indeed a form of inter-institutional cooperation. It is not a freestanding phenomemon that occurs in response to some separate set of motivating factors. Mergers occur and evolve in response to the same factors that lead, for example, to consortia.

The Paradigms of Merger

We now understand that there is only one continuum, and that that continuum includes merger. We also understand that while merger may be the predominant form that inter-institutional cooperation has taken in recent years, it is neither a unique nor an independent form. It shares a number of basic characteristics with other forms of cooperation – especially federation – and it evolved from those forms. This question then follows: How do individual colleges and universities respond to the various factors that motivate inter-institutional cooperation generally, and merger particularly? There are a number of paradigms that attempt to explain institutional behaviour that leads to institutional change and diversification; and to explain why, among the several forms that inter-institutional cooperation may take, some institutions choose merger.

The Drive to Compete

Various attempts have been made to explain diversity and differentiation among colleges and universities. Some scholars – principally Joseph Ben-David and Roger Geiger – have identified autonomy and competition, not cooperation, as the factors that influence most heavily the forms that institutions take, including the various forms that result from merger (Ben-David, 1972; Geiger, 1986). In other words, institutions cooperate in order to gain a competitive advantage in the educational marketplace. That advantage may take the form of lower costs, new programs, new modes of delivering programs, and opportunities for growth.

In the paradigm of competition, autonomy is not about having the discretion to resist various social demands and maintain the status quo. Rather, it is about having the authority to respond and adapt to the social and economic environments largely independently of government planning and regulation. However, the absence of government planning and regulation is not the same thing as an absence of public policy. Recent studies of the restructuring of public systems of post-secondary education demonstrate that the competitive paradigm can produce as good a fit between systems of higher education and the social and economic environment as is produced by prescriptive planning and regulation (MacTaggart, 1996).

The competitive paradigm is a powerful lens for looking at mergers and acquisitions in market systems. Indeed, terms such as 'acquisition' and 'take-over' are more closely associated with the idiom of corporate merger than with the idiom of cooperative arrangements among colleges and universities or among other not-for-profit institutions. To the extent that one views the cases described in this book as acquisitions of smaller institutions by larger institutions, they fit the paradigm of competition.

Natural Selection

In structural and organizational terms, colleges and universities can sometimes be understood as rational organizations that balance the demands for quality, scale, and so on with the need for economy. Sometimes they can be understood in competitive terms as businesses that struggle with one another for market position. But they can also be understood as organisms seeking to survive in an ecosystem. In this context, natural selection essentially involves applying a Darwinian model to institutions of higher education, or more precisely to groups of institutions (just as there are multiple organisms in an ecosystem). The most prominent proponent of the natural selection paradigm is Robert Birnbaum, who deployed it in his measurements of diversity in post-secondary education (Birnbaum, 1983).

How does the natural selection model explain mergers? Merger may be a means of institutional survival. Survival is a necessity. Like any species in an ecosystem, colleges and universities will seek to survive, and will choose change over the *status quo* in order to do so. The complexity of ecosystems, perhaps like systems of post-secondary education, is incomprehensibly great; at the same time, this complexity reflects the essential role that specialization and diversity play in maintaining the system's health. From this perspective, every system of higher education comprises a plethora of unique niches that are constantly changing. Merger in this sense can be regarded as the institutional equivalent of genetic variability. Each merger represents a unique combination of institutional characteristics that together enable the participating institutions to fill a new niche.

But as in an ecological system, not all species survive. Some fail to evolve, and die. Some evolve, but disappear into merger. Moreover, not all that survive do so by symbiosis: some evolve without cooperation with others. But in those cases which do involve merger, either in the biological sense or the organizational sense, the success of the merger depends on the compatibility of the two institutions. Success in mergers is not random: some institutions make a good fit, while others do not.

Resource Dependence

Yet another paradigm that sometimes explains merger as a manifestation of institutional behaviour is resource dependence. Resource dependence is superficially similar to the paradigm of natural selection: the fundamental objective of the organization is to survive. However, the resource dependence paradigm ties survival to a single factor: resources or money (Birnbaum, 1983; Goedegebuure, 1992). That factor includes as well the authority or franchise to raise or claim money, for example, under system-wide funding formulas (Goedegebuure, 1992). It should not be surprising, then, that in the case of public colleges and universities, the role and posture of government is paramount, because government is the source of the majority of funding on which the institutions depend. Nor should it be surprising that the language of merger often borrows from the idiom of monopolies. The analogy to economic monopolies is of course not perfect. But that is not the point. The point is that the purpose of forming monopolies through merger is to secure and control resources and then protect them from competition. Thus, while the competition paradigm and the resource dependence paradigm share a common ground in the marketplace, they explain the behaviour of merger quite differently: one depends on the marketplace to determine how institutions change and adapt through cooperation while the other seeks to insulate institutions from the marketplace, and in particular from the possible loss of resources.

The State as Ecosystem and Market

The final paradigm for merger may not be a paradigm at all, but it is important, especially in juxtaposition with the other paradigms. Unlike the natural selection paradigm, according to which evolution occurs without 'system' boundaries, and the resource dependence paradigm, which refers predominantly to funding, this paradigm recognizes that governments control not only money but also the conditions of the institutional ecosystem. A conundrum that confronts several of the other paradigms is that the political jurisdiction in which a given post-secondary educational system functions is not itself the product of, for example, natural selection or competition. History, culture, language, and geography are far more often the determinants of a political jurisdiction.

Any one of these factors can explain why certain institutions either merge or do not – for example, colleges and universities in remote, underpopulated areas or, conversely, congestions of institutions in other areas. Other paradigms cannot explain why. Inter-institutional cooperation under this paradigm is to a great extent determined by government policy, and is virtually synonymous with restructuring by government fiat. These circumstances lead more often to merger than to other forms of inter-institutional cooperation along the continuum.

The Two Cases in Context

The two mergers this study addresses demonstrate that there is an evolutionary continuum of inter-institutional cooperation, and that merger is part of it. They also demonstrate that although the motivation to merge is common to many colleges and universities, institutional behaviour in response to that motivation varies widely; and that various paradigms explain those differences in behaviour.

In each case study, the partners to what eventually became merger initially considered other forms of inter-institutional cooperation. In one of the cases – the Technical University of Nova Scotia and Dalhousie University – some of the participants believed for a time that what was being proposed was more a federation than a merger. In the other case – the Ontario Institute for Studies in Education and the University of Toronto – the participating institutions were already affiliated prior to merging. In both cases, then, merger was not only seen but acted on as occupying a place along a continuum of various forms of inter-institutional cooperation. Moreover, as the participants approached merger, they investigated various options for locating themselves on that continuum.

Once motivated to merge, all four institutions behaved in ways exhibiting the differences between the several paradigms. As the following chapters will show, TUNS and OISE were driven to varying degrees by concern for *institutional survival*. The government of Nova Scotia wanted to secure greater strength in a key discipline (computer science) and was skeptical that further *competition* among relatively small institutions could produce the desired result, whether or not any savings were realized. The government of Ontario, on the other hand, was concerned principally if not exclusively about resources – a fact that OISE, which was heavily *dependent on those resources*, reluctantly came to understand. The University of Toronto and Dalhousie University were relatively large, healthy, and autonomous institutions, but neither felt that it could approach merger without reference to the public *ecosystem and market*, which was controlled not only by the governments then in office but by their predecessors, which had shaped the systems so as to include the anomalies that merger finally resolved.

PART TWO

The Cases

THREE

The Merger of Dalhousie University and the Technical University of Nova Scotia

The Deep Background

Nova Scotian Higher Education in the 1800s

To understand the merger of Dalhousie University and the Technical University of Nova Scotia, it is necessary to know something about the history of higher education in Nova Scotia.

Nova Scotia's universities were founded at a time of fierce denominational rivalries in what was then a British colony. What came to be known as Dalhousie College was established in 1818 on the initiative of Lord Dalhousie, Nova Scotia's lieutenant-governor, as 'an institution at Halifax in which the advantages of a collegiate education will be found within the reach of all classes of society, and which will be open to all sects of religious persuasion' (Waite, 1994, 21). Accordingly, it languished for many years due to lack of interest.

By the early 1840s, four colleges had been established – King's (which was an Anglican institution), Dalhousie, Acadia (Baptist) and Saint Mary's (Roman Catholic). As Waite notes (1994, 61), many had reservations about the wisdom of so many colleges:

> The *Novascotian* put it in the context of the whole educational system of Nova Scotia: of a population of two hundred and fifty thousand, probably thirty thousand children were growing up without the basic rudiments of education, and here was the legislature squandering £1,800 a year on four colleges. And the worst of it was that everyone knew the Methodists and Presbyterians were waiting, thinking in due course that they, too, would get

their slice of the cake. Richard Nugent, the Catholic editor of the *Novascotian*, became more annoyed the more he thought of it:

> We must confess ourselves astonished at the credulity or infatuation of our Countrymen, and lament the mistaken policy of our public men which gave rise to the present deplorable state of the Educational affairs of the Province...
>
> What is to be done? Shall we go on *ad infinitum* creating College after College ...? Or, shall we pause here, and enquire seriously, where the evil will end?

Nova Scotia was by no means alone in experiencing a proliferation of denominational colleges in the mid-1800s. Some jurisdictions responded by creating federated institutions modelled on the University of London. Typically, they consolidated several colleges under one university examining body. The University of Toronto was constituted in this way in 1853 (Cameron, 1991). Although 1843 saw a movement to establish 'One Good College' in Nova Scotia, religious rivalries proved to be too strong for the idea to come to fruition.

In the mid-1860s, Dalhousie was revived under Presbyterian auspices. By 1875, eight years after Confederation, it had eighty-seven students in arts and science and thirty-three in medicine – a larger enrolment than Nova Scotia's other colleges combined. Facing straitened circumstances, it petitioned the legislature for a larger grant, urging the province to support it as a provincial university. (The Ontario government would pass legislation in 1887 making the University of Toronto the provincial university, to be funded publicly for teaching and research in the sciences and the professions.)

It was politically impossible to designate Dalhousie as Nova Scotia's provincial university because of the opposition of five other colleges and their supporters. Nevertheless, the government recognized the need to raise the standards of higher education in the province. In 1876 it created the University of Halifax – modelled explicitly on the University of London – with that goal in mind. It did not, however, give the new body real teeth by removing the existing colleges' degree-granting powers. The University of Halifax examined candidates for degrees for two years and then disappeared. But the act that created it was never repealed. The most immediate consequence was that public grants to Nova Scotia's colleges and universities ceased in 1881 for almost 80 years – with an exception being made for one institution, as we will shortly see (Waite, 1994).

By the early 1900s, Dalhousie had expanded greatly in numbers of professors and students and had added a law school. It decided to establish a program in mining engineering as well, and sought funding for it from the premier, George Murray. According to Dalhousie historian Peter Waite, 'Murray's response was ambivalent: interest and helplessness. The Nova Scotia government could not afford politically to give any commitment to develop engineering at Dalhousie, however desirable in practice the idea might be' (Waite, 1994, 191).

Dalhousie went ahead, raising funds and establishing a School of Mining Engineering in 1902. A program in civil engineering was initiated shortly thereafter, along with an extension program in Cape Breton, where King's also provided classes in engineering. Two other universities – Acadia and Mount Allison – offered the first two years of a four-year engineering degree, the last two years of which were to be completed at McGill.

In a letter to the editor of the *Halifax Herald* on 4 August 1906, James S. Carruthers commented on his experience as a teacher in Dalhousie's engineering extension program. His words reflected the growing perception that technical education was central to individual prosperity and industrial advancement:

> Sir, – For the past three summers my work in connection with Dalhousie College has been largely in industrial centres. During those months, I have met, conversed or discussed, both with the men and the management 'our present industrial advance'. Such conversations or discussions could not help but raise the question, 'What, so far as education is concerned, is the pressing need of the hour?' I need hardly say that there came to my mind a number of answers. But one crowded out all others – we must have more information on the question of technical education ...
>
> Why? Because [today's young men] are not yet awake to the fact that technical education means [in the words of] Professor F. H. Sexton of Dalhousie College: 'More salary and a comfortable living,' lack of it 'poverty and serfdom.' I trust these articles [submitted to the *Herald*] may result in awakening 'the hope of Nova Scotia.' Leading them to prepare now for the industrial advancement that is knocking at our door. To wait until the clock strikes is suicidal. Both from a patriotic and personal standpoint, the watchword for all young Nova Scotians is PREPARE.

The Creation of Nova Scotia 'Tech'

At the invitation of the Mining Society of Nova Scotia and the Halifax

Board of Trade, representatives of Dalhousie, King's, Acadia, and Mount Allison met in Halifax in 1906 to discuss the state of engineering education. The colleges acknowledged that with their slender resources, none of them could meet the need, and they agreed to recommend that the provincial government take responsibility for offering the third and fourth years of civil, mechanical, electrical, and mining engineering degrees. Frederick Sexton, who became the first president of the Nova Scotia Technical College, later described this joint recommendation as the first in which 'the colleges in Nova Scotia and New Brunswick, [which] were then strictly competitive and far from friendly [and which] clung to old established prejudices ... had ever been united' (Sexton, 1929, 1).

In 1907 the Nova Scotia legislature passed the Technical Education Act. Premier George Murray described it as 'one of the most important measures ever introduced into this legislature.' It provided for the establishment of the Nova Scotia Technical College (NSTC) in Halifax, and of industrial schools to provide technical training at other provincial centres. It also transferred to the Department of Education responsibility for provincial mining schools that already existed. To ensure the integration of the new system for technical education, the province's Director of Technical Education would also be the NSTC's principal. The NSTC board would include representatives from each of Nova Scotia's colleges and from Mount Allison University, as well as NSTC professors.

Funds were committed and facilities built, and on 29 September 1909 the Nova Scotia Technical College opened with twenty-three students. The *Halifax Herald* reported:

> Without any firing of guns or flourish of trumpets, the Nova Scotia Technical College began its work yesterday. The opening of this institution in its magnificent new quarters on Spring Garden Road is a notable event in the educational history of the province. This college stands at the head or apex of the whole unique system of technical education in Nova Scotia which marks this province as the leader of the whole of the Dominion of Canada in this direction ...
>
> This college is the people's college. In it any boy in Nova Scotia may get an engineering training in any of the four great branches, namely, civil, mining, electrical or mechanical engineering ...
>
> The professors in charge of the technical college are men of thorough education, wide practical experience, attractive personalities and high ideals ...
>
> The technical college intends to serve the industrial needs in more than

merely instructing students in engineering for a degree ... The college will also ... carry out industrial research as far as possible in connection with the industries now flourishing or struggling in Nova Scotia.

Under Frederick Sexton's leadership, the NSTC embarked on its mission. The early years were not easy. According to Sexton, 'some of the colleges expected that there would be some inefficiency on account of political patronage or meddling just because the government was responsible for the maintenance of the college. The first few efforts at co-operation were not whole-hearted. Slowly and painfully the standards of instruction were built up and maintained' (1929, 4).

That the new college had critics can be inferred from a wonderful briefing memorandum prepared for the Honourable R.M. MacGregor in 1916:

The Technical College in Halifax is the centre and head of the system of technical education from which the schools in various parts of the Province are controlled and directed ... In establishing the Technical College the Government worked out a plan of affiliation so that there should be no overlapping [with the colleges] of plant and staff. All the other colleges agreed to give the first two years instruction in the general studies of a four-year engineering course, and the Technical College undertook to provide the last two years of professional training in the four basic courses of civil, mechanical, electrical and mining engineering. This scheme of cooperation is a feat rarely achieved in the realm of higher education ...

The Technical College is an institution that every Nova Scotian may well be proud of. The buildings are substantial and dignified, but no money has been wasted in ornate decoration. The equipment has been carefully chosen for the purpose so that a comparatively small amount has been expended in comparison with other institutions of this kind ...

The Technical College offers the Nova Scotian youth with mechanical ability the opportunity to make the most of himself. The son of the farmer, the miner, the mechanic, the fisherman has the opportunity of securing the highest grade of professional training in engineering at comparatively little cost ... No better opportunities for the ambitious boy who is poor exist anywhere ...

The running cost of the College as is shown in the annual report of the Superintendent of Education is about $25,000 a year. A large part of this amount is spent on salaries to the staff and will be no more when the number of students increases to three times the number. There are no more instructors and professors than are absolutely necessary. The salaries paid to the professors are not as high as those paid to professors in some other colleges in the province, although the men at the Technical College have had long practical experience in industrial life and have shown their ability to success-fully manage large engineering undertakings. The men on the staff are re-quired to teach more hours per day than is the regular practice in the other colleges in the province.

Some ignorant or misleading critics have tried to charge the whole of the annual cost of the college up to the engineering students alone and make out that it costs $1,000.00 a year to train a student. This is malicious misrepresen-tation. The Provincial Museum and Science Library occupy more than one-fourth of the building and should have a proper amount charged against them. A part of the equipment is used for the coal mining schools and beside the regular engineering students there are a considerable number of men who come in for short courses who should be charged for their share of the expense. Then a large part of the apparatus in the College is used for special technical training for evening technical classes in Halifax which portion of the expense should not be charged against the engineering students alone. If those men who understand long division better than engineering education were to try to get the real truth of the matter, instead of perverting the surface indications, they would find that it costs very little more to train engineering students at the Technical College with its present small numbers than it does to train them in other large engineering colleges with hundreds of students. The fact that it does not cost more than it does now, with the high quality of the work done, is a tribute to the economical administration of this institu-tion.

There is another important function of the Technical College which must not be overlooked and that is the service it renders in facilities for industrial research and advice to people with industrial problems that can be solved only by the application of science. Every year there are more people turning to the College for assistance in helping them to test products or to solve difficulties that they meet in exploiting the rich resources of the Province. Ores, coals, woods, rocks, steels, cements, waters, and various other raw and manufactured products are analysed and tested ... This has been an important factor in assisting to develop the potential wealth of the Province ...

Then, too, the short courses which are carried on at the College should receive adequate accommodation for no other engineering college in Canada offers such facilities to men actually engaged in industry ... Recently, the College has developed a number of correspondence courses specially adapted for the needs of men and women in the province. By this means technical instruction can be carried into the homes anywhere in Nova Scotia and technical instruction be provided to anyone at a very nominal cost ... Every year sees the extension of the usefulness of the Technical College which has been so maligned and willfully misrepresented by some of the opposition members in the House of Assembly.

The Evening Technical Schools, the Coal Mining Schools, and the Engineering Schools are too well known to need much explanation and too well appreciated by all the people to receive any criticism except that they should be extended more rapidly ...

The system of technical education has been laid on broad, deep foundations. All of the gaps have not been filled in yet, to make it a rounded out whole, but this ideal will be fulfilled when money is available to complete the scheme adequately so that every Nova Scotian boy and girl will be trained efficiently to perform his or her life work in the best possible manner ... Any Nova Scotian of any political conviction should be proud of what has been accomplished and lend every effort to increase the scope and efficiency of this branch of education which is considered by every advanced nation as one of the most powerful influences known to man for promoting happiness and prosperity and diminishing vice, poverty and crime ('Memorandum re. Technical Education,' 1916).

The Attempt to 'Confederate the Colleges'

The success of the efforts of Sexton and his colleagues to provide solid technical education was attested to by a report commissioned by the Carnegie Foundation of New York in the 1920s. Lacking government funding, Dalhousie and other Nova Scotia colleges often applied to that source for funding. In 1921 the Carnegie Foundation decided that, instead of continuing to respond to funding requests on an *ad hoc* basis, it would commission an inquiry into the state of higher education in the Maritime provinces. The study was conducted by William Learned and Kenneth Sills. With respect to the NSTC, they reported:

The institution is well officered and adequately equipped for its strictly limited function, and adheres rigidly to it. The budget amounts to about $50,000 annually, and as students are few and the per capita costs are high, the school receives constant criticism in the legislature. The expenses are, of course, very much less than would be required to conduct anything like as efficient courses at each of the different colleges. Furthermore, the experiment of cooperation has been recognized as being completely successful, and has possibly helped to pave the way for something still better. (Learned and Sills, 1921, 26)

From the perspective of Learned and Sills, that something better would be a 'Confederation of the Colleges,' and that is what they recommended. Their overall finding was that, 'underfunded, undermanned, under-equipped, with no money at all from the Nova Scotian government, Nova Scotia's colleges were fundamentally in parlous condition, struggling not so much to meet national standards as to survive ... Thus, said Learned and Sills, "to seek to perpetuate present arrangements ... is foregone defeat"' (Waite, 1994, 261).

Concentration of resources was called for. Learned and Sills proposed that Nova Scotia's colleges and Mount Allison College (in Sackville, New Brunswick) move to the Dalhousie campus and federate into a larger university modelled explicitly on the University of Toronto. Each college would retain its name but would hold in abeyance its degree-granting powers (except in Theology). Some subjects would be taught by university faculties, others by the colleges.

The Carnegie Foundation embraced the scheme and was prepared to put $3 million into it. Representatives of the colleges prepared a plan for federation. It was approved by the boards of Dalhousie, King's, and Mount Allison, but turned down by those of Acadia and St Francis Xavier. The eventual outcome of the initiative was that King's moved from Windsor to Halifax and entered into an affiliation with Dalhousie, with the Carnegie Foundation providing an endowment of $600,000 for their joint benefit. The other colleges went their separate ways.

Postwar Plays

Up to the Second World War, the NSTC continued to carry out two functions: providing university-level engineering education, and overseeing technical education in the province. However, by war's end changes were in the wind. Sexton's retirement was imminent, the provincial government was contemplating a reorganization of vocational education, and the college had outgrown its existing facilities. President Kerr of Dalhousie consulted with Professor Copp of his Department of Engineering about these developments. Copp wrote in response:

As suggested by you, Dr. Sexton probably will be retiring in the course of a few years. You state that a suggestion has been made to you that Dalhousie approach the Nova Scotia Government with the suggestion that Dalhousie be permitted to grant these degrees and that it be understood that the present expenses in connection with the buildings and salaries of the staff be carried on as at present by the Nova Scotia government ...

I have talked with Professor Theakston, himself a graduate of Tech, because I felt that his reaction would be typical. He is opposed to the idea, because he fears that it would meet with tremendous opposition from many sources, including an influential Alumni.

Undaunted, Kerr proposed to Premier Angus L. MacDonald in January 1946 that the technical college become a Faculty of Engineering of Dalhousie, if and when changes were made in the organization and personnel of the college. By April he was having second thoughts. On 27 April he wrote to the premier that he had 'discussed the idea with a number of persons who are intimately concerned with engineering education and as a result of these conversations I would like to amend our original suggestion so that our proposal would simply call for the transfer of the Nova Scotia Technical College to the Dalhousie campus where it would carry on in close affiliation with the University.'

Among the advantages of such an arrangement, Kerr (1946) cited these:

- The study of engineering would be conducted in a university atmosphere. This is most important for the maintenance of high professional standards in the Engineering Course.
- The Technical College could retain its own identity and stand in an affiliated relation with Dalhousie on terms somewhat similar to those in which the University of King's College stands at present.
- This step would be in line with the ideal indicated by the Report of the Carnegie Foundation on Education in the Maritime Provinces (1922) ...
- It would permit of closer contacts between Engineering on the one hand and the Physics and Chemistry Departments of the University on the other ...
- Any scientific research which might be directly associated with the Technical College would have the stimulus of the other research activities of the University ...
- The transfer of the Technical College to the Dalhousie campus would be a step in the direction of giving Nova Scotia a university centre which would compare in impressiveness with the larger Canadian universities, without taking away the individuality of the co-operating colleges ...
- It would provide that Engineering courses, at the university level, be carried on in close physical contact with the larger and more varied interests of university life rather than on a small separate campus.

The letter was copied to Alan E. Cameron, then Deputy Minister of Mines for Nova Scotia. The arguments it advanced would be repeated many times in later decades.

In the spring of 1947, Frederick Sexton retired after forty years as the NSTC's president. At his last board meeting in March, the president-elect, Alan E. Cameron, proposed that the college move to the Dalhousie campus. Two months later, the original act establishing the technical college was repealed, and two new ones were passed, one with respect to the college, the other with respect to vocational and technical education. The college was removed from the control of the Council of Public Education and established as a body corporate under the control of a board of governors and a president. The new board consisted of the premier as chairman; the president of the college as vice-chairman; the presidents of associated colleges and universities (i.e., institutions offering the introductory years of the engineering program to students who would complete their degrees at the technical college); the president of the newly formed provincial research foundation; two alumni representatives; and five members appointed by the governor-in-council.

The new board met in September 1947 and considered the proposal to relocate. Dalhousie had offered to provide a site of approximately two acres on its campus, half a dozen blocks from the existing college. After a lengthy discussion, it was agreed that the premier would strike a committee to advise on the future requirements of the college; on alternative sites; and on their respective costs and advantages.

At the new board's second meeting in January 1948, the committee recommended that the college remain on its present campus and that new facilities be built. Should a move be deemed advisable, it should not be to the Dalhousie campus. The committee's report was accepted and forwarded to the Legislative Council. President Kerr of Dalhousie hastened to add, 'in referring to the proposed move to Dalhousie campus, [that he] wished it understood that the offer of the site was made in response to a plea for such assistance in the cause of engineering education and not for any benefits that might accrue to Dalhousie' (NSTC Board of Governors, 1948). He later complained to the premier that the committee's report had been sprung on board members at the meeting and that they had not had an opportunity to consider the alternatives seriously. However, the issue was apparently settled. Land adjoining the NSTC campus was secured, and additional facilities were built. The idea of a closer relationship between the college and Dalhousie lay dormant for some years.

The Nova Scotia government, having begun to provide ongoing funding to universities in 1958, established a University Grants Commission in

1963. This body's efforts to streamline engineering education caused such an uproar that Premier Robert Stanfield commissioned a report on engineering education by Dean R.R. McLaughlin of the University of Toronto. Among McLaughlin's recommendations were that 'NSTC becom[e] the faculty of applied science and engineering of Dalhousie University ... Such a union would be to the advantage of both institutions ... I believe [it] would greatly strengthen engineering education' (1966, 10). The 'associated university system,' in which other Nova Scotia universities offered the first years of the engineering program, would continue as before.

The recommendation did not go far. Dalhousie's president, Henry Hicks, was not surprised. He had been by turns Nova Scotia's education minister (1949–54) and premier (1954–56), so he knew the dynamics of the system and had anticipated resistance. In response to an expression of support for the proposed merger from a former head of the National Research Council, Hicks said that he doubted 'how useful or effective it would be for me, as President of Dalhousie, to become an active protagonist of the views you have expressed?' Then Premier Robert Stanfield shared Hicks's assessment of the small 'p' politics. He observed to Hicks: 'There may be very rigid and widespread views on this subject. Consequently I do not know that we are likely to see any change or not ... My guess is that not very much will happen unless the government is prepared to push people around pretty fiercely, and this might have unfortunate repercussions' (Waite, 1998, 255).

McLaughlin's report was discussed at the April 1966 meeting of the NSTC Senate. At that meeting, the college's president, George Holbrook, spoke against merger with Dalhousie: 'He felt that it was important that NSTC retain its autonomy. He had not originated the proposal for amalgamation and he did not favour it' (NSTC Senate, 1966). The NSTC Alumni Association and the senate (on which, like the board, the associated universities were represented) also opposed it, as did other universities. In short order, the idea was dead.

The NSTC did not wish to relinquish its autonomy. Even so, there was support, both within the college and on the part of the University Grants Commission, for closer cooperation between it and Dalhousie. In 1969 the two institutions signed a five-year agreement providing for cooperation in a number of areas, including Architecture and Graduate Studies. Earlier in the decade, the NSTC had established schools for both.

Dal/Tech Merger: The 1970s Round

In 1970 the NSTC was in financial crisis. A change in the NSTC Act in

1962 had made it an autonomous institution and given it responsibility for its own financial affairs. Although the board conducted a successful capital campaign, operating funding for the college was inadequate. By 1971 the situation had become so severe that the administration notified seven of its fifty-two professors that their contracts would not be renewed. There was an outcry. Students marched on Province House to demand that the government provide more funding for Tech. In the ensuing uproar, Holbrook and the Dean of Engineering resigned. Orest Cochkanoff was appointed acting Dean of Engineering, and the Director of Administration was appointed acting president.

The Faculty of Engineering failed to convince the government to act on the college's plight, and so launched its own review of engineering education in Nova Scotia. The seven-person faculty council conducted the review, which was assisted by P.A. Lapp, who had been engaged by the NSTC Alumni Association for that purpose, owing to his involvement in reviews of engineering education in a number of other provinces. The review committee consulted widely throughout the 'Tech system' and then met *in camera* to wrestle with the issues confronting it. Its members eventually reached the conclusion that the best course of action for Tech was to merge with Dalhousie.

Dalhousie had expanded tremendously during the 1960s in numbers of students, faculty, and staff, breadth and depth of programs, research activity, and physical facilities. To illustrate, student enrolment had stood at 1,496 in 1957–58, but had reached 7,335 by 1972–73. Growth continued apace in the early 1970s. In one year, seventy new faculty members were appointed to the Faculty of Arts and Science alone (Waite, 1998).

Before the Faculty of Engineering's review committee made its conclusions known to others, three of its members, including its chairman, Dean Cochkanoff, met with Dalhousie's president, Hicks. They laid out for him the process they had gone through and the conclusions they had reached. Hicks thought their proposal an excellent one, but – with the perspicacity that had served him well in politics of all kinds – he offered two observations: 'one, the politicians won't buy it,' and 'two, Dalhousie will be blamed.' Nevertheless, he would do what he could (interview with Cochkanoff).

Most of the action took place at Tech. The review committee produced its report, *Engineering Education in Nova Scotia*, in September 1972. It began with a lengthy foreword by Lapp, in which he presented his assessment:

- The engineering education system in Nova Scotia is moving into a state of crisis
- There has been a serious deterioration in the relations between NSTC and some of the Associated Universities
- Enrolments both at NSTC and the ... Associated Universities have been dropping
- by any standard [the writer] has seen across Canada, NSTC has been woefully underfinanced
- the cleavage of curricular powers between NSTC and the Associated Universities has resulted in uneven preparation of students entering their junior year at NSTC and it is a traumatic experience for some
- While the NSTC system provides a good educational program for the students, and there were no strong complaints either from students or employers of NSTC graduates interviewed by the writer, the staff at NSTC are seriously troubled and concerned. These concerns centre around matters of excellence, identification and morale.'

Lapp concluded that 'the NSTC system should consolidate into one large engineering school with access to a multi-faculty, co-educational campus. It is difficult to escape from this conclusion, certainly by anyone viewing the system from the outside. The degree to which this ideal objective can be achieved will be a function of the political realities prevailing within the Atlantic provinces university system' (NSTC Faculty of Engineering, 1972).

He indicated that he concurred with the review committee's conclusion that NSTC should become the College of Engineering of Dalhousie, but noted:

While the recommendations may well be ratified by the staff members of NSTC, there could be difficulties in obtaining unanimous approval from the Senate and Board of Governors of NSTC. This might be expected because of the constitution of these two groups which could lead to excessive delays, polarization of positions and varying degrees of acceptance. Under these circumstances, the government may well have to act independently to break the deadlock, and dictate the final outcome.

The findings of the review committee paralleled Lapp's. Their report described the founding of the NSTC and the establishment of the associated university system at the beginning of the century as 'one of the outstanding innovations in the field of higher education in Canada in this century.' But circumstances had changed. The college was seriously underresourced. Faculty salaries 'were amongst the lowest in the country, especially in the higher ranks.' Laboratory equipment was totally inadequate. The associated universities were now in competition with the NSTC for government funding, and this put them in a conflict of institutional interest on the NSTC board. The NSTC Senate was incapable of resolving issues of standards and curriculum and 'has been during the last decade largely ineffective, often divided.' In light of these problems – and of the desirability that first and second year students have access to upper-year students; that engineering professors be involved in education at all levels and in research; and that professional engineers be involved in the wider academic community – the review committee, 'mindful of our traditions, our predecessors and our ties with the past,' recommended 'with regret, rather than with rejoicing,' that the 'Tech system' be disbanded and that the NSTC be merged with Dalhousie (NSTC Faculty of Engineering, 1972).

The proponents of Dal/Tech merger gradually gained support for their proposal within NSTC and from professional bodies. A Dal/Tech negotiating committee was struck, consisting of Dalhousie's academic and financial vice-presidents and NSTC's board chairman and acting president. The task of building support for the proposed merger continued in parallel with negotiations. As Lapp predicted, it was not easy.

In an opinion piece published in the *Halifax Mail-Star* in November 1973, a past president of the NSTC Alumni Association wrote:

In the *Mail-Star* of October 30, under the heading 'Engineers' association in favor of Dal-Tech union,' it was reported that APENS [the Association of Professional Engineers of Nova Scotia] had, in arriving at its conclusions, studied the following:

- The NSTC faculty report
- The Saint Mary's University report
- The Acadia University report
- The sub-committee of APENS report
- Recommendations by the engineering faculties of the associated universities
- Recommendations of the presidents of the associated universities
- Recommendations of the Association of Atlantic Universities (AAU) executive

I believe it is an irrefutable fact that of these seven reports, only two, namely, the NSTC faculty report and the recommendations of the executive of the AAU, expressed opinions in favor of the merger.

I further believe that none of the associated universities in the Tech system has supported the merger, and all, at one time or another, with the exception of Dalhousie, have through your newspapers expressed opinions in opposition.

Dalhousie has, in fact, not publicly expressed any opinion. (Phillips, 1973)

In spite of the very considerable opposition, the Dal/Tech negotiating committee was able to state in its May 1974 report to the boards of the two institutions and the University Grants Committee that:

[The September 1972 report on *Engineering Education in Nova Scotia* which recommended amalgamation with Dalhousie] was approved in principle by the Faculties of Engineering and Architecture, by students, by the Senate and the Board of Governors of Tech. It was subsequently approved in principle by the Tech Alumni Association with some stated conditions, by the Association of Professional Engineers of Nova Scotia, and by the Nova Scotia Association of Architects. Subsequently the report was studied by the Association of Atlantic Universities ... The report on engineering was also approved in principle by the University Grants Committee ...

The Alumni Association of Tech proposed an alternate draft agreement which, in the opinion of Dalhousie negotiators, would have altered fundamentally the arrangements long under study and which Dalhousie was not prepared to accept. Dalhousie negotiators hope that the arrangements set out in the draft agreement attached to this report will prove acceptable to the alumni of Tech and that they will continue as individuals and as an association to play their long-important role in the life of Tech, with the opportunity provided to contribute also to the general government of Dalhousie as well as to Engineering and to Architecture students, staff and programs. (Dal-Tech Negotiating Committee, 1974, C-1)

The negotiating committee's report included two pieces of draft legislation. The first would amend the NSTC Act to enable the college's board to transfer responsibilities, assets, and liabilities to another institution; the second would enable Dalhousie to make additional appointments to its board in accordance with the draft agreement between the two institutions. The latter draft was a detailed, fifteen-page document dealing with organization; governance; administration; academic affairs; degrees; student affairs, services, government and fees; staff policies; alumni relations; finances, assets, liabilities, and succession; and – last, but not least – negotiations with the Province of Nova Scotia. The proposed date of amalgamation was 1 July 1974.

The agreement envisioned that the NSTC would become the Nova Scotia Technical College of Dalhousie University and would have faculties of architecture and engineering. The Dalhousie Department of Engineering would become part of the latter. The two faculties 'would have essentially the same autonomy as other faculties of Dalhousie, reporting to the Senate and to the President and to the Board of Governors of Dalhousie as other faculties do.' NSTC's Faculty of Graduate Studies would be subsumed by its counterpart at Dalhousie. The college would have an advisory council, which would be appointed by Dalhousie's president and would include students, faculty members, the professions, alumni, and government. The NSTC's acting president would become the administrative head of the new college and would facilitate and oversee complete integration for a year after amalgamation; following this, his position and responsibilities would be reviewed by the president of Dalhousie, in consultation with the faculties and the advisory council.

The draft agreement committed the NSTC and Dalhousie to negotiating jointly with the government for funding for the college. It included amendments to the institutions' acts and provisions for continued participation by NSTC staff in the provincial public service pension plan.

Dalhousie's board approved the draft agreement, and a special meeting of the NSTC board was convened to consider it. The minutes of that meeting – on 5 June 1974 – reveal that the amalgamation proposal was still contentious. A motion to approve the agreement having been moved and seconded, an amendment was moved:

WHEREAS this Board considers it desirable that it or some other autonomous body continue to be responsible for the administrative control of NSTC, that those portions of the draft agreement ... concerned with the granting of academic control over engineering and architectural education in Nova Scotia to the Senate and Board of Governors of Dalhousie be approved, and that the Negotiating Committee reconvene to negotiate the other portions of the Agreement to provide for administrative control of NSTC remaining in the Board of Governors of NSTC or some autonomous body other than the Board of Governors of Dalhousie University.

'After considerable discussion,' a vote was taken. There were six votes in favour of the amendment and seven against. A second amendment was then moved: 'That at Page 2, Item 2, of the report, the word "affiliated" be deleted so that the statement will now read "Tech shall become, and continue, as a college of Dalhousie etc." – In this way it is clear that there is to be a complete merger – and further that any other phrase within the document that includes the word "affiliated" or connotation thereof be deleted by the Negotiating Committee.'

This amendment carried.

When the vote on the main motion was taken, all of those eligible to vote voted in favour of the agreement, with the exception of two board members who abstained. (The depth of the latters' feelings are illustrated by the fact that one of them subsequently made a large bequest to the Technical College, a condition of which was that the college remain independent of Dalhousie. Should the college merge with Dalhousie, the endowment was to be transferred to Acadia. This occurred in 1997, after the amalgamation of the Technical University of Nova Scotia with Dalhousie.) The day after the board meeting, the Minister of Education said he would bring a resolution for amalgamating Dalhousie and NSTC to Cabinet in the near future. Bills 110 and 111 were introduced in the fall.

The opposition had not been quieted. The bills passed first and second reading. Then, at the Law Amendments Committee's hearing in November, they ran into what the chairman of the NSTC board later described as 'the spirited opposition of some of the Associated Universities and the Tech Alumni Association' (NSTC Board of Governors, 1974, 3). On the recommendation of that committee, a select committee of the House was struck to consider the matter further. It held hearings in January.

In the meantime, the debate continued to rage in the local newspapers. A series of excerpts from briefs to the select committee were published. For opponents of the amalgamation, the issue was no longer simply the quality of engineering education, but the future of the university system itself. A former head of St Francis Xavier University's engineering department wrote:

> I urge you not to be misled by the impression that the proposed Dal-Tech merger is a matter that concerns engineering education only ... It is my belief that the proposed merger would seriously weaken and eventually might well destroy altogether our present system of higher education ... To hand over to Dalhousie a monopoly on engineering at the urging of a portion of the Tech faculty is to hand over to Dalhousie a virtual monopoly of the sciences, and

would come dangerously close to giving her a monopoly of all university-level education. If this be not clearly understood, the proposed merger will not be seen in its true light, nor its consequences fully appreciated. (Fogarty, 1975)

The select committee of the House eventually recommended the merger, but it did so by only one vote, and one of its members was not present at the time of the vote. In spite of assurances to the contrary from the Minister of Education, the bills were never brought back to the House. Eventually, the minister wrote to advise the NSTC's acting president that 'it has been decided not to proceed with the Dal-Tech merger at this time' (MacAskill, 1976). The 1970s drive for amalgamation was over. There was deep disappointment at Dalhousie and, especially, at NSTC.

The two institutions went their separate ways. The associated university system continued. In 1980, Tech was renamed the Technical University of Nova Scotia.

Campus Relocation Revisited

The next attempt at Dal/Tech rapprochement came in the late 1980s. Compared to the previous effort, it was a flash in the pan.

On 1 December 1989 the presidents of Dalhousie and TUNS announced a study of the feasibility of relocating TUNS next to Dalhousie. The existing TUNS campus would be sold, and land adjacent to Dalhousie would be redeveloped into a new campus at an estimated cost of $150 million. It was anticipated that the two schools would achieve savings by sharing a heating plant as well as library, computing, and recreational facilities. The stimulus to education and research was expected to be great.

The first sign that the project was in difficulty came even before it was announced, when the presidents were advised half an hour before the initial press conference that the premier would not, after all, be attending. Things went downhill from there. Within days of the announcement, the Member of the Legislative Assembly for the area – who was also chairman of the province's Management Board – told the *Halifax Chronicle-Herald/Mail-Star* that the project did not have his support or that of the provincial government ('Halifax city council opposes ...,' 7 December 1989). Furthermore, Dalhousie's neighbours were outraged. Ward 2 Alderman Walter Fitzgerald exclaimed at a meeting of city council, 'Why not drop an atom bomb on the neighbourhood?!' The council passed a motion opposing the feasibility study. Only one alderman voted against it. Finally, a mere nine days after the initial announcement, TUNS announced that the universities would not proceed with the study.

The Attempt to Rationalize in the 1990s

The Nova Scotia Council on Higher Education and System-Wide Reviews

Unhappy with the advice of the Maritime Provinces Higher Education Commission, the Nova Scotia government established the Nova Scotia Council on Higher Education in 1989. In 1992 it gave the council the authority to allocate funding to the universities and appointed Janet Halliwell, former Chairman of the Science Council of Canada, as its chair. Her mission was to lead the process of rationalizing Nova Scotia's universities.

The challenge was outlined in a discussion paper issued by the council:

With economic recession and competing demands on limited public funding, our university system faces a steady state fiscal situation, at best ... [This], at a time when student numbers continue to increase ..., the costs of research are rising, the physical infrastructure established during the expansionary period of the 1960s is eroding, the costs of library acquisitions are increasing well in excess of inflation, equipment in undergraduate laboratories is outdated and out of touch with the realities of the workplace and there are increasing demands for more outreach to the private sector and increased expectations of accountability.

As a result, our university system, even with its rich heritage and pride in higher education, scholarship and research, is growing increasingly fragile ... The special characteristics of a Nova Scotia system – 13 degree-granting institutions, many of which are small or specialized in focus – are being challenged publicly as inefficient, wasteful and duplicative of effort. There is a new sense of urgency in calls for increased efficiency and effectiveness of our universities, calls for the system to do more and better with less ...

Rationalization/revitalization focuses on structuring and equipping the university system to meet the challenges of tomorrow, strengthening quality and the underlying capacity of the system to adapt and evolve as a vital and innovative instrument of society while retaining its essential intellectual character, all within the steady state budgetary conditions. (NSCHE, 1992, 2)

One of the tools for rationalizing the system was to be 'system-wide reviews' of programs replicated at various Nova Scotia universities. Education, Engineering, Computer Science, Business, and Earth and Environmental Sciences were identified as priorities for review. The reviews would be conducted by panels of experts from outside the province.

By this time, Nova Scotia's universities were experiencing relentless budget cuts. They feared that the worst was yet to come. Dalhousie's administration, having made an unsuccessful attempt at cutting programs, feared that its resources would soon be inadequate to sustain its programs at reasonable levels of quality. Rationalization – on the advice of independent expert consultants – appeared to offer a solution. Dalhousie was for it.

The first system-wide review – that of Education – recommended that teacher education programs in Nova Scotia be consolidated. The government passed legislation in 1994 to close the Education programs at Dalhousie and St Mary's in Halifax and at the Nova Scotia Teachers' College in Truro. Mount Saint Vincent University in Halifax assumed responsibility for teaching and research in Education.

The outcome of the second review (of Engineering) was less dramatic – it recommended continuing the Associated University system. Even so, Dalhousie was on its guard. It appeared to people at that university that a pattern was beginning to emerge – 'rationalization' of duplicated programs meant removing them from Dalhousie in favour of the other institutions at which they were offered. After all, Dalhousie was big and had lots of programs. What would the loss of a few programs matter to it?

Computer Science in Nova Scotia

The review committee for Computer Science established in 1993 studied programs at Dalhousie, TUNS, St Francis Xavier, Acadia, Mount Saint Vincent, and the University College of Cape Breton. Three of these schools (Acadia, Dalhousie, TUNS) offered degrees in the field. Saint Mary's University refused to participate. The committee described Dalhousie's program as follows:

> At Dalhousie, computer science remains a group within a Division of Mathematics, Statistics and Computer Science. Moreover, there are only eight faculty members in computer science, and we consider that some of them are natural scientists or mathematicians of one stripe or another, not computer scientists.
>
> Most importantly, the university's commitment to develop computer science, as measured by dollars, is entirely inadequate. The unit's operating budget was described to us as being about $600,000 per annum – a fraction of the minimum amount which would permit a respectable effort.

Although the senior administration stated repeatedly during our visit that they considered their computer science unit to be essential to the university's mission, and spoke of the important interdisciplinary ties which can exist between computer science, the sciences, psychology, neurosciences, etc., this warm verbal support has not been translated into either organizational clout or even minimally adequate dollars. (NSCHE, 1994, 24)

Computer Science at TUNS was described thus:

Computer science teaching and research began [at TUNS] in 1983. Unfortunately, TUNS has not yet achieved real distinction in computer science. The department is too small to achieve critical masses in research and the quality of faculty is uneven. Morale is not good and there are serious problems with interpersonal relations ... The computer science department is not a department in the Faculty of Engineering at TUNS, nor is it located on the main campus. Instead, it is an autonomous School, physically and organizationally isolated from the Faculty of Engineering, and the TUNS Computer Science department must therefore battle the Faculty of Engineering for scarce resources. There seem to be few of the mutually beneficial links which a computer science department should have with a modern Engineering Faculty. (NSCHE, 1994, 25)

The review committee recommended that Dalhousie be stripped of its degree programs and that only Acadia and TUNS be authorized to offer bachelor's degrees. Graduate education, research, and technology transfer would be carried out through a new Joseph Howe Institute for Computer Science, in which universities across the province might participate. Dalhousie went ballistic. The Halifax *Daily News* reported:

Infuriated, Dalhousie University president Howard Clark is calling for an end to the rationalization process under the guidance of Janet Halliwell, chairwoman of the council.
'Dalhousie will not, in the absence of any plan or strategic thinking, agree to give up programs vital to the academic and financial health of this province's major university,' he said in a release. 'Dalhousie calls on the government of Nova Scotia to demand that the council produce a strategic plan for the provincial university system which can be debated publicly. If the council cannot or will not produce such a plan, it should be disbanded.' ('A Smart Bomb,' 13 July 1994, 5)

Halliwell acknowledged that the rationalization process had hit a rough patch. 'We came into the process with a very good buy-in [by the universities], but we're seeing fragmentation of that now,' she said at a news conference ('Nova Scotia higher education ...,' 11 July 1994).

In its response to the review committee's report, Dalhousie pointed out that

the Review Committee's recommendations would involve:

• a major new expenditure commitment for the province; and
• the establishment of a fourteenth institution of higher education in an already complex, fragmented provincial university system ...

[The provincial government] has projected reductions in expenditures [on universities] of 12.8% ($26.6 million) over 4 years. The universities have been advised that actual reductions for 1995–96 may exceed these projections. The current rationalization process was initiated in order to strengthen the university system within this financial context ... The recommendation to commit additional funding of $2 million per year to a Joseph Howe Institute of Computer Science is inconsistent with the purpose of the rationalization process and with the financial challenges facing the province and the system. (Dalhousie University, 1995, 1)

Dalhousie instead proposed that a consolidated school of computer science be established in Metro Halifax, that would bring together faculty from Dalhousie, Saint Mary's, Mount Saint Vincent, and TUNS.

Meanwhile, TUNS applauded the review committee's report and lobbied for the proposed institute and for the two million dollars that had been earmarked for it. In 1993, the director of its School of Computer Science and its industrial Advisory Board had prepared a plan titled 'Creating a World-Class School of Computer Science at TUNS.' Action on the review committee's recommendations – with a few appropriate modifications – might enable the School of Computer Science to fulfil this plan.

TUNS regarded as both dangerous and ridiculous Dalhousie's suggestion that consolidation of existing resources could obviate the need for an infusion of new funds. It refused to have anything to do with the idea of a consolidated school.

Rationalization Unglued

Meanwhile, the so-called rationalization process was spinning out of control. Early in 1995 the NSCHE held a public forum on higher education, as well as hearings on campuses across the province. Dalhousie proposed that the universities in Halifax be consolidated, along with the Nova Scotia Agricultural College, in order to achieve critical mass in education and research, as well as administrative savings. In support of its proposal, it released a study by Ernst & Young which showed that consolidation of the metro universities would achieve annual savings in the order of $10 million in administrative costs alone. TUNS advocated federation. Other Halifax universities countered with a proposal for 'partnership'. The *Halifax Chronicle-Herald* editorialized:

> For a decade now, Nova Scotia's university presidents have had a mandate to rationalize programs, control costs, and collectively prepare their institutions for the next century.
>
> And, for the most part, they've failed.
>
> Neither a royal commission, nor the 'get-your-acts-together' threat of two governments, nor a worsening financial crunch has convinced the universities to take action ...
>
> Dalhousie has given some legitimacy to its proposal for a merged University of Halifax by working to cut some programs and get its financial house in order over the past two years. Dal's view seems to be that big savings – $9 million in administrative costs alone – can be realized in amalgamation.
>
> This seems like an idea worth talking about, unless you happen to be one of the city's smaller universities. One major, and legitimate, fear among smaller universities is loss of identity. They are also worried about getting saddled with some of Dal's outstanding debt of $22 million or so.
>
> Still, Dal's proposal is surely worth discussing. It could lead to elimination of redundancies and to the creation of first-rate joint faculties. It could, in short, actually be of benefit to those consumers known as students.
>
> What Dal got instead was a more or less summary rejection from other institutions, four of which came up with a counter option last week.
>
> Saint Mary's, Mount Saint Vincent, the Atlantic School of Theology, and the Nova Scotia College of Art and Design want more collaborative efforts. The fearless four estimate they could collectively save $4 million through bold joint efforts on course scheduling, applications, registration, academic programming, food services, marketing of university facilities and services, and career counselling.
>
> To many Nova Scotians, such proposals seem to have been around since shortly after humankind discovered it was possible to build a fire by rubbing two sticks together. ('Power to the Students,' 22 February 1995).

Relations among the Halifax university presidents were barely civil. Concerned that the situation had gotten so far out of hand that the government might, as promised, 'do something,' the chairman of Dalhousie's board, with Howard Clark's foreknowledge, invited his Halifax counterparts to a meeting. They acknowledged that the universities' infighting was damaging and fraught with risk. They discussed how their institutions' differences might be overcome. They agreed that it would be useful to meet again. These meetings continued. On one occasion, the board members were joined by the minister; on another, by Halliwell. After a couple of months, the presidents joined the discussions.

Into this picture came a fresh, young face, Dalhousie president-elect Tom Traves. The other presidents found him flexible and easy to deal with, unlike his predecessor. Under his leadership, Dalhousie decided to give partnership a try. Dalhousie's apparent conversion was a great surprise to the other Halifax universities – and initially a little unnerving. The newfound partners began work on a joint plan for meeting anticipated funding reductions with savings to be achieved through collaboration. The plan envisioned the establishment of a Metro University Consortium. In return for their commitment to implement the plan, the universities sought a guarantee from the government that their funding would not be reduced by more than 12 per cent over three years.

Dal/TUNS Amalgamation

Getting to 'Yes'

The government – by now circumventing the Council and dealing directly with the universities – liked the Consortium plan. But from its perspective, the Consortium was not enough. For one thing, it didn't address the perceived duplication of Business Education programs at Dalhousie and Saint Mary's. Also, it didn't resolve the Computer Science issue. The government was convinced of the vital importance of information technology for Nova Scotia's development and, hence, of the need for a strong school of Computer Science in Halifax. The creation of yet another institution of higher education (the proposed Joseph Howe Institute) was clearly not the way to go. Government officials sounded TUNS out on the joint school proposal, but TUNS remained opposed.

In the meantime, the NSCHE issued a report, 'Shared Responsibilities in Higher Education.' It observed:

Recent reviews in Engineering and Computer Science commissioned by Council have identified serious problems with the *status quo* [i.e., the existing relationship between Dalhousie and TUNS] in terms of effectiveness and cost-efficiency.

The Engineering review identified the need for more access by engineering students to advanced non-technical courses in business, the humanities, social sciences, etc ...

Despite the controversy surrounding some of the recommendations of the report from the external review team, the review of Computer Science identified the central importance of getting more for our current investment ... Computer Science is an expensive, but key, discipline for the health of educational and research activities at both Dalhousie and TUNS and for the Nova Scotia economy ...

Students and the relevant industry sector are not well served by the fragmentation of Computer Science education and research between Dalhousie and TUNS and the lack of critical mass at either site ...

A strong research and research training environment requires the establishment and maintenance of the infrastructure essential to a research capacity ... Additionally, the policy infrastructure for this activity, e.g., graduate education policies, procedures for animal experimentation ... is expensive and specialized. These physical and policy infrastructures should not be duplicated.

With a larger taxation base, continued separation of Dalhousie and TUNS might well be viable, even desirable, to obtain the full benefits of a polytechnical institution in metro. However, Council judges that this would not be feasible or sustainable.

Recommendation: That there be a commitment by universities and government to effect a functional, if not structural, consolidation of Dalhousie and TUNS with a view to creating a coherent research-intensive nexus that can better underpin the diverse needs of the growing knowledge infrastructure in Nova Scotia. (NSCHE, 1995, 45)

TUNS's response was that it wasn't interested in any form of consolidation with Dalhousie. To be part of a larger consortium or federation was one thing; to amalgamate with Dalhousie was quite another.

In February 1996 the Halifax university presidents met with the education minister, John MacEachern, and his staff to discuss their Consortium proposal. He advised them that he would consult his colleagues in Cabinet concerning the Consortium proposal and the NSCHE's recommendations and would advise them of Cabinet's views. Shortly thereafter, he reported back that the Cabinet saw the Consortium plan as a worthy initiative that should proceed.

With respect to the Dalhousie – TUNS 'nexus,' the Cabinet accepted the NSCHE's reasoning and supported its recommendation. Amalgamation was seen as a means of enhancing efficiency, improving academic interconnections, developing critical mass, and stimulating research capacity. MacEachern and his Cabinet colleagues did not see how these objectives could be met except through an amalgamation of Dalhousie and TUNS. Amalgamation was also seen as an effective way to develop Computer Science programming in accordance with the objectives set out in the review committee report. There was great concern about the future of Computer Science in Nova Scotia.

Little of these discussions had been public, but a reporter got wind that a Dal/TUNS merger was on once again and began calling people at TUNS for reaction. TUNS president Edward Rhodes quickly issued a bulletin to his faculty, students and staff: 'It is apparent that the media and in particular ATV are attempting to prepare a feature on the possibility of a TUNS/DAL merger as a result of the ongoing rationalization process. Because of this, I wish to further inform the University community of the current status of the rationalization discussions.' He described the current status of the Consortium plan and quoted at length from a letter from the Minister of Education that conveyed to the university presidents the Cabinet's response to the plan and to the NSCHE's report. He continued: 'As can be seen from the above [quotation], the question of a TUNS/DAL consolidation is still considered to be an option by the Government ... In ongoing discussions with both Government and sister universities, TUNS is continuing to pursue the concept of the Metro Consortium and at the same time attempting to ascertain what advantages and disadvantages the Cabinet-desired TUNS/DAL consolidation could have for advanced technical education in Nova Scotia' (Rhodes, 1996).

By this time it was crystal clear to the leadership of TUNS that the provincial government was not going to provide the additional funding the university needed to realize its aspirations in Computer Science. And more deep cuts were coming. Rhodes and the board chairman, Andrew Eisenhauer, did not believe that TUNS's academic programs could withstand further cuts. In their view, it was not a question of institutional survival: TUNS could certainly survive additional cuts. Rather, it was a question of academic quality. Any further cutbacks would prevent TUNS from offering sound education and rob it of its capacity for innovation. Whether or not Rhodes and Eisenhauer were aware of it, some employers already felt that quality had declined to unacceptable levels. According to the NSCHE's then-chair, the NSCHE had received some complaints from the private sector about the poor quality of TUNS's engineering graduates.

The government wanted a merger. If TUNS did not amalgamate voluntarily with Dalhousie, it might be forced to do so. Conversely, if TUNS agreed to merge, it might secure a commitment to additional funding in return. By relying on Dalhousie's administrative services, TUNS could also save money on administration and put it into academic pursuits.

Rhodes and Eisenhauer decided that TUNS should seize the initiative and seek to negotiate amalgamation on its own terms. Rhodes proposed to Tom Traves that the universities consider amalgamating. The two presidents began to draft the terms of an agreement. The provincial government was delighted. It wanted badly to bring the acrimonious rationalization process to an end and, on the eve of a new legislative session, to announce some good news. The premier and the minister were ready to announce approval of the Consortium plan and a number of other post-secondary initiatives. They wanted to do so before the House reconvened. A press conference was scheduled for 4 April. Would a Dal/TUNS agreement be ready in time to be included in the announcement? It was dicey. The government was keen to include a Dal/TUNS merger in the announcement and might therefore be presumed to be generous. On the other hand, it would be impossible to negotiate and sign an agreement between the universities and the government in a matter of weeks.

Rhodes and Traves sought and obtained approval from their respective senates and boards for amalgamation in accordance with a set of terms. The order in which the terms were presented and their wording differed slightly between the two institutions. For example, the first item in the list presented to the Dalhousie Senate was: '1. The amalgamated University will be known as Dalhousie University. All assets and liabilities of Dalhousie and TUNS will become the property of the amalgamated university.' Yet the list of terms that Rhodes presented to his senate and board was as follows:

1. The Government declares a strategic policy that advanced technical education and research as well as a strong college/institute of applied science and technology (TUNS) are fundamental cornerstones of the economy of Nova Scotia.

2. TUNS is amalgamated with Dalhousie as a constituent college/institute of Dalhousie. An appropriate name for TUNS will be sought.
3. TUNS will contain the professionally accredited Faculties of Architecture, Computer Science and Engineering.
4. Academic and administrative structures will be reorganized.
5. Current collective agreements at both institutions will be honoured until such a time as new ones are negotiated.
6. The target date for amalgamation is March 31, 1997, or as soon thereafter as possible.
7. TUNS will have a 'Principal' who is also a Vice-President of Dalhousie.
8. In order to enable the realization of the above-stated public policy, over a period of three years TUNS will be allocated a total of $3.0 million of additional funds, and in addition, the use of the monies allocated for off-campus space. The academic operating budgets of TUNS will, at steady state, be increased by $2.4 million.
9. A research contract between TUNS and the Government for support of cooperative research with industry is confirmed. The total value of the contract over three years is $2.8 million.
10. TUNS in collaboration with Dalhousie, UCCB and the Agricultural College will receive $130,000 per annum support for the new technology transfer centre named UTECH Inc.
11. Transition costs will be provided by the Government in the same way that the so-called Halifax Universities Consortium is dealt with.
12. After amalgamation, TUNS will have a small Board which is a sub-committee of the Dalhousie Board. Five members of TUNS Board will be made members of the Dalhousie Board.
13. Current students will complete their programs in the existing universities.
14. Academic and administrative support staffs in Engineering and Computer Science at the two institutions will come together in the new Faculties at TUNS.
15. Relationships with the other Associated Universities will continue unhindered by the amalgamation.
16. TUNS will have an Academic Council which will include a number of TUNS academic members who will be eligible to sit on the representative, expanded Dalhousie Senate.
17. TUNS will become active in an expanded Dalhousie Capital Campaign.
18. The Government will assign the Halifax Infirmary and adjacent lands free of physical or other encumbrance to the amalgamated institution for the purposes of redevelopment.
19. All parties agree to best efforts.

TUNS's senate met on 1 April 1996 to consider a motion to recommend amalgamation with Dalhousie on the above terms. Few of the senators were enthusiastic about it, but they saw their president's logic. They knew all too well how poorly resourced their programs were and what impact additional cuts in academic budgets would have. Some perceived that the growth of TUNS's administration had gotten out of hand and that amalgamation would enable them to use monies spent on administration for better purposes. Though no one was wild about the prospect of being part of Dalhousie, they would do it if it meant additional funding – especially if, as foreseen, TUNS would continue to exist as a college within Dal. By a wide margin, the TUNS senators approved the motion to amalgamate. The board members did likewise later in the afternoon.

On the whole, TUNS's computer scientists were less sanguine than the engineers and the architects. They had been pitted against their Dalhousie counterparts in the system-wide review process, and the outcome of that process had in their view confirmed the superiority of Computer Science at TUNS. Many professors felt that they had little to gain from merger with Dalhousie. As one of them observed, '[to us] it was kind of a joke that you'd have a computer science department as a sub-sub-unit of Mathematics and Statistics.' They regarded the perspective of their engineering colleagues on amalgamation as simplistic: 'They had a typical engineers' logical constructivist way of looking at the issue: 1) we need resources + 2) amalgamation will bring resources = 3) let's amalgamate.' But there were many more engineers and architects at TUNS than computer scientists, so the feelings of the latter did not prevail.

The Announcement

On 4 April 1996, the premier and the education minister announced 'a plan for university renewal that builds on the individual strengths of Nova Scotia's universities, builds a better future for students, and will propel the province and the economy into the 21st century' (NS Department of Education and Culture, 1996, 1). The press release endorsed the Metro University Consortium:

> Government also stated, as a matter of strategic public policy, [that] advanced technical education and research and a strong institute of applied science and technology are fundamental cornerstones of the economy and future of Nova Scotia. Therefore, TUNS, Dalhousie and the government

agree the public benefit in this regard can be advanced by an amalgamation of the two universities, with TUNS becoming a constituent part of Dalhousie. TUNS will have a new Faculty of Computer Science, an amalgamated Faculty of Engineering and a Faculty of Architecture.

The province will provide $3 million in new funding over three years to support these priority initiatives. Additionally, the government has agreed to transfer to TUNS the $1 million currently spent by government to lease off-campus space [for TUNS]. By this means, TUNS intends to redirect more than $400,000 per year into academic programs (Department of Education and Culture, 1996, 1).

Also included in the announcement was a new doctoral program in Business at Saint Mary's University and $1 million in capital funding for its new Commerce building; $ 1 million each for Acadia University and the University College of Cape Breton; and $250,000 for St Francis Xavier University.

The Amalgamation Agreement

Rhodes and Traves expected the tripartite agreement drafted prior to the announcement to be finalized in a matter of weeks. In the event, once the announcement had been made, it proved to be difficult to get the government's attention. Weeks, then, months, passed. Drafts went back and forth between the presidents and the minister's office. Changes crept in. There was a Cabinet shuffle. A new education minister was appointed. The loss of momentum was such that it began to appear that the process might unravel.

It was July before the government returned to the matter of amalgamation. When it did so, its lawyers unwittingly made a number of changes that were unacceptable to the presidents. Finally, on 10 July, the new minister, Robbie Harrison, sat down with the presidents, the deputy minister, government lawyers, and other officials and hammered out a final version. It was signed by the presidents that day and by the premier and the minister following a Cabinet meeting the next morning. (The text of the amalgamation agreement is reproduced as Appendix 1.)

The Merging Institutions

In 1996, Dalhousie had approximately 11,000 students in the following faculties: Arts and Social Science, Science, Management, Law, Health Professions, Dentistry, Medicine, and Graduate Studies. Henson College of Public Affairs and Continuing Education provided a wide range of continuing professional education and outreach programs. External funding for research and international activity at Dalhousie was approximately $37 million annually.

The university employed approximately 990 full-time faculty (including clinical faculty and librarians); 800 part-time faculty and teaching assistants; 380 grant-paid staff; 960 unionized staff; and 278 administrative staff and managers. There were six bargaining units (faculty, part-time faculty and teaching assistants, clerical and technical staff, trades, custodial staff, and security staff). The annual operating budget was approximately $145 million. As of the same year, Dalhousie had had a succession of balanced budgets and had reduced its accumulated deficit and debt to approximately $10 million from a peak of almost $40 million in 1982–83. The value of its endowments was approximately $180 million.

TUNS had approximately 1,450 students, 93 full-time faculty, 60 part-time faculty, 45 grant-paid staff, 150 full-time unionized staff, and 30 administrative staff and managers. There were two bargaining units, one for full-time faculty and one for staff. External research and project funding amounted to approximately $5.5 million per year. There was a very active continuing education department. TUNS's operating budget was approximately $23 million. Its operating deficit was $1.9 million, and its long-term debt was approximately $550,000. The value of its endowments was almost $5 million.

The cultures of the universities were very different. Although small by national standards, Dalhousie had the more impersonal feel of a large institution. It comprised many diverse worlds. By and large, its faculty, students, and staff identified with their units rather than with the institution. They took pride in their university, but that sentiment was ordinarily far from the surface. TUNS, in contrast, had many of the cultural characteristics of a small college. There were strong institutional attachments and close personal ties. A 'no nonsense' engineering ethos dominated. The Faculty of Architecture's vibrant culture was by and large confined to its historic building. At Dalhousie, rules abounded and 'management rights' were few and far between. In contrast, at TUNS individuals in positions of authority enjoyed wide discretion. The relative lack of rules and procedures made possible swift administrative action, but also provided little recourse for those who didn't like it.

Many at TUNS had little time for the type of shenanigans that went on at Dal. An engineering student who had come to TUNS from Dalhousie mused in TUNS's student newspaper:

> The students at TUNS are dedicated to excellence and trying to find a meaningful career. Ours is a quiet, reserved school. We don't get tied up in the great debates about plastic versus paper bags at the grocery stores ... We won't scream too loud when they take their hatchets to our fine institution. You may wonder why I like many other Dalhousie graduates feel such trepidation about the merger. It is not the Engineering faculty at Dalhousie. They did a great job preparing us for TUNS. It is the atmosphere as a whole. The suffocating environment of special interest groups and cliques. And don't get me started on all the 'elite' yuppie and hippie wanna-bees. TUNS was a refreshing breath of fresh air. Students and staff in pursuit of academic excellence, developing practical solutions to real world problems. No special interest groups who think the world owes them something, no yuppie or hippie cliques, no. p.c. wanna-bees; just plain ordinary students who want to learn. ('From the mind of Abbi,' 1996, 3)

Many TUNS professors would no doubt have expressed much the same sentiment, albeit differently. Conversely, some students and faculty members at Dalhousie perceived TUNS as parochial.

The Transition

The amalgamation agreement called for the universities to merge on 1 April 1997. (That date was chosen so that TUNS could close its books at the end of its fiscal year, minimizing the complexity of accounting.) There was an immense amount to be done in eight-and-a-half months.

An Amalgamation Planning Committee (APC) was established consisting of the two presidents, the universities' vice-presidents and directors of public relations, TUNS's dean of engineering, and an executive coordinator of amalgamation. The executive coordinator, who was seconded from a position in the President's Office at Dalhousie, reported to both presidents and was responsible for assisting them in planning and managing the transition. A couple of subcommittees of the APC were established. The steering committees of the two Senates formed a joint committee to address Senate matters. The presidents had an initial meeting with union representatives. A vehicle for communicating with people on the two campuses was created. A search for a Dean of Computer Science was initiated. A committee was struck to recommend a name for the college that would succeed TUNS.

There was some initial confusion about roles. For example, Senate officials initially objected to the formation of an Academic Coordinating Committee, co-chaired by Dalhousie's academic vice-president and TUNS's dean of engineering, on the grounds that its role, relative to that of the joint Senate committee, was unclear. (The former was concerned mainly with academic administrative matters.)

Although all official communications conveyed forward momentum, at times during the summer and early fall of 1996 the two institutions' conceptions of what would flow from amalgamation were so far apart as to render the outcome doubtful. By and large, people at Dalhousie envisioned the college as more or less a grouping of faculties; people at TUNS expected continued autonomy. These differences in expectations played out in discussions between the universities' senates, faculty associations, student unions, and so on. In the first couple of months, few governance issues were settled.

The two presidents were at the centre of the process. On most issues, they themselves reached a preliminary agreement which they then proposed jointly to the appropriate university bodies. The manner in which the central issue of governance was resolved was typical. In October 1996, Traves drafted, and revised in collaboration with Rhodes, a statement concerning the role and responsibilities of the college board. After obtaining input from the APC, he presented the statement to a meeting of several senior board officials from each institution. With a few revisions, it was approved by the boards of both universities. This marked a watershed: it put to rest any doubt about whether amalgamation would happen, set a pattern for agreements at other levels, and led to a request for government legislation in November. The universities' lawyers prepared a proposal for legislation, on which there was consultation within the institutions. Bill 44 was introduced soon thereafter and passed on 13 December 1996. In contrast to events twenty-two years earlier, only the two universities' lawyers showed up to speak to the bill at the Law Amendments Committee.

In the meantime, the universities had announced in November which units of the two universities would merge and who would head them. Those selected to head merged administrative units were assigned to develop organizational plans. The future relationships of two units – Graduate Studies and Libraries – were controversial and were not resolved at this time.

Apart from Dalhousie's small Department of Engineering, which would disappear into TUNS's Faculty of Engineering, the academic units most affected by amalgamation were TUNS's School of Computer Science and Dalhousie's Division of Computing Science of the Faculty of Science. Many of TUNS's computer scientists had been opposed to amalgamation, but once it was clear that it was going to happen, the director of the school stepped aside and both units worked to implement it. Even before the amalgamation agreement was signed, the two groups of computer scientists elected a joint transition committee (JTC), composed of three faculty members and one student from each group, to negotiate with the administrations and to look after their mutual interests. As one computer scientist put it, 'While the administrations were still floundering, we got on with it.'

The presidents and vice-presidents had anticipated that the computer science units would remain separate for a year after amalgamation, until the new dean arrived, but the JTC made the case late in 1996 that the new faculty should come into being upon amalgamation and that its members should be in a single location by September 1997. The presidents accepted these arguments, Dalhousie's Senate approved the new faculty, and the JTC began planning for the Dalhousie people to move to the other campus and for the two faculties to begin functioning as one.

At the beginning of January 1997, the universities applied to the Nova Scotia Labour Relations Board for rationalization of the bargaining units. The universities proposed that the number of bargaining units be reduced from eight (six at Dalhousie and two at TUNS) to three (representing full-time faculty; part-time faculty and teaching assistants; and staff) after amalgamation. They agreed with the unions in March that there would be four. (Instead of one union for all staff, there would be one for clerical and technical staff and another for tradespeople.) This arrangement was approved by the Labour Relations Board in March, along with an agreement between the parties on bridging provisions. (The latter was necessary because existing collective agreements were to continue in force until 1 November 1997, due to provincial wage restraint legislation.)

Draft operational plans were approved in February, and in March staff were assigned to new or changed jobs, as applicable. There were only four staff layoffs.

By the beginning of 1997, agreement had been reached on the role of the College Academic Council *vis-à-vis* the three faculties and the University Senate, but the composition of the council had not been decided. This proved to be a thorny issue. The membership of the TUNS Senate consisted of all full professors, academic administrators *ex officio*, and several representatives of the students, the Associated Universities, and various professional bodies. The Senate's planning committee had originally been asked to propose a much smaller body. However, it proved to be difficult to reduce the size of the body while preserving an acceptable balance between *ex officio* and elected members. Deans and department heads were adamant that they should serve on the smaller council, but many senators argued that if they did so, it would be reduced to a 'management body'. No one wished to be disenfranchised. The Senate resolved in February that the council should include the members of the former Senate as well as all associate and assistant professors (for an estimated membership of approximately 130!). Then, in March, the Senate decided to leave well enough alone: the composition of the council would be the same as that of the TUNS Senate.

Meanwhile, the committee established to recommend a name for the college had sought and considered suggestions from students, faculty, staff, and alumni and made several recommendations to Dalhousie's president and to the executive committee of TUNS's board. A 'new name' was recommended to and approved by the two boards. The name – Dalhousie University Polytechnic – was unveiled by the lieutenant-governor at a ceremony on 6 March. In the face of vociferous complaints from the faculty, it was quietly withdrawn at the end of March. Pending review of the name question, the college was referred to by an informal name that had gained wide currency, DalTech.

It was agreed in February that the DalTech library would become part of the Dalhousie system. An agreement on graduate administration was reached at the eleventh hour. On 1 April 1997 – in the middle of an unseasonable snow storm – TUNS became part of Dalhousie.

Amalgamation: Why in 1997?

One cannot help but ask why this merger – long conceived of and often attempted – came to fruition when it did. Leadership was certainly a vital factor. Tom Traves, with his fresh, pragmatic approach, disarmed many who had been skeptical of Dalhousie, and he proved to be an astute and forceful negotiator. Ted Rhodes' genuine commitment to quality led him to take up the politically unpalatable challenge of negotiating amalgamation. Both presidents were relatively new to their offices and enjoyed the confidence of their universities' members. Their leadership in the amalgamation process was crucial. But both Dalhousie and NSTC had had willing and capable leaders in 1974, and internal support for merger had been present that year as well. And financial duress was hardly a new experience for either institution.

Some things *had* changed, however. One was the power of the Associated Universities within TUNS. They had proportionately fewer representatives on TUNS board and senate in 1996 than they had had at NSTC in the mid-1970s. Arguably, this made it easier to obtain and sustain internal approval to proceed with merger. Another difference was in the attitude of alumni. The intense partisanship that Tech alumni had exhibited in the 1970s had dimmed by the mid-1990s.

Even more significant was the change in the attitude of the provincial government. Premier Stanfield had been reluctant to 'push people around' in the late 1960s, and the Regan government had been willing to bend in the face of opposition in the 1970s; in contrast, the government of Premier John Savage had strong public policy reasons for wanting amalgamation to happen. On a less elevated plane, it needed something to show for all the turmoil of university rationalization. The Metro Consortium was something, but it was something pretty amorphous. Dal/TUNS amalgamation had more substance. It was more likely to convince people that something had been achieved.

Finally, the Savage government had become more or less inured to protests. In its efforts to get the province's expenditures back under control, it had closed and merged hospitals, merged municipalities, and cut budgets left and right. It was not easily dissuaded. Nor were other Nova Scotia universities disposed to make a fuss. They too knew that something had to come from rationalization. If TUNS took the hit, so much the better. Furthermore, weren't the metro universities all partners now? The Consortium was the key to securing a three-year funding commitment from the government and to getting the council off their backs. They couldn't very well undermine it by objecting too loudly to the merger of TUNS with Dal.

Quiet objections there no doubt were. Historic patterns of behaviour rarely change overnight. But Nova Scotia's universities had learned from the rationalization process the danger of allowing themselves to be pitted against one another. Furthermore, there was a *quid pro quo* for silence in the face of the Dal/TUNS merger. Though (as one newspaper headline declared) 'Dal absorb[ed] TUNS,' Saint Mary's University got its long-desired PhD in Business (in complete circumvention of the procedures of the NSCHE and its Maritime counterpart), Acadia and the University College of Cape Breton each got $1 million, and St Francis Xavier got

$250,000. The provincial government's April 1996 plan for university renewal contained something for almost everyone.

By 1996, changes in the dynamics of the university system, the structure of TUNS, and the circumstances and attitudes of government had enabled the right leaders to bring a venerable idea to pass.

FOUR

The Merger of the Ontario Institute for Studies in Education and the University of Toronto

Students at G.S.E.'s [graduate schools of education] are unlike those of any other graduate school. On many campuses, the feeling I detected outside the G.S.E. is that some odd animals (not necessarily dangerous or offensive) were being let into the zoo.

Judge, 1982, 37

The school of education has always had to fight for its rightful share of the fiscal pie and it has often been treated as a pariah among the other, more prestigious faculties.

Morris, 1985, 61

The stories of the Ontario Institute for Studies in Education (OISE) and the Faculty of Education of the University of Toronto (FEUT) and their eventual integration and merger within the University of Toronto highlight the problematic status of faculties of education in the academy. The merger of OISE and the University of Toronto is also an illustration of what can happen when social forces collide with organizational design. As with Dalhousie and the Technical University of Nova Scotia, the forces that eventually led to merger had deep roots.

Teacher Training and Educational Research in Ontario, 1900–1965

In the 1800s, preparation for elementary school teaching in Canada was provided by 'normal schools.' Toward the end of the century, universities, particularly in Ontario, began to contribute to the preparation of secondary school teachers (Harris, 1976, 179). In 1907, faculties of education were established at the University of Toronto and at Queen's University in Kingston. In 1920 the Queen's program was discontinued and the University of Toronto's faculty became the Ontario College of Education (OCE). The latter was affiliated with the University of Toronto and had a very close relationship with the provincial Department of Education, which provided its budget and appointed its dean (Academic Integration Task Force, 1995). For the next forty-five years, all prospective Ontario high school teachers studied at the OCE. Elementary schoolteachers were still trained at normal schools, which were renamed 'teachers' colleges' in the early 1950s (Harris, 1976, 545).

By the end of the 1920s, educational testing was common in the United States. American tests began to attract the interest of Canadian educators, who soon sought their own Canadian tests. In 1931, with the assistance of a grant from the Carnegie Corporation, OCE established the Department of Educational Research (DER), which was the taproot in the evolution of OISE. Despite its official name, the department's main role was test development (Fleming, 1972).

After the Second World War, the DER became *de facto* the provincial Department of Education's educational research bureau. In return for regular government grants, the expanding DER not only conducted studies for the Department of Education, but also assisted in the administration of grade 12 tests and in the development of formulae for allocating funds to school boards. It had closer relations with the Department of Education than with the rest of the OCE. There was a gulf between educational research and teacher preparation (Fleming, 236). This legacy would continue until 1996, when OISE and the Faculty of Education were integrated as part of the merger of OISE and the University of Toronto.

The Boom Years

The Davis Reforms

In the postwar period, educational systems expanded at a phenomenal rate everywhere in Canada. Nowhere was the growth more rapid than in Ontario, where a high birth rate, coupled with strong in-migration and rising participation rates, drove tremendous expansion at the elementary, secondary, and post-secondary levels. William Davis, who became Ontario's Minister of Education in 1962 (and later its premier), oversaw much of that growth. He initiated major reforms: colleges of applied arts and technology were established; the Department of Education was restructured; small school boards were amalgamated; curricula were reformed; and responsibility for teacher education was transferred to the universities (Fleming, 1972).

Growth and reform were inspired not only by need to accommodate larger numbers of students, but also by the conviction that education is fundamental to social well-being, industrial and technological development, and economic prosperity. The public expectations that surrounded the birth of OISE were thus similar to those which attended the establishment of Nova Scotia Technical College (NSTC) decades earlier. In a speech to the legislature, Davis described the changed role of education in society:

> Until relatively recently ... education beyond elementary school was thought to be necessary for only a few rather than for everyone ... In such an environment the students tended to be assessed on their ability to conform to the existing program with little regard for its relevance to their needs. There have been two developments which have radically changed this conception of education. The first was the unprecedented development of the economy which has continued for over twenty years. With full employment and the increasing technical complexity of the world, it became evident that education had to fill a much larger role in enabling all citizens to realize their full potential ... The second important development was the realization that if indeed all citizens must be highly educated it was no longer possible to have only one type of education program. (Ontario Legislature, 1967, 3527–8).

The government's plans for education thus went beyond finding ways and means to accommodate growth. They came to include broad educational reforms and an implicit belief in education as a means of enabling Ontarians to realize their individual, social, and economic potential. As an almost immediate consequence, Davis, as the minister responsible, sought a critical mass of highly qualified researchers skilled in educational development who would focus on the needs of the province's schools. According to Fleming:

> The minister was actually attracted to [the] possibility [of] the establishment of an independent research and development agency, unattached to any university, and with no responsibility for a program of graduate studies. Presumably it would have been operated in close association with the Department of Education but, in controlling its own program, would have been able to demonstrate more initiative and vitality than a departmental [research] branch. Davis was persuaded by his advisers that active participation

in a program of graduate studies would not only be an important contribution in itself, but would also constitute a major source of strength for the
research program. (1972, 239)

The concept of OISE was born.

The Establishment of OISE

The bill to establish OISE was introduced on 6 May 1965. It described the
functions of the institute as follows:

1. to study matters and problems relating to or affecting education, and to
   disseminate the results of and assist in the implementation of the findings of
   educational studies;
2. to establish and conduct courses leading to certificates of standing and graduate degrees in education.

Bill 127 also made OCE's Department of Educational Research part of
the institute. It was especially significant, both then and later, that the bill
did not bestow degree-granting power on the institute; instead it authorized the board, 'with the approval of the Minister, [to] enter into agreements of affiliation with one or more universities relating to the
establishment and conduct of programs leading to degrees in education.' In
response to a comment from a member of the opposition, Davis indicated
that the institute's degrees would initially be granted by the University of
Toronto (Ontario Legislative Assembly, 1965, 2953). It is important to
understand two things about this arrangement. First, it was not an oversight; rather, it was the deliberate intention of the government. Second, it
was a fundamental anomaly that from the start marginalized OISE.

Another noteworthy feature of the bill was that it gave greater authority
to the institute's director and board of governors, relative to its academic
bodies, than is usual in academic settings. It put 'the affairs of the Institute ... under the management and control of' the board and provided that
'the Board shall establish an academic council composed of any class of
instructional staff and officers of the Institute with such powers and duties
as may be prescribed by by-law of the Board' (Ontario Legislative Assembly, 1965, 2878).

The first assistant director of OISE, W.G. Fleming, who by his own
account 'had the main responsibility for devising the structure of the
Ontario Institute for Studies in Education during 1964–65' (Fleming, 1972,

239), suggested later that this departure from academic tradition was no accident. It was an attempt to design an institution of higher education that would serve the needs of Ontario's education system, much as the Nova Scotia Technical College was established to serve the industrial and technical needs of that province.

Bora Laskin, the OISE board's first chairman, described the institute's mission in his foreword to its first annual report:

> The Institute is ... a public body, in the best sense of that overworked phrase, established deliberately by the government as part of its overall long-range policy to foster, particularly through its very substantial efforts in education at all levels of the school system, the social and economic growth and development of our province ... The government has brought into existence the instrument by which we may, through research and development, continuously and systematically evaluate and improve the education system of this province.' (OISE Annual Report, 1966, 5)

Fleming, in considering what design would best enable the institute to fulfil this mission, had observed:

> Research programs conducted by graduate faculties of education had not proved to be major sources of strength for public education systems anywhere in the world. Students had a way of demanding first priority in terms of staff time and effort ... The professor, who required a large amount of freedom for the adequate performance of his teaching duties, tended to engage in small, independent research studies as a sideline. Since there are innumerable ways of defining almost any problem in education, the results obtained by different individuals very seldom added up to anything important ...
>
> [A number of features of OISE's design were intended to overcome] these disadvantages ... 1/ Control of the institute was vested in a board of governors with wide representation from the university community, the Department of Education, the teacher training institutions, the Ontario Teachers' Federation, school trustees, and other groups, including members of the institute staff ... The board would have a strong influence in shaping the institute's program of research and development ... It would be in a position to assure itself that the OISE program was broadly acceptable to the educational community. For this purpose, it would have to have a decisive voice in the determination of priorities. 2/ The internal structure was supposed to be such that administrative power could be exerted to ensure that certain objectives could be achieved ... As the institute was first

set up, the director had the unrestricted right to recommend the employment of certain personnel for limited periods to perform specified functions. He was also in a position to secure the board's approval for the assignment of funds to meet defined obligations ... The division (later department) heads were also supposed to have sufficient authority to ensure that balanced programs were developed within their own spheres of operations. (Fleming, 1972, 239)

In the Ontario Legislature, the Leader of the Opposition expressed concern that authority was being concentrated in the hands of the director, the board, and ultimately the minister. Robert Nixon told the House that 'this new institute will be very much under the control of the Minister ... entirely the hon. Minister's baby' (Ontario Legislative Assembly, 1965, 2876). These concerns were, however, outweighed by recognition of the need to strengthen the province's educational research capacity. The bill to establish OISE was passed with the support of all parties.

R.W.B. Jackson, former director of OCE's Department of Educational Research and a close adviser to the minister (Fleming, 1972), was appointed as OISE's first director. Like that of his counterpart at NSTC, Jackson's vision for his institution was one of service to the needs of his province. In one of the institute's early Annual Reports, he wrote:

The Institute is designed to recommend and help make changes in our schools so that what is taught and how teaching is carried out consistently reflect the most advanced thinking in education ...

The meaning of research and development as they apply to education may require some explanation. Perhaps the best way to illustrate them is to show how they work in a field where they have had a longer history and where their results are better known: ... agriculture. Research stations are set up where agricultural scientists bring together their knowledge and that of others, all derived from basic research in plant genetics, chemistry and other fields related to agriculture. This knowledge provides the basis for development of a design or product, such as a new variety of commercial crop. The product is then field-tested on experimental farms to determine how it will grow under a variety of soil conditions, fertilizers, climates and methods of cultivation. If the field tests are successful, district agricultural representatives encourage local farmers to demonstrate the product on their farms. The representatives then continue to offer advice on cultivation and harvesting of the new crop, and report on developments and improvements.

Research and development in education proceed in much the same way. (OISE Annual Report, 1967, 1)

By no means all of Jackson's colleagues at OISE understood their collective mission in this way – if indeed they acknowledged such a mission at all. Some would probably have regarded his choice of metaphor as at best unconventional, and at worst offensive.

OISE's Heyday

In a special 1995 issue of *OISE News*, Malcolm Levin, a member of OISE's faculty – and at the time also of its senior administration – described coming to the institute in 1968:

> I received a letter from a Professor T. B. Greenfield inviting me to OISE for an interview. I accepted the invitation and soon found myself standing in front of 102 Bloor Street West, wondering if I had the right address. It looked more like a new office building than a graduate institute of educational studies. Thinking that I was being interviewed for a faculty position in Curriculum, I was surprised to learn that T.B. Greenfield was the Chair of Educational Administration. As a former high school history teacher ... and curriculum developer/evaluator with no background or manifest interest in school system administration ... I wondered aloud why I was being interviewed for a position in Ed. Admin. We need someone to teach and co-ordinate our core course in Program Organization, I was told.
>
> After lunching in style at Le Provençal with a few interesting potential colleagues ... and learning that I would be expected to teach only one (full) course, would have access to as much secretarial and research assistance as I might need, and that my starting salary would be nearly equivalent to that of some of my Harvard professors, any qualms I may have had about moving with my family to Toronto evaporated ... I suspect that my introduction to OISE was not unique. (Levin, 1995)

Levin's was among a burst of new appointments. As he observed, 'The flood in 1970 of new (mostly) young academics who settled into OISE's custom-built new headquarters across the street from Varsity Stadium brought with them enough ideas and energy to launch several new research and development institutes' (1995). They had other ideas, too. Perhaps not surprisingly, given the prevailing social climate and the trend toward democratization of university affairs in the wake of Duff and Berdahl's Report on University Government in Canada (1996), the vision for the institute spelled out in the OISE Act was never actually followed. According to Fleming:

After little more than a year's operation, it became evident that a large proportion of the faculty were determined that the institute should develop into a kind of internal democracy ... Perhaps it was inevitable, in view of the rapid initial growth of the faculty, that a resolute stand was taken against 'status hierarchies' ... As time went on, there was at least superficial acceptance of the idea that all employees of the institute, regardless of training or function, had a right to a voice in the basic decisions of the organization. Thus in the fall of 1970 all students and employees, including research assistants, librarians, finance officers, and stenographers were assembled to discuss priorities among the institute's operations. (1972, 421)

In Levin's words: 'As a new institution, OISE had few traditions to draw upon so it created its own participatory one: every-one who wished to could participate in just about every committee or assembly' (1995). Administrative authority was so deeply circumscribed as to be almost non-existent. By Fleming's account:

The kind of participation that the faculty were determined to have meant going much further than the privilege of having representative faculty members advise the director or other administrative officials. It had to be established that the director, except in unusual circumstances, acted upon the advice of advisory bodies ... When [the director, R.W.B. Jackson] stepped out of line during the summer of 1968 by recommending the reactivation of the position of assistant director without full consultation with the Academic Council, there was such a storm of protest that this type of independent action on his part was never repeated ... Thus most of the powers he was entitled to exercise according to the act and regulations were soon in abeyance. (1972, 241)

The OISE environment was 'a climate of possibility with few constraints on individual choice' (Levin, 1995). In this climate, there was a profusion of academic offerings and research initiatives – of widely varying quality and relevance to education in Ontario.

This phenomenon – a lack of academic focus and integration – was by no means unique to OISE. As Harry Judge observed in his 1982 report to the Ford Foundation on American graduate schools of education, such schools tend to distance themselves from the low-status profession of teaching and attempt, usually unsuccessfully, to seek academic prestige by imitating the arts and sciences: 'They have, in intention but not always in performance, ceased to be professional schools without ever quite becoming anything else' (1982, 40). The result is that:

> It becomes difficult to link scholarship with a unifying set of concerns –
> something that simply is not true of any other professional school of any size
> or stature. [As Malcolm Levin's account of his appointment to OISE's fac-
> ulty attests], a clear priority is attached to winning for the GSE [graduate
> school of education] able scholars of established reputation or certain prom-
> ise, and questions about the nature of their interests or background experi-
> ence inevitably are of secondary importance. If GSE's are latitudinarian, they
> are also atomistic ... Those drawn in by a GSE are given – and have every
> right to expect – an unusual degree of freedom in defining their interests and
> developing their work. For a GSE under pressure or in decline, it is a short
> step to fall into intellectual anarchy. (1982, 48)

The Last Years of OCE

Its research and graduate education functions having been subsumed by
OISE in 1965, the Ontario College of Education in Toronto became the
College of Education of the University of Toronto. As part of the Davis
reforms, responsibility for preparing elementary school teachers was being
transferred from teachers' colleges to the province's universities (Academic Integration Task Force, 1995).

Teacher education faculties tended to be relegated to the lower ends of
the universities' political and fiscal priorities. Their low status arose in part
from the discrepancy between their members' credentials and those of
members of other university faculties (Awender, 1986).

Ironically, the establishment of OISE with a province-wide mandate for
graduate education and research exacerbated education faculties' difficulties in securing respect within universities. Walter Pitman, an opposition
MPP in the Ontario Legislature, who would later become OISE's director,
foresaw this and questioned the education minister about it:

> I think that the only way that education is going to receive proper status at
> any universities is if we can associate a degree of research. Now there is some
> feeling, I think, on the part of university people that with the establishment
> of the Ontario Institute for Studies in Education there might very well be an
> overabundance, an overemphasis, and perhaps an overconcentration of re-
> search in that institute, and that teacher education will then no longer be able
> to achieve status in the individual university ... I suggest ... the possibility of

setting up research and development centres in each of the universities. (Ontario Legislature, 1968, 4051)

The implication of Pitman's comments – that instead of raising the stature of programs in education, the existence of OISE was contributing to their decline – was not lost on Davis, who replied that 'it has been brought to my attention, I will put it this way, that several of the universities would like to get involved in educational research ... but I think it is a shade premature to be saying that every university that has a faculty of education or a teachers' college integrated into it will have a massive program of educational research thereto.' Thus, other university faculties of education came to envy OISE's near monopoly on doctoral education and on special provincial research funding in education (only one other Ontario university – the bilingual University of Ottawa – was authorized to offer a doctoral program). This coloured their reactions to later attempts to merge OISE with the Faculty of Education of the University of Toronto. There was a widespread sentiment that if OISE's mission and resources were 'up for grabs,' other universities' education faculties should be able to grab too.

Years of Retrenchment

The Faculty of Education of the University of Toronto

In 1972 the College of Education was renamed the Faculty of Education of the University of Toronto and became fully a part and responsibility of the University of Toronto. Compounding the difficulties arising from its low prestige among the university's faculties was the drop in the demand for teachers associated with the leveling off of growth in the province's school system. The mid-1970s marked the beginning of a long decline in the resources available to FEUT. In 1974, it had 132 full-time equivalent faculty members, including the teaching staff of the faculty's two schools. Fourteen years later, in 1988, its full-time equivalent faculty complement had dropped to under 100. Not one new tenure-stream faculty appointment was made during these years (Fullan, 1998).

The End of OISE's Golden Age

Malcolm Levin observed in the 1995 Commemorative Issue of *OISE News* that 'for most members of the OISE community who have lived through the recent years of stress and turmoil as OISE reluctantly adapts to the Nasty Nineties, [OISE's] early years are coloured with the rosy hues of a mythical golden age ... However, [the] honeymoon was rather short-lived.' By 1970 the institute was beginning to face trouble on a number of fronts, one of which was financial. .

In 1971, responsibility for OISE was transferred from the Minister of Education to the Minister of Colleges and Universities. Henceforth, OISE would be funded in the same way as the province's universities. The government also announced that the R&D grants it had previously made exclusively to OISE would be reduced by successive stages to 80, 60, and 40 per cent of the total provincial funds available for this purpose. However, the funds would continue to be provided by the Ministry of Education (Fleming, 1972).

At first, because the province's university system was being funded relatively generously, the switch to the higher education funding regime was not especially problematic for OISE. It did not occur either to OISE or to the government that the formulas and regulations by which universities were funded might not be appropriate and realistic for an institution like OISE, which was unique in terms of its organization and cost structures. Soon enough, problems arose.

By the mid-1970s the institute was beginning to suffer financial predicaments, including a series of operating deficits and the loss of 30 per cent of its support staff (OISE Board, 1976). These financial problems were arguably symptomatic of a much deeper problem – a mismatch between OISE's mission, as understood within the province's education system and legislature, its governance, culture, and demographics.

Levin suggests that 'as faculty and research staff pursued their own projects and interests with only partial regard for the agendas and policies of the Ministry of Education, influential people in government began to question the value of Bill Davis' investment.' One of those who questioned the investment was Stephen Lewis, leader of the province's New Democratic Party. In April 1971 he told the house:

OISE is not performing the function for which it was intended. That is the great pity about OISE. It has become a self-serving institution. It does not serve the people of the Province of Ontario ... It was designed largely to work through programs which would be appropriate for the Province of Ontario and the school system. But there is very little to show for the money which we have put into OISE – which now exceeds something like $100 million, Mr. Speaker, a very considerable investment ... There are legitimate post-graduate activities at OISE which should be sustained by members of this House. There are extraordinary problems which OISE could analyse. OISE should be doing work on the cost of extending aid to the separate school system to the end of grade 13. OISE should be analysing the saving that might be introduced if grade 13 were eliminated from the school system ... Instead, OISE is often fraught internally with irrelevant and fratricidal battles (Ontario Legislature, 1971, 316).

Levin confirms that 'while alliances shift[ed at OISE], internal struggles over resources and symbolic power [were] ubiquitous.'

Governance, culture, academic socialization, infighting, demographics (OISE was often criticized for having appointed too many American scholars) – all of these made it harder for OISE to meet the expectations placed on it (i.e., to be a teaching and research institution focused on Ontario's needs). OISE's remoteness from the education system it was established to serve, whether real or perceived, was not unique. Harry Judge contrasted Education to academic Medicine.

There is in medicine a subtle, complex relationship between practice, training and research. At the centre of this relationship lies the teaching hospital ... The work of training new doctors, the treatment of patients, the dissemination to the field of the results of research, the even more rapid incorporation in training procedures of the results of research, the generation of more research, the involvement in it of theoretical scientists who work in a spirit neither of arrogance nor of undue deference to immediate utility – to none of this can I find an analogy in education ...

Whenever I contemplate the working of G.S.E.'s [graduate schools of education] and, at a contrived distance from them, the rest of the educational world, I am afflicted by a curious sense of free-floating, of rootlessness, of the separation of what should properly be parts of a whole. (1982, 41)

That seems to have been the implicit view in Ontario as well. The province's Special Program Review Committee recommended in November 1975 that OISE's graduate programs be transferred to FEUT, and that its block grant for R&D be phased out over three years. (The block grant was officially called a 'transfer' grant and was in practical effect a means by which the Ministry of Colleges and Universities compensated OISE for the inadequacy of its formula-driven operating grants and fees.) Although lobbying against the adoption of this aspect of the Henderson Report was successful, the issues underlying the initiative were by no means put to rest. As Walter Pitman observed in 1994 in an opinion piece in the *Toronto Star*, 'in its relatively short history covering only a quarter of a century, [OISE would] face extinction three or four times' ('Meeting of Minds,' 1994).

The End of Affiliation?

By the late 1970s, OISE had recovered to some degree from its early problems and growing pains. After a series of constraint measures in the latter half of the decade, it was financially back in the black. Its relations with its stakeholders had improved as well. In 1979 the institute's second Director, Clifford Pitt, cited the following statement, by the Ontario Teachers' Federation to a committee of the provincial legislature, as evidence of support for OISE:

> The general feeling is that the research of the Institute has over the last several years been moving steadily in the direction of more practical help to the teachers of the province. In earlier years, there was a feeling ... that the Institute was insensitive to the practical needs of the educational system and teachers throughout the province ... However, from a practical point of view, it is felt that research should be as immediately applicable as possible. The Institute has moved dramatically in this direction in recent years. Such a move has been welcomed. (OISE, 1980, 8)

There was similar testimony from the Ontario Association of Education Administrative Officials: 'There has been a distinct trend [at OISE] away from esoteric research to study topics with high potential for application to current problems'; and from the Ontario School Trustees' Council: 'The Institute has become a valuable resource to the school boards of the province' (OISE, 1980, 9).

However, OISE's relationship with the University of Toronto continued to be difficult. Because it lacked independent authority to grant degrees, OISE was bound to the university. OISE functioned officially as the university's Graduate Department of Educational Theory; as such, it was required to abide by the rules and regulations of the university's School of Graduate Studies, as were all of the university's faculties, schools, and colleges. The arrangement was frustrating for both parties.

One indication of the extent of the difficulties was the amount of time the two institutions spent negotiating and renegotiating their affiliation agreements (Guttman, 1988). Some aspects of the affiliation agreements were pragmatic, involving for example the compensation payable by OISE for the registrarial services provided by the university. But other issues were more fundamental – for example, admission, grading, standards of appointment for faculty, and degree requirements. On topics such as these, the university (as represented primarily by its School of Graduate Studies) and the institute found agreement difficult. From OISE's point of view, affiliation both reduced its autonomy and gave rise to instability because of uncertainty about the terms under which the university would be willing to renew the agreements. The institute found itself negotiating from a position of systemic weakness because it lacked the power to grant degrees and was required under the terms of its mandate to affiliate with a degree-granting institution. As OISE's third director observed to the Social Development Committee of the Legislature some years later, 'despite the Institute's formal autonomy, negotiations with the University cannot be imagined as a negotiation between equals' (OISE, 1986).

In 1976, OISE's director, Clifford Pitt, 'issued a statement raising the possibility of ending the [affiliation] agreement and presenting what he saw as the advantages and disadvantages of affiliation' (OISE, 1977, 1). An institute task force established to look into the matter recommended in 1977 that affiliation continue, but that a number of OISE's concerns be addressed.

Two years later, in May 1979, U of T's president, James Ham, notified Pitt that motions were being submitted to the university's governing bodies which, if approved, could result in OISE being disaffiliated from the university. The motions came from the School of Graduate Studies. In response to representations from faculty members at OISE, the motions were withdrawn and a university committee (called the Mettrick Committee after its chair) was established to review the relationship between the two institutions.

The committee expressed a number of predictable concerns. It was concerned about the size of OISE's graduate program (which accounted for a disproportionately large share of the university's graduate enrolment). It identified administrative problems relating to admissions and finance, and, less tangibly, 'philosophical differences,' which seem to involve mainly the practices of thesis committees. Although the Mettrick Committee's recommendations antagonized the institute (calling as they did for transfer of responsibility for graduate degrees in Education to other units of the university as a condition of continued affiliation), the two institutions succeeded in reaching a new affiliation agreement.

It is arguable that the logistics of affiliation were not the real issue in the tensions that were arising between OISE and the University of Toronto. Harry Judge reported to the Ford Foundation:

> Students at GSE's [graduate schools of education] are unlike those of any other graduate school ... They tend to be older than most graduate students, and more of them are women or belong to minority groups. An unusually high proportion not only have full-time jobs but unusually demanding jobs. These students, quite understandably, tend to take longer to fulfil their course requirements, and they present more special cases for consideration. More of them than in any other graduate school are taking courses for specific, limited professional reasons: to acquire a new credential, secure the renewal or extension of a teacher's license, advance a step or move along a salary scale. Their scores in the Graduate Record Examination are lower than those secured or required for entry into other graduate schools ... It's only too easy for other departments to quip that GSE's, even some good ones, will take any bodies, provided they're warm. (1982, 37)

In other words, precisely the same perceptions that coloured relations between U of T and OISE were fuelling difficulties between American universities and their graduate faculties of education, where affiliation was not an issue.

Integration: The 1980s Attempts

The Marsden Report

By the early 1980s, relations between the institute and the university were running more smoothly. The second affiliation agreement was considerably more comprehensive than the first. Whereas the first addressed the administration of graduate programs in Education, the second also provided for cooperation between OISE and FEUT. The new agreement established a Joint Council on Education to foster collaboration between the institute and the university at the undergraduate and the graduate levels.

OISE's 1981–82 Annual Report described the establishment of the Joint Council on Education as having 'already ushered in a new era in terms of cooperation and interaction between the two institutions.' Its success was such that a subcommittee of the council was established to explore the possibility of integrating FEUT and OISE. The subcommittee, chaired by Lorna Marsden, a vice-provost of the university responsible for professional faculties, included senior faculty and administrators from the university, the institute, and the Faculty of Education. It recommended that FEUT and OISE be merged and remain affiliated with the University of Toronto. The merged institution would have its own board of governors and direct funding from the province. OISE was not enthusiastic about the recommendation, nor was FEUT, and it was not pursued (Academic Integration Task Force Report, 1995). Whether or not the Marsden task force ever had any real chance for success, it was a valuable learning experience that laid some groundwork for eventual merger.

The Nixon Bombshell

In May 1985, Ontario's Progressive Conservatives gave way to a Liberal minority government, after governing Ontario for forty-three years. Robert Nixon, former Liberal leader and a long-time critic of OISE, became Ontario's treasurer. In his budget speech to the Legislature that year, he stated that 'as a step toward eliminating duplication in the public sector, the government will transfer Ontario Institute for Studies in Education to the University of Toronto' (Guttman, 1988, 227).

According to Malcolm Levin, 'For the first time in OISE's history, several faculty members and support staff set aside (temporarily) their personal agendas and political infighting over resources to mount a campaign to maintain OISE's political autonomy.' The campaign was effective. OISE's defenders succeeded in mobilizing an impressive array of friends of the institute and in enlisting the support of the New Democratic Party, which held the balance of power in the legislature at the time. According to a report in *News & Notes*, at a rally for OISE on 5 December 1985:

> Bob Rae, NDP leader, reminded ... the unrepentant Treasurer of the Liberal minority government, Robert Nixon ... of the voting arithmetic at Queen's Park. 'Twenty-five plus 51 is more than 48,' he said ...
> Cornered by the media after the rally, [Nixon was] asked if he still thinks of OISE as a 'sacred cow.' Mr. Nixon's reply – 'That would be an inappropriate remark for me to make in the OISE building.'

That OISE was able to marshal such broad-based support – especially from a political party that had previously questioned its role and value – was evidence that by the mid-1980s it was viewed more favourably by the several constituencies that it had been founded to serve.

The government was eventually forced to call legislative hearings on the proposed merger. Various school boards, faculty associations, teachers' federations, and other groups presented 154 briefs in support of OISE's position. The legislative committee recommended that OISE not be transferred to the university. The government's attempt to forcibly merge the two institutions was dead.

The 1986 Attempt

In the aftermath, OISE and U of T returned to the negotiating table. By this time, the university had decided that its Faculty of Education was becoming increasingly unviable as it was – that is, with minimal resources and a mandate restricted to undergraduate teaching. It wanted a faculty that was also engaged in graduate teaching and research – as were the university's other faculties.

Enlarging the mandate and resources of FEUT in competition with OISE would involve unnecessary and unaffordable duplication of resources and effort, even if the province were to allow the university to offer separate advanced degrees in Education. Merger of OISE and FEUT appeared to be the only solution. The university by this time was willing to agree that FEUT become part of a merged OISE/FEUT, affiliated with U of T. Nevertheless, the merger negotiations failed, mainly because the university and the institute were unable to reach an agreement about how long funding for the merged faculty would be stabilized.

It would be too simple to say that money was the only reason why the institute and the university failed to reach agreement at this stage. Because of the reductions in government funding to both institutions, and the implications of those reductions for FEUT, which had suffered budget cuts higher than the university average, OISE was seeking more long-term budget stability than the university was able or willing to guarantee. The interest of FEUT in the merger cooled at this point too, and for the same reason. By this time, OISE evidently had come to understand how anomalous its financial position was under the province's funding formulas, and that without guarantees from the university, FEUT might become similarly vulnerable.

Reversal of Fortune

Renewal at FEUT

In the wake of the failed 1986 merger negotiations, U of T initiated a review of FEUT – a step that routinely precedes a search for a new dean.

The review committee's report contained a damning assessment of the state of FEUT, a condemnation of the university for having starved the faculty, and a call to reinvest. Its recommendations informed the subsequent search for a new dean.

Before accepting the position, Michael Fullan, a professor at OISE, negotiated with the university a multi-year commitment to faculty renewal. On assuming the dean's position in February 1988, he discovered a faculty culture 'characterized by a strong commitment to teaching and students, and a willingness to cooperate, along with a sense of hurt pride at not being respected in the university or valued more widely in the field' (1998, 33).

FEUT embarked on a program of rebuilding that involved the following: faculty renewal; the development of partnerships with school boards and other agencies; program innovation; research development; cultural change; and the development of closer relationships with the university as a whole.

Between 1988 and 1995, FEUT hired around thirty-five new faculty members, while a slightly larger number retired. It developed a Learning Consortium with OISE and four school boards, and developed a plan for restructuring the entire teacher education program. It made research a priority, hired to this end, and gave its members incentives and support for research. In 1992, thirty-five of FEUT's faculty members gave papers at the meetings of the Canadian Society for Studies in Education and its American equivalent; five years earlier, only two had done so (Fullan, 1998). Most of the faculty's new appointments were eligible for membership in the university's School of Graduate Studies.

By 1994, FEUT was a much stronger, more vibrant faculty – one with good relationships with the school system and rapidly improving standing within the university. But problems remained. Notwithstanding the progress that had been made, 'faculty [were] doing too much with too little' (Provostial Commission, 1994, 9). Teaching loads remained heavy – too heavy to be consistent with the faculty's objectives in research. Young faculty members – 'carrying extraordinary teaching and administrative assignments in collaborative, school-based teacher education programs' – were constrained in their professional development by lack of time for research and lack of involvement in graduate programs (20). Moreover, the academic renewal of the faculty had involved substantial cultural change, with all of the anxiety and tension that such change engenders.

Atrophy at OISE

The late 1980s and early 1990s were not as kind to OISE. Like universities

across the country, it suffered the effects of deep cutbacks in public funding for post-secondary education. Because of OISE's small size and
narrow range of specialized programs, some of those cutbacks were proportionately greater for the institute than for other post-secondary institutions in Ontario. In the April 1989 edition of *News & Notes*, Walter
Pitman, OISE's fourth director and former NDP MPP, wrote: '[The OISE]
community faces a time of decision ... having successfully assured our
institutional survival, it now becomes a first priority to determine our
academic future and plan for our financial health.'

But OISE was by nature poor at making strategic institutional decisions.
Like many graduate faculties of education, it was atomistic, lacked a
collective mission, and was highly decentralized. As Malcolm Levin observed: 'Despite the lipservice we pay to the OISE Community, OISE has
never really been a community in the strong sense of that concept. Rather
like other academic institutions, it has been a loose collection of individuals and shifting groups with diverse, often competing, interests' (Levin,
1995).

Lacking a shared mission or shared priorities, the OISE community
responded to funding cutbacks by intensifying its internecine rivalries.
Typically, the battles were fought along constituency lines. Malcolm Levin
noted in 1995:

In recent years ... fewer meetings [have been] held as more people find that
they have less time to spare from their day-to-day responsibilities to attend
meetings. One consequence is that a small influential core of staff and
students have come to represent OISE's constituencies. Thus, over the past
three decades OISE's culture of participatory democracy has evolved into a
more formal system of constituency representation where most of the key
issues are dealt with at the bargaining table' (Levin, 1995).

Many of those who weren't 'at the table' seem to have 'checked out' in a
psychological sense. One has the impression that year after year of institutional instability, aimlessness, and conflict – with no end in sight – had left
them exhausted. They no longer bothered to participate. The strategic
planning committee established to recommend a way out of OISE's predicament commented woefully in its May 1994 report on participation in
its consultations: 'The consultation involved approximately seventy
participants. Most were support staff. Fewer than ten were external
stakeholders. The Committee's inability to elicit responses to its work
from a larger number and range of stakeholders remains a piece of "unfin-

ished business" in the opinion of committee members' (OISE, Strategic Planning Committee, 1994).

The prolonged internal battles over resources damaged OISE's relations with its external constituents. Never closely connected to the province's education system, the institute became even more self-absorbed over the course of its last decade.

In 1991 a new director was appointed: Arthur Kruger, known for his labour relations expertise. But OISE remained in political deadlock, incapable of moving forward, and no major decisions were made (Levin, 1995). Meanwhile, the institute's financial health kept deteriorating. In 1994 it declared a state of financial exigency, having incurred a deficit approaching $4 million on an operating budget of $45.7 million the previous fiscal year. This, at a time when Ontario's education minister was touring the province extolling the virtues of doing more with less!

Integration, '90s Style

The Invitation

OISE's financial predicament was all the more embarrassing to the minister because it was a Schedule 3 institution. In other words, the minister was directly responsible for it. Among other things, this meant that OISE did not own and operate its own building – the government did.

A bailout for OISE was politically impossible; at the same time, the ministry had no confidence that the institute could solve its own problems. It had accumulated a large deficit, it was facing major funding cuts, and it had no apparent plan for solving its problems. The situation was untenable for both parties.

The University of Toronto's president, Robert Prichard, had longed believed that it made no sense for the university to have two faculties of education (FEUT and, by affliation, OISE). Neither was as strong as it should be. Although FEUT had made substantial progress under the leadership of Michael Fullan, it would remain weak and underfunded as long as it was shut out of graduate studies and research. At the same time, OISE had become increasingly marginal and vulnerable. It was not seen to be at the centre of public debate on education, to be serving the educational community, or, generally, to have its house in order. In Prichard's view, OISE was running a real risk – in the cold and unforgiving climate of the early 1990s – of being shut down and its resources dispersed. If that were to happen, the University of Toronto would never achieve excellence in

Education, and Ontario would be without a critical mass of research expertise in the field. This renewed the university's interest in merger, depending on the course that OISE chose to take and the willingness (or unwillingness) of the government to support that course.

Still under formal financial exigency, OISE sought special financial assistance from the Ministry of Education and Training, and was refused. In addition, and to make matters worse, the ministry made clear its intention to discontinue the special $1.5 million transfer grant that the institute had regularly been receiving. Merger with U of T was raised as a possible solution to OISE's predicament. The ministry, through its deputy minister, Charles Pascal, offered to support a merger and to broach the subject to the University of Toronto.

Late in January 1994, the Minister of Education and Training, David Cooke, invited the University's president and OISE's executive director to meet with him and his deputy. At the meeting, the minister invited the two institutions to enter into discussions about the possible integration of OISE and FEUT within U of T. Two days later, he wrote to the chairs of the governing bodies of the two institutions, inviting them formally 'to lead [their] respective institutions in a formal exploration of fully integrating the Ontario Institute for Studies in Education and the University of Toronto.' The institutions were to set their own terms of reference for the discussions and were to report back to ministry by the end of June 1994.

Cooke expressed the hope that 'by combining the objectives and academic resources of the Ontario Institute for Studies in Education and the Faculty of Education within the context of the University of Toronto as a whole, ... it will be possible to enhance your work in the important areas of educational research, graduate instruction, teacher training, the dissemination of knowledge, and the improvement of educational practice among professionals in the field.' He commented on the need for 'the greatest possible effectiveness and efficiency in the expenditure of public funds' in light of the 'fiscal challenges' facing the province and observed: 'Given the limited public dollars, an integrated institution might be better equipped to meet the challenges of preparing for the twenty-first century and realizing the missions of your respective institutions than would be the case if you stay apart.'

It appears that this invitation was understood differently by the leaders of the two institutions. In U of T's February *Bulletin*, Prichard was reported as saying that the university's position going into the talks was that OISE would become part of the Faculty of Education, not vice versa. The University's provost was reported as saying that while professors in the university's education faculty would not lose their jobs, some OISE faculty might not be offered positions at U of T. In fact, the provost did not go quite that far. What he did say was that 'our position will be that faculty at OISE may explore employment opportunities at other universities or with the ministry itself.' In other words, U of T's leaders initially construed the negotiations to be about building a new Faculty of Education – an end to which merger could be a means.

The provost's printed comments, whether they were reported accurately or not, inspired outrage at OISE. The 28 February issue of the *Bulletin* reported Kruger, OISE's executive director, as saying that whatever support there had been for merger at OISE had evaporated when 'it looked like the U of T was telling us "you folks close down the place and we'll hire whoever we like."' Although he himself believed the university's position to be 'quite different from that,' the perception had 'created panic and hostility' at the institute. It also led to concern, at both the institute and the university, that the government might be persuaded to allow other universities to 'cherry pick' OISE faculty.

At OISE, the minister's invitation was understood to mean that the provincial government wanted OISE to agree to become part of U of T. Many at the institute felt that it should not cooperate with either the government or the university. Their voices were outweighed by members of the institute's board and administration, who argued that to refuse even to negotiate would simply antagonize the provincial government – something that OISE could by then ill afford to do.

The Negotiations

Both parties assembled negotiating teams. Before they met, the teams' leaders shared with each other their respective instructions.

Angela Hildyard, Assistant Director of Research and Field Studies at OISE and team leader of its negotiations, advised her university counterpart that OISE's board had passed the following resolution on 22 March 1994:

BE IT RESOLVED ... :

- That OISE shall retain its name, mandate, own Board of Governors, and control over its revenues, either under the current OISE Act or as it may be amended.
- That central OISE shall retain a distinct physical location.
- That OISE shall continue to study education in a broad sense, maintain its Provincial presence, and retain its emphasis on issues of access and equity.

- That the academic contracts with all students shall be honoured.
- That all union contracts shall be honoured.

In reply, Stefan Dupré, a political science professor and chair of the university's negotiating team, informed Hildyard that his instructions were:

- That there shall be an integrated graduate and professional Faculty of Education under the Governing Council of the University of Toronto.
- That all academic commitments to students currently enrolled in the School of Graduate Studies of the University of Toronto shall be honoured.

The teams met for the first time on 11 April.

In the meantime, the university's provost had established a commission, consisting of three distinguished professors of education – one Canadian, one American, and one British – to advise him on the potential for merger and the form that an integrated faculty of education might take. OISE's leaders decided that since the university had its experts, they should have experts, too. They engaged a professor of education at Columbia University's teachers' college to advise them on the optimal relationship between OISE and the university and its Faculty of Education.

While the negotiating teams were meeting, some faculty and staff at OISE renewed their campaign to save the institute. The president of the faculty association wrote to its members encouraging them to identify clients, alumni, and colleagues at other universities who might be prevailed on to write to the education minister on OISE's behalf. A pamphlet published by the association described OISE as 'a world leader in the study of education,' and the crisis confronting it as follows:

> On Feb. 3, 1994, Dave Cooke, Ontario Minister of Education and Training, requested OISE to negotiate a possible merger with the University of Toronto ...
> Since that time, the U of T has moved to dismantle OISE. If the merger proceeds as planned, OISE could disappear, its education funds would be funnelled to other parts of the U of T, and many of OISE's programs would be shut down.

The pamphlet included quotations from twenty-seven 'supporters of OISE.' The quotations were anonymous. In contrast to 1985, when OISE was able to enlist many prominent people to defend it openly, the silence was deafening.

The *Toronto Star,* which had railed against Nixon's 1985 plans for OISE, editorialized on 7 February 1994:

> The two institutions have flirted with the idea [of merger] before and, when he was provincial treasurer in the former Liberal government, Robert Nixon tried unsuccessfully to bring OISE under the control of U of T.
>
> But times were different in 1985. Now, the funding crunch is much more severe ...
>
> Charles Pascal, deputy minister of education and a former senior administrator at OISE, is right when he says the new proposal to join the two institutions should be seen as an opportunity.
>
> 'There comes a time and a place when it becomes obvious that integrating the best of what scholarship and research can offer with teachers and real on-the-ground practice is a smart thing to do,' he says.
>
> This is the right time and place.

With many of their former allies – in the NDP, the unions, the education system, and the media – failing to rally to save OISE, some at the institute decided to turn to York University. U of T was perceived as arrogant, authoritarian, and right-wing; in contrast, York was perceived as a kindred spirit. It had strong unions, its faculty's collective agreement had served as a model for OISE's, and it seemed to share OISE's values of openness and equity.

After some preliminary soundings, OISE's senior officials did meet with their counterparts at York. OISE wanted to try to negotiate an agreement with York, but – according to OISE personnel – the latter's leaders were unwilling to enter into such negotiations without the minister's permission. It was not forthcoming.

The negotiating teams met throughout the summer. No progress was made. In August, both sides made their negotiating positions public. OISE's position was as follows:

> OISE and FEUT ... be integrated into a new professional Integrated Institution, affiliated with the University, subject to notice given by either OISE or the University to review the agreement, such notice not to occur prior to June 30, 2000.
>
> The name of the Integrated Institution ... be the Ontario Institute for Studies in Education at the University of Toronto.
>
> The new institution have its own Act (the OISE Act, revised in accordance with the proposed agreement) and Board of Governors. The President of the University would select just over half of the Board's members.

Funding for the new institution flow through the University.

The new institution be headed by a Director 'appointed by the Board ... taking into account the recommendation of the President,' and retain a distinct physical location.

The new institution retain a distinct physical location, a broadly-defined provincial mandate, and a commitment to equity and access.

The terms and conditions of employment of current OISE and all new faculty and staff be determined by OISE's collective bargaining agreements.

The university's negotiators had initiated the release of the parties' positions because they believed that faculty members at OISE would view integration more favourably if they knew what merger would mean for them. The university's proposal included the following major points:

OISE and FEUT ... be integrated into a new professional faculty of education under the Governing Council of the University of Toronto.

The name of the new faculty be the Ontario Institute for Studies in Education of the University of Toronto.

The new faculty have all the rights and responsibilities and guarantees belonging to other faculties at the University of Toronto.

The new faculty be headed by a dean, appointed in accordance with [U of T's] procedures.

The new faculty have a Faculty Council and an Advisory Board, appointed by the University's Governing Council on the advice of the Dean.

The new Faculty's budget 'be the sum of (a) the resources available to OISE at present from all sources modified by projected reductions and additions arising from government decisions, program changes and other factors and (b) the current budget of FEUT modified by the University-wide budget reductions already announced for 1994–2000. The University would be prepared to assure that (b) will not be reduced for a fixed period of time except by the average of any reductions (beyond those already announced) applicable to all academic divisions of the University.

The extent of applicability of existing OISE collective agreements following integration of OISE and FEUT within the University of Toronto may be determined by the Ontario Labour Relations Board. With respect to OISE faculty, assuming the discontinuation of the current collective agreement, the University of Toronto will ... grant tenure at the University of Toronto to faculty members holding tenured appointments at OISE ... and all faculty members will be subject to the terms and conditions of the Memorandum of Agreement between the University of Toronto and the University of Toronto Faculty Association.

The University's proposal was silent regarding the arrangements that would apply to staff, should their collective agreements be discontinued.

In mid-September the chair of OISE's board requested that the education minister appoint a mediator acceptable to both parties. The chair of the university's Governing Council concurred with the request. Early in October the minister announced that John Stubbs, President of Simon Fraser University, had accepted the assignment.

Mediation

Stubbs conducted the mediation at a local hotel. The administrative leaders and lawyers of the two institutions were present to advise their respective teams. The mediator shuttled between them.

The university's president was prepared to go to substantially greater lengths to secure an agreement than were his colleagues. Dismayed by the lack of progress in the first mediation session, he assumed a more direct role in the process. The members of the institute's team, committed to functioning by consensus, weighed the stark alternatives open to their institution. With Stubbs's patient assistance, the parties eventually came to a tentative merger agreement.

The agreement to merge was especially tentative with respect to a number of provisions requiring the government's support and approval. In the view of OISE's negotiators, it was the university's responsibility to secure the support and approval of the government. The provisions in the agreement that involved the government were mainly about funding:

- A guarantee about the maximum amount by which the funding previously available to OISE would be reduced. The amount was to be based on a rough analysis of potential economies of scale.
- A transitional fund to meet the costs of merger ($10 million, which was one-half of the reduction in government funding over ten years).
- A guarantee that the province's operating grant formula would not be amended to reduce the weight assigned to graduate programs in Education.
- An initial reduction in the special transfer grant to OISE of only 50 per cent, with the remaining 50 per cent to be reduced in phases.

• A guarantee that the university would assume all the assets and liabilities of OISE.

University officials met immediately with the minister and his officials, briefed them on the outcome of mediation, and negotiated the government's commitment to the agreement, subject to Cabinet approval.

Early in November, the agreement was announced. It was greeted with pleasure – and a tad of apprehension – at FEUT. The OISE community was stunned.

The Agreement

The tripartite agreement is reproduced in Appendix 2. In contrast to the agreement between Dalhousie and TUNS, the agreement was very specific about funding and resources and contained instructions for planning and implementing the merger.

In an article in *OISE News*, Hildyard addressed the question on the minds of many people at OISE: Why? She wrote:

'Since ... we reached the tentative agreement with the University regarding the creation of OISE/UT, many members of the OISE Community have asked us why we recommended merger as a faculty under the Governing Council of the University of Toronto when our previously stated position had been opposed to this outcome. In other words – what caused us to change our minds?'

Hildyard reviewed the course of the negotiations over ten months, the reasons for the request for mediation, and the progress made during that process. Having secured the university's agreement to a broadly defined mandate for OISE/UT and an attractive financial offer:

We debated long and hard about the potential implications of merger upon support staff ... and loss of our separate legal identity. But we kept coming back to a real concern that as a stand-alone institution in the anticipated financial climate, we would be placing the Institute in jeopardy as we might be unable to hire sufficient new faculty to continue support for all of our OCGS [Ontario Council of Graduate Studies] programs. This would lead to loss of students and income and set us in a downward spiral that would be difficult to halt.

In the final analysis, the negotiating team was 'convinced that we had struck the best possible deal under the circumstances' (1995). Integration looked much less auspicious for staff than for faculty members at OISE. Nevertheless, some staff members took the view that – especially given the transition funding for severance and other purposes provided for in the agreement – it offered them a better future than could an independent but impoverished OISE.

OISE's board approved the agreement on 22 November 1994, with eighteen board members voting in favour, one against, and four abstaining. The university's governing body approved the agreement shortly thereafter, and it was signed by the education minister and the institutions' heads on 16 December 1994. The only unresolved issue was the ownership of the OISE building, which was finally transferred to the University of Toronto in 1999.

The Merging Institutions

At the time of its merger with OISE, thé University of Toronto – the largest university in Canada – had about 50,000 students on three campuses. Approximately 80 per cent were at the university's St George campus in central Toronto, on which FEUT was located. The latter had about 3,100 enrolled students, not including those at its two laboratory schools. OISE, with about 2,500 students, was located just over a block up the street from FEUT.

FEUT, with just over $20 million in annual expense, was the university's sixth-largest academic division (out of nineteen in total). The faculty had 121 full-time academic staff, of whom thirty-five were teachers in its laboratory schools. There were five part-time members of the faculty. There were seventy-four administrative staff positions, none of which was unionized.

FEUT was a relatively large division, almost as large as OISE as an independent institution. But within the overall scale of the university, neither FEUT nor OISE was unusually large or predominant. For example, the university's largest faculty – the Faculty of Arts and Science – was five times larger than either.

In the year prior to merger, the university's total operating expense, exclusive of ancillary operations and sponsored research, was $600 million. Ancillary operations and sponsored research added roughly $200 million to the figure. The university's budget supported just over 6,600 full-time staff – 2,942 academic and 3,685 administrative. Only 871 of the staff were unionized, and almost all of these were either library technicians or skilled tradespeople in physical plant operations.

The year prior to merger – 1995–96 – was a pivotal year for the university's budget plan. Six years earlier the university had introduced a regime of multiyear planning and budgeting, which at the time was very unusual among Canadian universities. Under its multiyear plan the university had deliberately incurred deficits in order to support long-term academic planning and transition and to smooth out 'boom and bust' funding cycles. The multiyear plan allowed the accumulated deficit to rise as high as $16.2 million in 1993–94. The 1995–96 budget plan called for a surplus sufficient to eliminate the accumulated deficit, which by that time had been reduced to $11.8 million. The university had an endowment of just over $500 million. Under the multiyear planning and budgeting process, all unrestricted investment revenue was taken directly into the operating budget and regarded as general university income. This accounted for $2.6 million of the university's income in 1995–96. But also under the multiyear scheme, the accumulated deficit was fully debt-serviced as foregone investment income. Thus much of the advantage of the endowment was neutralized.

In terms of vital statistics, OISE looked more like one of U of T's large to medium-sized faculties than like the university itself. OISE had just over 300 full-time staff, of whom 128 were faculty members and librarians. Virtually all were unionized. This was perhaps the single greatest difference between the cultures of the two institutions in the merger.

OISE's annual budget was just over $33 million. Its accumulated deficit – depending on which auditor's report was used – was between $2.7 million and $4.9 million. In proportional terms, OISE's deficit (roughly 10 per cent of revenue) was far more serious than U of T's (which at its peak was less than 3 per cent). OISE's endowed funds amounted to about $400,000. Just under 5 per cent of OISE's annual revenue was generated by research funding, the bulk of which came from an annual 'transfer' grant from the provincial government. As part of its affiliation agreement with U of T, OISE purchased about $675,000 in administrative services (mainly registrarial) from the university.

Caution should be exercised in comparing OISE to either U of T at large or to FEUT specifically. As a free-standing, independent institution, OISE faced some costs that FEUT did not – to be more precise, FEUT faced costs that were not attributed to it because the university did not allocate indirect costs and overhead costs to its faculties. Had those costs been allocated, OISE and FEUT would have looked more alike in terms of overall expense.

As an independent institution, OISE was in a unique position with regard to the cost of operating and maintaining its premises. The Government of Ontario held title to OISE's building and met about two-thirds of its annual $3.7 million operating costs. So in one respect, OISE's overall operating costs were considerably understated.

Another area in which comparisons should be made cautiously is the composition of the academic staff. The university had made retirement mandatory at age sixty-five. OISE had no fixed mandatory age of retirement. At the time of merger, OISE had about a dozen academic staff over sixty-five. Its age profile was very different from that of FEUT. It was projected that in the ten years after merger, 34.8 per cent of OISE's academic staff would turn over through attrition based on age. The comparable figure for FEUT was nearly 55 per cent.

In terms of capacity to respond to the cutbacks that merger would necessitate, there were major differences between OISE on the one hand and the university and FEUT on the other. There are different estimates for the optimal size of universities, but by any measure, U of T was so large that it would not have been reasonable to expect it to realize further economies of scale in those of its operations that would be affected by merger. Those economies, logically, were to be found principally in the operations of OISE.

The Transition

In accordance with the integration agreement, OISE and U of T established two task forces early in 1995. The first, the Academic Integration Task Force, was co-chaired by FEUT's dean and OISE's assistant director (academic), and consisted of six representatives each (four faculty members, one staff member, and one student) from OISE and FEUT. It was charged with:

(a) reviewing academic programs, research and field development activities of OISE and FEUT with a view towards establishing closer linkages among preservice, inservice and graduate programs, research and field development; (b) exploring possible linkages between OISE/UT and other departments and faculties of the University; (c) determining an appropriate departmental structure for OISE/UT; and (d) making recommendations on the appropriate constitution for the Faculty Council of OISE/UT. (Academic Integration Task Force, 1995)

This task force was to report in six months, and its report, once approved by the provost, was to constitute a complete academic and budget plan for OISE/UT. The integration agreement invested OISE/UT with considerable budgetary autonomy and 'flowed through' to the new faculty the income that OISE would previously have generated.

Initial progress was slow. Jane Knox, the last chair of OISE's board, observed: 'I had thought that people would accept the inevitable and get down to work. Unfortunately, that didn't happen. Many people continued to deny and resist.'

Others involved in the process suggested that the fact that the future leadership of OISE/UT had not yet been chosen made it difficult to move forward. No one person had authority to lead the process, and this made compromise and delay inevitable.

Nevertheless, the Academic Integration Task Force pressed forward, establishing working groups, striking advisory groups, issuing questionnaires, developing models, holding open meetings, and seeking feedback. It then drafted a report, which it submitted to the provost in July 1995. The report proposed a mission, an organizational structure, and a constitution for OISE/UT. Under the proposed organizational structure, there would be seven academic departments, each led by a chair; these seven departments would contribute to three major functions – preservice, graduate studies, and research and field studies – each led by an associate dean. The report also identified the level of funding that would be available to OISE/UT in its first year of operation (in accordance with the integration agreement) and showed the extent to which the current expenditures at OISE and FEUT exceeded that level. It indicated that a second task force, the Administrative Integration Task Force, would design OISE/UT's administrative structure within that budget framework.

The first task force's proposals were modified in response to the provost's feedback – for example, the number of academic departments was reduced (for academic reasons) – and approved by the university's governing bodies early in 1996.

The provost chaired the search for a dean, which was launched soon after the integration agreement was signed. By that time, Arthur Kruger had resigned as OISE's executive director and Michael Fullan's term as FEUT's dean had been foreshortened. It was announced in July 1995 that Fullan would be OISE/UT's first dean. He appointed associate deans early in 1996. Once the departmental structure was approved, searches were conducted for chairs. At the same time, faculty members were invited to decide which of the new departments they would join.

In the meantime, the Administrative Integration Task Force, consisting of co-chairs Angela Hildyard (now executive director of OISE in the wake of the previous director's resignation) and Anne Millar (associate dean of FEUT), and one other management representative from each institution, wrestled with the task of designing the administrative organization of OISE/UT. Its task was complicated, first, by the need to await the results of the deliberations of the Academic Integration Task Force, and, second, by the new Progressive Conservative government's announcement that operating funding for post-secondary institutions would be cut by 15 per cent in 1996–97.

Since the integration agreement and the province's budget together entailed a cut of $5.1 million in the resources jointly available to FEUT and OISE, and since the integration agreement provided for no loss of faculty, it was evident that deep cuts in staff positions would be required. Through a process described in more detail below, the task force designed an administrative organization for OISE/UT within the established budget parameters.

Severance packages were negotiated, and offered to staff early in 1996. The deadline for applications was extended a number of times. Ultimately, almost 115 staff – most of them from OISE – took severance. The costs of the packages were met from the transitional fund provided by the integration agreement.

The spring of 1996 was a very difficult time at OISE. The 22 April issue of the *Bulletin* reported that 'uncertainty over layoffs, the prospect of union decertification and exit package deadlines at the Ontario Institute for Studies in Education are definitely affecting morale, say faculty and staff groups.'

The OISE community was also in the throes of profound cultural change. As the date of integration approached, the dean-designate and the university administration increasingly took charge. Some members of the OISE community, accustomed to virtual co-management of their institution, did not like the university's more traditional approach to management. A group called The Coalition issued a newsletter 'to provide members of the FEUT and OISE Communities and members of the Press with the real story about the union busting, layoffs and secretive decision-making processes now taking place.' For many 'old hands' at OISE, an empowered administration was an unwelcome change.

Meanwhile, at FEUT, apprehension grew. Though the announcement of the integration agreement had been greeted with pleasure there, concerns about what merger with OISE would really mean increased as the date approached.

The OISE Act was repealed just days before OISE and the university merged. In the absence of the education minister, Toni Skarica (PC, Wentworth North) moved third reading of Bill 45 – An act to repeal the Ontario Institute for Studies in Education Act and transfer assets to the University of Toronto – at a night sitting of the House on 17 June 1996. In doing so, he said he wished to make four points:

- This legislation will save Ontario taxpayers some $10 million over the next 10 years.
- I would like to quote from the budget presented in 1985 by the Honourable Robert Nixon, Treasurer of Ontario, 'As a step towards eliminating duplication in the public sector, the government will transfer the Ontario Institute for Studies in Education to the University of Toronto.' Five years later and $10 billion in debt later, it did not occur ...
- The NDP government took over in 1990 and Mr Cooke, the Minister of Education, stated, 'Given the limited public dollars, an integrated institution might be better equipped to meet the challenges of preparing for the 21st century ... ' Five years later and $50 billion of debt later, no integration.
- Finally, our government took over in power one year ago and now in one year we're at the point where all that is needed to complete the integration is the passage of Bill 45. Every day this bill is delayed costs the taxpayer $2,700, and the only question I have is, why did it take 11 years for us to get here?

Although members of the two opposition parties corrected this highly partisan account of the measure's origins, they did not oppose the legislation. OISE – a political football for most of its life – ceased to exist as an independent institution on 1 July 1996, with all-party support.

FIVE

The Cases in Context

The Cases Compared

What are we to make of these two cases? It may be useful to begin the analysis by comparing them on a number of dimensions.

Context and Structure

The Similarities

Jurisdiction: First, both mergers took place in Canada, within the same broad constitutional, cultural, and socio-political framework. Each involved publicly funded institutions in the same province. Hence, the merging institutions were subject to common policies on post-secondary education, funding regimes, and labour legislation. All four had been established by acts of their respective provincial legislatures.

The fiscal context was one of constraint: the governments of Nova Scotia and Ontario had accumulated large deficits, and were reducing their expenditures dramatically.

Institutional histories and structures: Both cases involved one larger, more comprehensive university (U of T; Dalhousie) and one smaller, more focused institution (OISE; TUNS). In each case, the larger institution was the province's major university. The University of Toronto was historically Ontario's provincial university; Dalhousie had sought to be Nova Scotia's.

In each case, the smaller institution had an explicit provincial mandate. The Nova Scotia government of 1907 was convinced that technical education and research were keys to the industrial and commercial development of the province. Almost sixty years later, the Ontario government perceived research and graduate studies in Education as means to ensure that the province's rapidly expanding education system would advance individual and social well-being and prosperity. Both institutions were founded to serve their provinces' needs in direct and specific ways.

For some time, the governments of Nova Scotia and Ontario funded NSTC and OISE (respectively) differently than they did universities. Both institutions were initially subject to criticism from provincial opposition parties. Both were eventually brought under the same funding regime as the universities in their jurisdictions, but retained some distinctive financial ties with the government (e.g., OISE's transfer grant; the payment by government of rent for some of TUNS's premises).

Physical proximity: Both sets of institutions were in close physical proximity – a factor that is associated positively both with the success of merger negotiations and with the extent of post-merger integration (see, for example, Rowley, 1997; Mahoney, 1995). Merger partners separated by large distances tend to remain separate both administratively and culturally. Institutions that are close to each other can capture much more readily the intellectual, educational, and operational benefits of coming together. Dalhousie and TUNS were separated by half-a-dozen city blocks; OISE was across the street from U of T's main campus.

Degree complementarity: The degree programs of the merging institutions were largely complementary. FEUT offered undergraduate degrees in Education; OISE offered graduate programs. Dalhousie's Department of Engineering offered the first two years of an undergraduate program; TUNS's Faculty of Engineering offered bachelor's, master's, and doctoral degrees. Only in Computer Science, in which both Dalhousie and TUNS offered bachelor's and master's degrees, was there duplication. However, TUNS also offered a PhD. Even in Computer Science, there was less duplication than it first appeared, in that TUNS's Bachelor of Computer Science was an accredited, professional, co-op program, whereas Dalhousie's BSc was a multidisciplinary program with an optional co-op element.

In both cases, in the disciplines duplicated at the merging institutions, there was greater emphasis on undergraduate studies at the larger institution and on upper-year undergraduate and/or graduate education at the smaller institution.

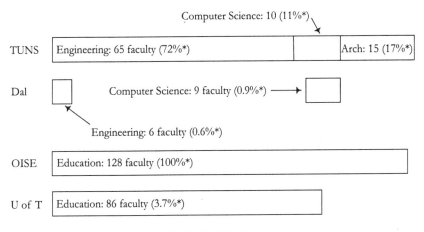

* Disciplinary faculty as a % of total institutional faculty

Figure 5.1 Disciplinary overlap in merging institutions

Disciplinary overlap: There was no duplication of degrees except in Computer Science; that being said, the merging institutions were active in many of the same fields. Dalhousie offered programs in two of the three disciplines represented at TUNS (architecture, computer science, and engineering). OISE and FEUT were both dedicated to Education. Furthermore, OISE had departments of Applied Psychology, History and Philosophy of Education, and Sociology of Education; the teaching and research activities of these overlapped to some extent with those in various departments at U of T.

The overlap in fields of study and research at OISE and U of T, and at TUNS and Dalhousie, is illustrated in Figure 5.1 in terms of the approximate numbers of faculty members by discipline at the smaller institution and at the corresponding disciplinary unit of the larger institution in the year prior to merger. (The percentages in brackets represent the number of faculty members in the discipline in question as a percentage of the total number of faculty members at that institution.)

It matters a great deal whether merging institutions are active in the same field or in different fields. Mergers of institutions that offer programs in the *same* fields present different challenges and opportunities than do mergers of institutions in *complementary* fields. Mergers of the latter type can extend the breadth of institutions' offerings without great disruption to academic departments. In contrast, in mergers of the former type, programs, personnel, and facilities are typically combined. The goal may be to strengthen programs, to maintain them in the face of budget cuts, or to achieve economies of scale. Whatever the case, there is far-reaching change for the affected academic units as programs, personnel, and facilities are integrated. For this reason, it has often been suggested that mergers of institutions active in the same fields are more difficult to negotiate and implement than mergers of institutions that specialize in different areas. (For a discussion of this, see Geodegebuure, 1992.)

Institutional missions: Although the merging institutions had different cultures, their missions were similar insofar as graduate and professional education and research were central to each.

There is much evidence that when missions and associated values are similar, mergers are easier to negotiate and integration is easier to achieve. Thus, for example, the Australian experience was that greater integration was achieved by 'redesignated' universities (universities created out of the merger of two or more colleges of advanced education) than by 'incorporated' universities (universities created by the merger of a university and one or more colleges) (Mahoney, 1995).

Prior linkages: OISE had pre-existing institutional ties with U of T, as did Dalhousie with TUNS. OISE was affiliated with U of T and was part of its School of Graduate Studies. The university granted its degrees. By virtue of the fact that it offered the first two years of the undergraduate Engineering program, Dalhousie was one of TUNS's associated universities.

Financial predicaments: Both TUNS and OISE were in serious financial trouble. In this respect, both cases were typical: the literature on higher education mergers suggests that the smaller partner is almost invariably in financial duress (see Millett, 1976; Geodegebuure, 1992).

Previous attempts: Finally, both mergers had been attempted several times before.

Differences

The provinces: The mergers took place in different provinces, and those provinces had different histories, different political cultures, different policies on post-secondary education, and different labour legislation.

Relative size: The difference in size between OISE (1994–5 enrolment: 2440) and U of T (1994–5 enrolment: 50,893) was far greater than that between TUNS (1994–5 enrolment: 1,449) and Dalhousie (1994–5 enrolment: 10,910).

It has been speculated that differences in size and power actually facilitate merger. The argument is that organizations avoid uncertainty; and that the outcome of a merger of relatively equal institutions is more uncertain than that of a merger of institutions which differ in size and power, and thus less likely to occur. Empirical evidence about this is mixed. Goedegebuure and Vos found that this hypothesis was borne out in the wave of mergers that took place in the Netherlands between 1984 and 1987 (Goedegebuure and Vos, 1988). Goedegebuure subsequently found circumstantial evidence that the Australian mergers inspired by the Dawkins revolution followed this pattern, but also found indications that post-1987 Dutch mergers tended to involve participating institutions that were very much balanced in terms of size and resources (Goedegebuure, 1992). In her econometric study of private college mergers in the United States, Chambers found that the effect of dominance (measured in terms of difference in institutional income) depended on whether the partners' academic programs duplicated each other (in which case dominance negatively affected the success of merger negotiations) or were complementary (in which case dominance sometimes facilitated agreement to merge) (Chambers, 1986).

Structural fit: OISE, though it contained departments of psychology, sociology, and other disciplines, was devoted to teaching and research in the field of Education. Merged with FEUT, it thus fit into the pre-existing structure of U of T as a faculty.

TUNS, in contrast, comprised three faculties. If, after amalgamation, TUNS had retained a distinctive identity as a multifaculty unit within Dalhousie, it would have been an anomaly within the university's faculty-based structure. TUNS did not fit as neatly into Dalhousie's structure as OISE did into U of T's.

Degree-granting authority: OISE did not have independent degree-granting authority; TUNS did.

Unionization: Faculty members and most staff at both TUNS and Dalhousie were unionized. In contrast, whereas OISE was overwhelmingly unionized, the faculty and most staff at U of T were not. The university's administration wished to avoid increased unionization – especially faculty unionization.

Players and Motivations

What about the players and their motivations? To what extent did they differ?

The Similarities

In each merger, the provincial government played a major role. In both cases, the government favoured merger. In both cases, provincial officials made it clear to the smaller institution that the government would not solve its financial problems. Neither government ruled out legislative action, but both wanted the mergers to be voluntary.

The presidents of U of T and Dalhousie saw merger as a means of extending their universities' offerings in accordance with their missions. Robert Prichard, U of T's president, regarded it as an anomaly that U of T was not involved in graduate studies and research in Education – a field of utmost social and economic importance. He did not believe that U of T could 'grow' FEUT into a strong, comprehensive faculty, in isolation from OISE's resources. Dalhousie's Tom Traves, like many of his predecessors, believed that amalgamation would help Dalhousie fulfil its destiny as a comprehensive, research-intensive university.

In some respects, the smaller institutions' motivations were also similar. Both OISE and TUNS were seeking to secure sufficient resources to maintain their programs, while preserving as much autonomy as possible. If TUNS could not get an infusion of funding as an independent institution, it was prepared to federate with Dalhousie. If the *status quo* could not be maintained, OISE might absorb FEUT and accept closer ties with U of T.

Both small institutions valued their provincial mandates, their applied research, and their relationships with their professional and other constituencies, and were concerned that these might be adversely affected by merger.

Nevertheless, alumni, professional bodies, and other groups that had rallied to the defence of the autonomy of OISE or TUNS in the past, were not inclined to do so in the 1990s. Some professional and other constituencies supported the mergers. In the same vein, other provincial universities did not strongly oppose the mergers.

In neither case was reducing the number of faculty members an objective.

Differences in Players and Motivations

The Nova Scotia government and the Ontario government favoured the mergers in question, but they differed in terms of how they were prepared to treat the mergers financially. As an inducement to amalgamate, the Nova Scotia government was prepared to offer additional funding to TUNS and Dalhousie for Computer Science and other programs. It was not, however, willing to give the universities transitional funding. In contrast, the Ontario government was insistent that a merger of OISE and U of T save it money in the medium-term. The reduction in funding upon which the Ontario government insisted was mitigated by its willingness to provide (1) transitional funding; (2) a guarantee that OISE/UT would be treated no worse than the rest of the university system; and (3) mitigation of some planned financial cutbacks to OISE.

From the outset, Dalhousie understood the rules of the game (i.e., voluntary agreement) and the desires of its potential merger partner (e.g., distinct identity, continued autonomy). In contrast, U of T's senior officials initially sought to acquire not OISE itself, but rather some of its resources for the purpose of building a stronger FEUT. Very quickly, the university's leaders realized that this objective was unattainable by voluntary agreement. The university then sought to acquire OISE as a faculty.

Dalhousie was seeking mainly to extend its range of offerings, and was prepared to be somewhat more flexible – that is, to accord to TUNS's successor some prerogatives unavailable to other faculties.

More dissimilar than their presidents' intentions were the desires of others at Dalhousie and U of T. Most deans at Dalhousie were in favour of amalgamation – provided, of course, that their faculties did not have to pay for it. In contrast, within the administration at U of T there was initially vehement opposition to integration. According to the chief negotiator for the university, calming the internal opposition was much more time-consuming than negotiating with OISE.

Perhaps the greatest differences were in the desires of members of the smaller institutions. By 1996, TUNS's president and most of his colleagues had accepted that TUNS would have to join Dalhousie in order to secure additional resources for its programs. Though it was by no means their first choice, they sought amalgamation – on the right financial and other terms. In contrast, the weight of opinion at OISE was against integration – *strongly* against integration – in spite of the executive director's personal openness to the concept. Many felt that OISE should not even agree to negotiate with U of T. In their view, for OISE to become a faculty of the university would be anathema. If merge they must, York University would be a much more acceptable partner.

As noted in Chapter 4, OISE did in fact meet with York officials. TUNS, in contrast, did not have other potential partners.

In sum, the contextual and structural similarities between the two cases were remarkable. Two large, comprehensive, publicly funded institutions. Two small, focused ones. Both pairs of institutions located close together in their respective provincial capitals. Shared disciplines, but little duplication in degrees. Prior attempts at merger. The smaller institutions in financial duress.

There were similarities in some of the players' motivations, as well. The provincial governments wanted the institutions to merge voluntarily. The leaders of the two large universities sought to round out their institutions' offerings by acquiring their smaller neighbours.

There were also motivational differences. The prevailing sentiment on the Dalhousie campus in the mid-1990s – as it had been in 1966 and 1974 – was that a Dal/TUNS merger would be a good thing. In contrast, many opinion leaders at U of T could not fathom why their president wanted anything more to do with OISE.

An even more fundamental difference was in the smaller institutions' motivations: TUNS was prepared to amalgamate – on the right terms. OISE strove to avoid merger with U of T, but it lacked viable alternatives.

What, then, were the similarities and differences in how the two sets of institutions reached and implemented their merger agreements?

The Process of Merger

There are three basic stages in a higher education merger (see Figure 5.2). The organizational status of the parties changes during the process. The first stage involves *negotiations* between two or more separate institutions, usually with different interests. With publicly funded institutions like those in our cases, government may also be a partner. Once the institutions agree to merge, they enter a *transition* period, during which they plan and prepare for merger. Though committed to a common future, they continue to be separate legal entities. On the agreed date, the merger is implemented and a single new organization comes into being. This is the *implementation* phase. It is usually months or years before the remnants of the former institutions disappear and the merged institution functions as an integrated whole. In some types of mergers – for example, semiautonomous and subsidiary arrangements – former merger partners retain some of their distinctness indefinitely.

Next, we compare the process by which TUNS and Dalhousie merged with the one followed by OISE and U of T.

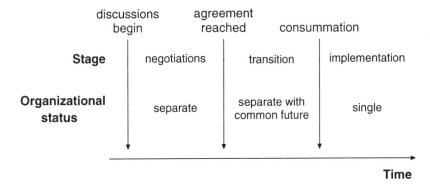

Figure 5.2 Stages in the process of merger

Timelines

One striking difference is in the amount of time it took. In the case of TUNS and Dalhousie, fourteen months elapsed between the beginning of negotiations and amalgamation; for OISE and U of T, merger was achieved twenty-nine months after negotiations began (see Figure 5.3).

The pace of the OISE/U of T merger appears to be more the norm – or perhaps somewhat faster than the norm, given some of the complexities and difficulties this merger faced. Gillian Rowley studied thirty recent mergers in the United Kingdom and found that the merger itself typically took more than a year but less than two (Rowley, 1997). The eighteen-month transition period at OISE and U of T is consistent with this; the eight-and-a-half months that elapsed between the Dal/TUNS agreement and amalgamation itself was exceptional. Rowley also found that exceptionally rapid mergers tended to 'be associated with extremes of positive or negative satisfaction with outcome' (1997, 258).

The Negotiations

The two mergers also were negotiated in strikingly different ways. Presidents Rhodes and Traves negotiated the Dal/TUNS agreement themselves. It was a relatively personal process, with little formality or bureaucracy.

The education minister's senior policy adviser at the time, who is a

OISE/U of T

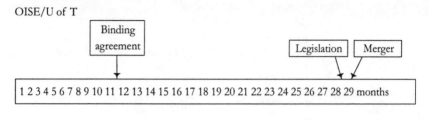

Dal/TUNS

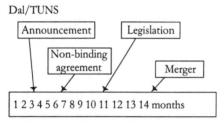

Figure 5.3 Time lines of the two mergers

lawyer, observed afterwards during an interview that when he first saw the presidents' draft agreement, he realized immediately that it wasn't a legal agreement. Asked what it was, if not a legal agreement, he replied: 'It was a good faith agreement. There was lots of good faith in this process.' Apparently so, given that amalgamation was announced at the beginning of April 1996, before a formal agreement had been signed!

In contrast, the process by which OISE and U of T negotiated integration was formal. Each side struck a negotiating team and provided it with instructions. The teams met. After months of no progress, the parties made their negotiating positions public. It was classic adversarial bargaining. Six months after negotiations began, mediation was requested. In contrast to the other case, it was only during the mediation process that the president of the university and the executive director of OISE became involved in the discussions.

The Agreements

The OISE/U of T agreement was legally binding. The Dal/TUNS agreement was not; rather, it was simply 'a statement of intent to amalgamate TUNS and Dalhousie substantially in accordance with this Agreement.' The OISE/U of T agreement was considerably more comprehensive and detailed. The Dal/TUNS agreement was silent on many of the issues its counterpart addressed – for example, the structure of graduate administration and the terms of reference of the administrative head of OISE/UT. Dalhousie and TUNS resolved such issues later.

The agreements also differed in the clarity and duration of the financial and budget commitments to the smaller institutions' successors, and in the nature of the provincial governments' commitments.

The Transitions

As soon as the OISE/U of T agreement was signed, the president of U of T ceased to be directly involved in the merger process. Arthur Kruger, OISE's executive director, resigned shortly after the agreement was signed, and Angela Hildyard, the assistant director who had led OISE's negotiating team, was appointed director in his stead. She continued to be very deeply involved in the merger process.

At OISE and U of T, the bulk of the activity during the transition period took place within and through committees. As specified in the agreement, the Academic Integration Task Force recommended a plan and structure for OISE/UT. The Administrative Integration Task Force made administrative plans and arrangements, including those for staff severance and redeployment. At the same time, a search was conducted for a dean. On his appointment, the new dean began to put together a new administrative team.

In contrast, the presidents of TUNS and Dalhousie continued to play a central role during the transition. They issued joint communications to both campuses throughout this period. Most issues were resolved by them or by other relevant university officials – and subsequently approved by the universities' governing bodies, as appropriate – rather than by committees.

Decision making at OISE and U of T tended to be formal, staged, and rational/bureaucratic; at Dalhousie and TUNS it was more informal, centralized, and *ad hoc*.

The Role of Governments

For all the striking similarities in the backgrounds of the two cases, and in the relationships between the institutions that were merging, the processes by which the merger agreements were actually reached and implemented were vastly different. However, the two mergers were very similar in one noteworthy respect: the role played by government. In each case, the provincial government at hand:

- impressed on the smaller, financially troubled institution that there was no prospect of financial relief from government. It would have to look elsewhere for answers.
- encouraged and (in the Ontario case) initiated discussions between the potential partners.
- discouraged other universities from intruding into the negotiations, by expressing public support for the process (and, in the case of the Ontario government, by asking another university not to enter into discussions with OISE while negotiations with U of T were continuing).
- encouraged the institutions to negotiate with each other in the first instance (instead of initiating trilateral negotiations).
- negotiated formally with the institutions once the latter had formulated a draft agreement.
- became a party to the merger agreement.
- provided transitional funding and medium-term funding guarantees, while exacting savings (Ontario).
- did not exact savings, and provided additional funding (without guarantees) (NS).
- agreed to transfer land to the merged institutions. (In the Nova Scotia case, this transfer has not yet taken place.)
- accepted the merging institutions' proposals for legislation.
- introduced and eventually passed the necessary legislation.

A final point of similarity relates to the role – or lack thereof – of provincial intermediary bodies. The Nova Scotia Council on Higher Education paved the way for amalgamation with its reviews of Computer Science and Engineering and its recommendation that Dalhousie and TUNS be consolidated; however, neither it nor the Ontario Council on University Affairs helped negotiate or implement the mergers.

In sum, the cases are similar in that they suggest that governments can in some circumstances (e.g., where at least one institution is financially hardpressed) foster particular higher education mergers that advance their public policy objectives, without undue intrusion into university affairs.

Negotiators' Perceptions of Outcomes

And what about the outcomes?

In the course of our research interviews, we asked the 'principals' to both agreements how they perceived the outcomes of merger. The presidents of Dalhousie and U of T declared themselves highly satisfied. Both indicated that their institutions' objectives had been – or would be – fulfilled.

OISE's last director, who had chaired its negotiating team, also spoke very positively of the outcome of merger. Hildyard told us that although integration had had very real short-term costs in terms of uncertainty, distress, and loss of staff jobs, the longer-term outcome was entirely positive. OISE/UT now has financial stability and access to a formidable fund-raising machine. It is among the university's 'Big Five' faculties and can work much more closely than before with other faculties. OISE has kept its name, and the university now understands its culture and values. She went on to say that the university had been generous with OISE/UT and had more than fulfilled the agreement. In her view, the outcome of the agreement had exceeded expectations. OISE's last board chair – who had also served on OISE's negotiating team – also spoke very positively about the outcome of integration. Although OISE/UT had not yet stabilized, she expected the eventual result of integration to be a better-funded, more efficient, higher-quality institution.

TUNS's last president, Ted Rhodes, and board chairman, Andrew Eisenhauer, were much less sanguine about the outcome of amalgamation. In separate interviews, they said it was not what they thought they had agreed to, nor did it reflect the spirit of the negotiations.

That Which Might Have Been: Types of Mergers

It is instructive to consider briefly what might have been – in other words, the different forms merger can take. One way of classifying mergers is in terms of the activities they bring together. As in the corporate sector, higher education mergers take place within and across fields of study (industries) and types of programs (product lines). A *horizontal merger* involves higher education institutions in the same field that provide similar offerings (e.g., a merger of two dental schools). The merger of Dalhousie and TUNS was a horizontal merger insofar as both institutions offered bachelor's and master's degrees in computer science before the merger took place.

A *vertical merger* involves institutions that are in the same field but provide different offerings (e.g., a merger of a degree-granting engineering school with a college that trains engineering techologists). The merger of U of T and OISE was a typical vertical merger in that prior to the merger, one offered undergraduate programs in Education while the other offered graduate programs in the same field. The Dal/TUNS merger also had a vertical dimension, in that it brought together distinct programs in Computer Science (first- and second-year programs at Dalhousie, a doctoral program at TUNS) and Engineering (first- and second-year programs at Dalhousie, upper-year and graduate programs at TUNS).

A *diversification* merger is one between institutions that are in different fields of study but offer similar types of programs. The merger of TUNS with Dalhousie was a diversification merger insofar as both institutions offered programs from the undergraduate to the doctoral level, most of which did not overlap.

A second way of classifying mergers is in terms of organizational outcome – that is, how the former institutions fit together to form the new one. The possible outcomes – consolidation, transformation, acquisition, and so on – are described in some detail below. From this perspective, the most fundamental distinction between mergers is whether the outcome results in a new institution or the absorption of one of the partners by the other.

Consolidation

The joining together of Institution A and Institution B to form a new Institution C is known as *consolidation*. Both parties to such a merger cease to exist in their former incarnations. The outcome is a melding of their features with new ones to form a genuinely new entity. When members of merged organizations say – as did some of those interviewed for this study – 'This wasn't a merger, it was a take-over!' they are equating merger with consolidation.

There is sometimes a tendency to take a romantic view of consolidations – to regard them as 'marriages of equals' that bring out the 'best of both.' That is one possible outcome of consolidation – if there are high levels of commonality of purpose, mutual understanding, and good will between the parties, and *if* there is effective communication throughout the process. Just as often, however, consolidation mergers give rise to confusion and conflict. Precisely because no party dominates, issues may proliferate, fester, and remain unresolved. A study of the financial services industry by the American Bankers Association and Ernst & Whinney (cited in Buono and Bowditch, 1989) found that cultural blending strategies associated with mergers of 'equals' often precipitated severe conflict between merger partners. Buono and Bowditch illustrated what can happen, with reference to the case of two law firms:

The two firms appeared initially to be a model for law-firm combinations. The union was friendly, a managing partner was assigned as a mediator to help resolve internal disputes and each firm's partners admitted that the time had come to 'inculcate some new values.' Within a year after the merger, however, instead of 'blending together,' postcombination interactions were described as tension laden and confrontational. As a result, the billing system broke down, the managing partner who was supposed to resolve internal disputes quit, a number of other partners left the firm, taking millions of dollars' worth of clients with them, and long-term clients began using other law firms. Ironically, it seems that many of the problems were related to the cultural blending strategy: since neither firm emerged as dominant after the merger, virtually everything – from pay scales and whose clerks and secretaries would be dismissed to which associates would be asked to leave – had to be negotiated. Instead of exchanging values and selecting the best features of each firm, the process broke down as the cultures repeatedly clashed with each other. (145)

Pure Acquisition

Whereas consolidation consists of the 'combination of two or more institutions to form a new institution ... an acquisition is where one institution absorbs another without being substantially affected in the process. For example, the absorption of specialist institutions for agriculture, law or medicine into a major university could be described as an acquisition, whereas combination of two or more colleges of advanced education to form a new institution would be a consolidation' (Harman, 1991, 178).

Acquisitions take many different forms. They can be characterized by the extent to which the acquired organization is integrated into the acquiring organization – that is, comes to share its structure, systems, resources, and culture. In cases of *pure acquisition*, the aim is complete integration – that is, that the acquired organization become a unit like any other of the acquiring institution (e.g., become a new faculty within a multifaculty university). The acquiring institution emerges greater in size or breadth, but fundamentally unchanged.

Transformative Acquisition

Acquisition can, however, change the acquiring institution as well as the acquired one. In transformative acquisition processes, one partner absorbs the other but changes substantially as a result. It seizes on the merger as an opportunity to bring about internal change, and its structure, policies, processes, and culture all change – albeit to a lesser extent than those of the subordinate partner.

Semiautonomous Acquisition

Acquisition can enable a dominant institution to change in desired ways; in the same vein, it can permit a subordinate one to retain a measure of autonomy. Clearly, a defining characteristic of merger is that it involves a loss of autonomy for at least one of the participating institutions. But within mergers, various organizational arrangements can be made that allow for considerable degrees of local autonomy for the previously independent institutions. This is especially relevant when the merger involves institutions of significantly different sizes or when one institution becomes a faculty or college of a university with many faculties and colleges (i.e., an identifiable unit of the larger institution). Although the larger unit's governing body and chief executive officer will have overall responsibility for the institution, the acquired unit may have a board, a chief administrator, and/or an academic council with delegated powers unavailable to other units.

Geography influences greatly the extent of an acquired institution's autonomy. Where two institutions were geographically separate before the merger, and neither one moved after the merger, there is *de facto* semiautonomy simply because of the distance separating the two campuses. This was characteristic of some of the mergers in Australia, where the two institutions were physically far apart. For example, about 900 kilometres separated the University of Western Australia in Perth and the Kalgoorlie School of Mines in Kalgoorlie.

One budgetary mechanism for according a measure of continued autonomy to academic units acquired through merger is responsibility centre budgeting (RCB). Adopted in the last decade by several major universities in the United States and Canada, RCB is also called responsibility centre management (Toronto, UCLA, Indiana), value-centred management (Michigan), incentive-based budgeting (Ohio State), mission-focused budgeting (Illinois), and revenue-centred management (USC). RCB also bears a close relationship to total quality management (TQM) and to school-based budgeting. Whatever the term used RCB does much to foster decentralizaiton and local autonomy (Lang, 1999).

RCB involves calculating all revenue generated by a faculty or other academic unit (e.g., tuition fees, revenue from endowments, share of government operating grants), and then assigning to it centrally budgeted indirect and overhead costs (e.g., costs of administrative and support services including libraries, payroll, research administration, physical plant). These calculations result in a revenue base and a cost base for each faculty or unit. Any net difference accrues to it. Very significantly, because the allocation of indirect and overhead costs is transparent and systematic, the faculty or unit can adjust its operations to reduce those costs. Just as significantly, it receives the full and immediate benefit of any steps it takes to generate additional revenue.

For this reason, RCB has relevance for mergers in which at least one partner wishes to retain some degree of local or premerger autonomy. The integration agreement between OISE and U of T had a strong element of RCB.

Relationships with governments, even when they are not direct parties to merger, can result in semiautonomy within a merger. For example, when the Osgoode Hall School of Law merged with York University in Ontario, the government continued to provide an operating grant for the school as if it were still autonomous. For the first ten years of merger between OISE and U of T, comparable funding arrangement will be in place.

Subsidiaries and Ancillaries

Many colleges and universities have subsidiary operations. In Canada these operations are usually called ancillaries. In the United States they are typically called auxiliaries. University presses and bookstores are usually operated as ancillaries. So are conference centres, student residences, and intercollegiate athletic programs. Somewhat more relevant to the issue of semiautonomy within merger is the status of museums, art galleries, and conservatories of music within universities. These units often are treated as ancillaries.

An ancillary is, in effect, a wholly owned subsidiary of its host or parent institution. Sometimes the employees of the ancillary are members of a separate collective bargaining unit and a separate pension plan. Also, the pay scales in the ancillary may be different from those of the host institution. The different pay scales recognize the uniqueness of the ancillary's role within the host institution. For example, conservatories often apply a hierarchical pay scale to compensate performance instructors.

When a merger takes the form of an ancillary or subsidiary, the smaller partner in the merger may continue to enjoy a distinct identity and considerable local autonomy. But this form of merger is not universally applicable. It is most applicable when one of the partners in the merger is distinctly different from the other partner – for example, when a museum or conservatory of music merges with a college or university. The work of a museum or conservatory is so specialized that semiautonomous status will be a *de facto* if not a *de jure* result of merger. The partners in the Dal/ TUNS and OISE/U of T mergers were post-secondary educational institutions offering baccalaureate and post-baccalaureate degrees. In each merger, the institutions involved were part of the same public system of higher education and were funded under the same formula. In other words, they were not so different that subsidiary or ancillary status would have been a necessary or appropriate outcome of merger.

Ancillary or subsidiary status can pose very significant challenges for management. To begin with, such a status is most appropriate when the smaller institution is sharply different from the host institution. Because the smaller institution is so different, the host institution may have no expertise for managing it. This adds to the complexity and diversity of the host institution. Complexity and diversity are difficult to manage.

A second challenge is debt. The usual rule in mergers is that one partner assumes all of the assets and liabilities of the other institution. Legally, that is the case in all mergers: the debt of one institution becomes the debt of the other institution. If ancillaries and subsidiaries are to manage their own financial affairs on a self-funded basis, the host institution may have to allow them to raise capital by incurring debt and the risks that go with it. Sometimes the host institution is the banker for the ancillary or subsidiary. At other times, it is the guarantor or co-signer of real loans. In all cases, however, the host institution bears the final responsibility for the debt. Few colleges and universities have experience or expertise with this form of financial management.

Figure 5.4 summarizes the post-merger organizational attributes that tend to be associated with each type of merger.

Mergers as Partnerships in Change

One way of distinguishing between types of mergers is in terms of the amount of change experienced by members of the merging institutions (see Figure 5.5). (Although consolidation does not involve 'acquiring' and 'acquired' partners, it is diagrammed as well for purposes of comparison.)

Consolidation entails a high level of change for both merger partners. In contrast, a pure acquisition concentrates change in one partner: the acquired institution is profoundly changed, while the acquiring institution carries on much as before. A subsidiary arrangement enables the acquired institution to retain a distinct identity and very substantial local autonomy. Within the triangle formed by these models are transformative acquisitions

FIGURE 5.4
Common organizational attributes of major merger types

	Consolidation	Pure Acquisition	Transformative Acquisition	Semi-autonomous Acquisition	Subsidiary
Institutional name	New/Combined	Acquiring institution's	Acquiring institution's, possibly modified	Acquiring institution's	Acquiring institution's
Name of acquired institution	n/a*	n/a*	Modified version of acquired institution's	Modified version of acquired institution's	Acquired institution's
Institutional governance	New or best of both	Acquiring institution's	Modified version of acquiring institution's	Acquiring institution's	Acquiring institution's
Systems, policies, and procedures	New or best of both	Acquiring institution's	Modified version of acquiring institution's	Acquiring institution's; local policies for unique purposes	Local, except for certain institutional requirements

FIGURE 5.4.–(Concluded)
Common organizational attributes of major merger types

	Consolidation	Pure Acquisition	Transformative Acquisition	Semi-autonomous Acquisition	Subsidiary
Budgetary status of acquired institution	n/a*	Faculty/unit budget status	Faculty/unit or special budget status	RCB	RCB/RCM
Bargaining units	Unified	Unified	Unified	Unique units for unique groups	Separate
Extent of integration	High	High	High	Medium-High	Low

*Former institutions are no longer recognizable.

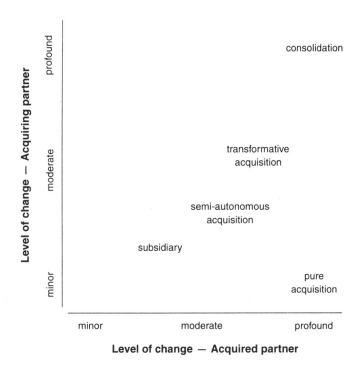

Figure 5.5 Model of magnitude of change for merger partners

(which involve a measure of planned change for the acquiring party, as well as change for the acquired) and semi-autonomy within acquisition (which enables the acquired partner to maintain a measure of autonomy).

The Cases as Partnerships in Change

How then should we classify the Dal/TUNS and OISE/U of T mergers in terms of organizational outcomes? In addressing this question, it is worth looking at what happened in each case both at the institutional level and at the faculty level.

The Institutional-Level Mergers

OISE and U of T

At the institutional level, the OISE/U of T merger was clearly an acquisition, insofar as the university absorbed OISE and did not change

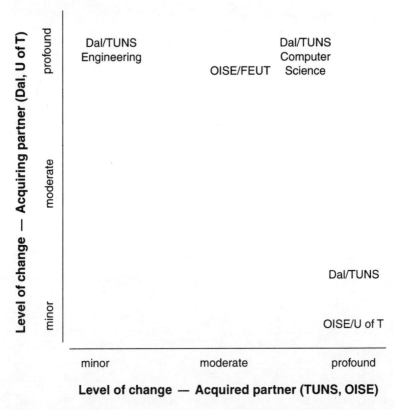

Figure 5.6 Magnitude of change for merger partners: The two cases

significantly. The institutional outcome was not expected to be otherwise. No one at OISE had expected to change the U of T.

The merger's location in Figure 5.6 reflects the fact that it changed the lives of members of the university infinitesimally if at all, whereas it resulted in very substantial change for the people at OISE.

At the same time, the merger did not extinguish OISE's identity and autonomy completely. Although the merged OISE/FEUT is governed by university policies and procedures, it still carries OISE's name (the Ontario Institute for Studies in Education of the University of Toronto, or OISE/UT), enjoys a strong element of responsibility-centred budgeting, and retains two bargaining units with no equivalents elsewhere at the university. In other words, the OISE/U of T merger was an acquisition that gave OISE's successor somewhat greater autonomy than other faculties enjoy.

Dalhousie and TUNS

The agreement to amalgamate Dalhousie and TUNS and the subsequent legislation implied consolidation insofar as they called for the establishment of an 'amalgamated university' (even if it was to 'hav[e] the name Dalhousie University'). At the same time, they suggested that the 'constituent unit' of the university that would succeed TUNS would be very distinctive and autonomous. The amalgamation agreement described 'a college/institute of applied science and technology' with 'at least three closely located professionally-accredited Faculties with strengths appropriate for an internationally renowned research-based university such as Dalhousie. These faculties will initially be Architecture, Computer Science and Engineering.'

In addition to a principal and an academic council (with powers to 'include, but not be limited to, provision for inquiry into all academic matters that might enhance the usefulness of TUNS'), the college was to have a board, the terms of reference of which would include 'to provide the necessary degree of autonomy to TUNS to sustain, protect and advocate the integrity of the TUNS professional programs.'

The references to 'the college/institute ..., amalgamated with Dalhousie,' with a board, a principal, and an academic council, sounded almost like federation, suggesting that the successor to TUNS would be at least semiautonomous.

The legislative act described TUNS's successor in similar terms:

(5.1) The amalgamated university shall create a College of applied science and technology devoted to the advancement of technical education and research;

(5.2) The College shall be an academic unit of the amalgamated university, bearing a unique name, having a College Board and an Academic Council, and headed by a Principal.

This was a statement about the future. In fact, 'the College' did not become reality.

As noted in Chapter 3, even naming the unit that would succeed TUNS proved to be difficult. In February 1997 the boards approved the name 'Dalhousie University Polytechnic.' Opposition to this choice soon surfaced, and the DalTech board undertook to review the choice. The opinions of faculty, staff, students, and alumni were sounded. Although most respondents preferred a suggested alternative – Dalhousie University Institute of Applied Science and Technology – many didn't like either name. The board therefore decided that the informal name by which everyone referred to the college, 'DalTech,' would be its official name.

The bodies that were to govern the college's internal affairs also failed to take root. Although DalTech's academic council had the same composition as TUNS's senate, its operations were different. Few people attended meetings. On several occasions in the first year after amalgamation, a quorum was lacking. It seemed that the academic council was being circumvented, both by deans and others at DalTech and by university bodies, which tended to deal directly with faculties. The council struggled to define a new and meaningful role for itself within the university.

Meanwhile, plans were proceeding for a new building at DalTech for the Faculty of Computer Science and a small number of other units. By late 1997 the Faculty of Computer Science had had several months' experience of teaching on both the old Dalhousie campus and the DalTech (formerly TUNS) campus, from the latter location. This arrangement was necessary because junior undergraduates required access to classes offered by the Arts and Social Sciences and Science faculties, which were located at the opposite end of the combined campus. The logistical headaches proved to be immense. Furthermore, it was less than desirable that junior undergraduates be isolated from senior students and faculty members.

At the end of the year, the Faculty of Computer Science voted virtually unanimously to recommend that its building be on the so-called 'Studley' campus (part of the former Dalhousie campus). The DalTech board accepted the recommendation, and the university administration relocated the site. The anger and outrage of some engineers and architects at DalTech was great. But it wasn't clear at whom to be angry: at Dalhousie for failing to live up to the agreement, at the DalTech board for failing to uphold it, or at colleagues for betraying the college!

In January 1998, Ted Rhodes, principal of DalTech and former president of TUNS, resigned. Tom Traves assumed the role of acting principal. Although there were calls from some quarters at DalTech for an immediate search, there were countervailing views. The main reason for amalgamating with Dalhousie had, after all, been to put more resources into academic programs. The deans and others wanted to put money into the faculties, rather than the principal's office.

In the wake of the principal's resignation, there was a great deal of concern and debate within DalTech about what was happening and what should be done. Some argued for acknowledging that circumstances had changed and moving on – as part of Dalhousie. Others called for people at DalTech to reassert themselves to ensure that both the letter and the spirit of the amalgamation would be fulfilled. Yet others called for the development of a new vision and structure for DalTech that would work in the Dalhousie context. There was bewilderment, confusion, and malaise. It was most notable in the Faculty of Engineering and among active alumni.

A faculty member from DalTech reported to his colleagues on a Dalhousie senate committee that 'in light of the perception that the Amalgamation Agreement was being violated, and the autonomy of the College increasingly undermined, morale [at DalTech] had nose-dived. As autonomy evaporated, disenchantment grew' (Dalhousie Senate, 12 February 1998).

In March 1998 the Faculty of Engineering voted to secede from the college, taking with it its share of resources for the administration of the college. The Faculty of Computer Science followed suit shortly thereafter. The engineers rescinded their motion to secede the following month.

How the college would be administered was discussed at length by the DalTech board and the academic council, as well as by the president and the deans. There were different views. Eventually, the DalTech board agreed that the deans would report to the university's academic vice-president, and that the college's administrative affairs would be attended to by a management council, consisting mainly of the deans – one of whom would also serve as principal.

Shortly after approving this administrative arrangement, the DalTech board reconsidered its own role. In the late spring of 1998, it voted that it be replaced by an advisory board.

Little more than a year after amalgamation, many of the trappings of the college had disappeared. A merger that had been expected to accord TUNS's successor distinctiveness and autonomy looked very much like the acquisition by Dalhousie of three additional faculties.

And, what of Dalhousie? To what extent did it change? The short answer is, not much. In spite of the earlier rhetoric of 'the amalgamated university' – a 'new Dalhousie' built on 'best practices' – its culture and systems did not change, at least not in the short run. The addition of the DalTech faculties, with their experience of other ways of doing things, did lend weight to forces for change within Dalhousie. It is therefore likely that amalgamation will hasten change at the university in the medium and longer term. In the short run, however, the acquisition of TUNS did not change its larger partner. The location of the Dal/TUNS merger in Figure 5.6 reflects this.

The Faculty-Level Mergers

Mergers take place at multiple levels. The Dal/TUNS and OISE/U of T mergers took place both at the institutional level – at which the governing, executive, and central administrative bodies of the smaller institutions were subsumed into those of the universities – and at the disciplinary level, at which OISE merged with FEUT, TUNS's School of Computer Science merged with Dalhousie's Division of Computing Science, and Dalhousie's Department of Engineering merged with TUNS's Faculty of Engineering. Where would these unit-level mergers be depicted within the change framework depicted in Figure 5.6?

The Merger of OISE and FEUT

The integration agreement between OISE and U of T stated that:

> OISE and FEUT ... will be integrated effective July 1, 1996 into a new professional Faculty of Education ... The name of this new Faculty will be the Ontario Institute for Studies in Education of the University of Toronto (hereinafter OISE/UT) ...
> OISE/UT will be established as a Faculty dedicated to national pre-eminence and international distinction in graduate studies, research and field development in education, and preservice and inservice teacher education, providing exemplary leadership within and outside the province, building on the reputations and accomplishments of the current OISE and FEUT ...
> Each aspect of the mission should reinforce the others, and faculty members should be encouraged, so far as possible, to contribute to all aspects.

So, how did it turn out?

A year and a half after it happened, the merger of OISE and FEUT was perceived by former members of FEUT whom we interviewed as more of an acquisition (of FEUT by OISE) than a consolidation – at least for the moment. Michael Fullan, the dean of OISE/UT (and the former dean of FEUT), observed at that time: 'At present, both parties feel that they've been swallowed up. OISE feels that it's been swallowed up by U of T. FEUT feels that it's been swallowed up by OISE.'

Our interviews with other former members of FEUT confirmed this statement. They perceived that OISE had not changed, whereas life was radically different for them. One member of the dean's office described OISE as 'carrying on more or less as before.' Asked how this was possible, given that the university's policies prevailed, another observed, 'The university's policies govern, but OISE's culture is more powerful.'

Asked how the transition to university policies and procedures had been accomplished, a former OISE administrator commented: 'It hasn't. That's part of the problem. The chairs [all of whom are former members of OISE] don't see themselves as part of the university. They just carry on as before ... There isn't a shared vision. There are two opposing cultures.'

A senior member of FEUT observed that no one had fully appreciated beforehand how different the cultures of OISE and FEUT were. Asked to characterize the two cultures, she described FEUT's as collegial, student-oriented and respectful; OISE's as confrontational, competitive, faculty centred, and pseudo-democratic. Other adjectives used to describe OISE – by members of both former institutions – were 'big,' 'inward-looking,' 'otherworldly,' and 'factionalized.' The impression one received was of OISE as a juggernaut that had overwhelmed the small, collegial, practical, teacher education–centred FEUT.

Former FEUT members perceived that preservice education was being devalued within OISE/UT. Although one of the principal objectives of integration had been to bring together preservice education and graduate education to the enrichment of both, the perception was that – at least initially – the latter had swamped the former. This wasn't simply at the level of principle. Three of those we interviewed commented independently that (in the words of one of them), 'people involved in preservice education are treated like second-class citizens by colleagues from OISE who think that only graduate teaching and research count.'

The dominance of OISE's values was reportedly such that junior faculty members from FEUT were concerned about coming up for tenure and promotion in departments that did not value contributions to teacher education.

Views were mixed about whether OISE's dominance of FEUT was temporary or permanent. Some of those we interviewed were confident that it was transitory and that a truly integrated faculty would eventually emerge. Others were more frustrated and pessimistic.

Early in the third year of OISE/UT's existence, Fullan identified achieving genuine integration of undergraduate and graduate education as a high institutional priority. In a 1998 memo to the OISE/UT community, he wrote: 'In the merger we have set out to place teacher education and graduate programs on an equal footing. This is not yet the case.'

He proposed seven measures to raise the prominence of teacher education. These measures ranged from providing additional rewards to undergraduate program coordinators, to implementing an equitable work load policy (to address the disproportionately heavy work loads of faculty members involved in teacher education), to facilitating greater involvement in teacher education by faculty members and students engaged in graduate programs. Participation in both undergraduate (teacher education) and graduate programs subsequently became a requirement in all new faculty appointments.

Clearly, the merger of OISE and FEUT did not result immediately in true consolidation. More than two years after the merger, achieving the sought-after synergy of undergraduate and graduate education, of teaching, research, and outreach, was a work in progress.

The location of the merger of OISE and FEUT in Figure 5.6 reflects this.

The Dal/TUNS Computer Science Merger

In contrast, the merger of the School of Computer Science at TUNS and the Division of Computing Science at Dalhousie was perceived – a year and a half after amalgamation – as having produced a truly new faculty. In the words of a former Dalhousie computer scientist, 'We have formed a new faculty – unquestionably formed a new faculty.' As a former TUNS professor explained: 'Everybody got it into their heads that it wasn't one unit taking over another unit. It was a bunch of people building a completely new program from scratch, from the bottom up ... It was a bunch of resources – programs, regulations, students – being pushed into the middle of the table and a group of people sitting around and rebuilding something completely new out of the good bits that they started with.'

There were elements of a take-over insofar as the former TUNS curriculum became the faculty's core curriculum. But the former Dalhousie computer science faculty members we interviewed said that this came about with their agreement and was not imposed on them. One of them explained:

> We [the two pre-existing CS units] both offered bachelor's programs and we both offered master's programs. TUNS also offered a PhD that we did not.

The Dal people wanted the merger and the TUNS people were not initially keen. What happened was, when it came time to decide which program was going to be our 'Cadillac' – the bachelor of computer science or the bachelor of science – the Dal people stepped aside rather than get into a fight ... We said, 'You want the BCS? Fine.' We did the same thing at the master's level. There was no conscious decision on our part, but I think that's what happened.

In other words, to the extent that the merger of the CS units was a take-over, it was a take-over by consent.

Asked if there were still two groups within the faculty, the four professors and one lecturer whom we interviewed all said 'no.' They all described a cohesive unit ('way more cohesive than a lot of departments that have been around for much longer') in which traces of the former cultures were still perceptible, but fading fast.

Although those whom we interviewed differed regarding the importance of an external appointment to the deanship of the newly merged faculty, all the professors said that the integration of the two groups had taken place very early in the process. One identified the first joint meeting of the faculty (in the spring of 1996) after the amalgamation announcement as the turning point. Another said: 'The unifying thing happened when we all had to start teaching together.' But all agreed that the faculty was functioning as an integrated unit before the new dean's arrival.

The outcome of the merger of the two Computing Science units is shown as akin to a consolidation in Figure 5.6.

The Dal/TUNS Engineering Merger

Predictably, the members of Dalhousie's tiny Department of Engineering were absorbed into TUNS's much larger Faculty of Engineering. As one of their number observed, 'It could not have been otherwise.' After amalgamation, they ceased to function as a unit, and joined the departments of the new faculty appropriate to their particular areas of specialization.

The members of Dalhousie's Department of Engineering were in favour of amalgamation, because it would create a comprehensive (first-year undergraduate to doctoral) Faculty of Engineering and would enhance their opportunities to participate in graduate education and research. They were nevertheless somewhat chagrined by how quickly Dalhousie entrusted issues pertaining to their discipline to TUNS's faculty. As soon as the amalgamation agreement was signed, Dalhousie's administrative leaders began treating engineering issues – including the post-merger delivery of undergraduate engineering education and the revision of the undergraduate curriculum – as matters within the purview of TUNS's faculty and dean, rather than as issues to be addressed through joint transition planning.

The location of the merger of the two Engineering units in Figure 5.6 reflects this.

Overview of Outcomes

In sum, both mergers were acquisitions at the institutional level. At the discipline level, one merger (Computer Science) resulted in a genuine consolidation of the pre-existing units; a second (Education) in the initial dominance of one by the other; and the third (Engineering) in the acquisition by the larger unit of the functions and resources of the smaller.

The next chapter reflects on what we can learn from all this about the forces that shape the outcomes of higher education mergers and how mergers can best be planned and managed.

PART THREE

Reflections on Experience

SIX

On Dynamics and Structure

In this and the following two chapters, we make observations about aspects of the two cases, and offer associated suggestions for planning, negotiating and managing higher education mergers.

Size and Power in Higher Education Merger

In *Merging Colleges for Mutual Growth* (1994), James Martin and James Samels advocate higher education merger as a strategy for achieving academic excellence, strengthening financial health, improving administrative efficiency, achieving economies of scale, stabilizing enrolments, realizing synergies, and securing other desirable outcomes. They contrast an emerging model of 'mutual growth mergers,' through which these outcomes can be achieved, with earlier 'bankruptcy-bailout mergers.'

> Traditional American bankruptcy – bailout merger plans were often driven not by a harmony of institutional missions, but rather by the coincidence of a financially secure, aggressive institution located near a weakened, even failing, college that was vulnerable to takeover. These were mergers in the barest sense of the word ... A pro-active, mutual-growth merger begins from a distinctly different perspective ... Two or more post-secondary institutions join in a common endeavour for the mutual benefit and advancement of both organizations. This agreement demonstrates a shared vision and a stake in collaborative growth and development.

In other words, a modern-day mutual growth merger is about shared vision, not about power.

The Dal/TUNS and OISE/U of T cases suggest otherwise. Even in mergers based on mutual interest, power shapes outcomes in profound ways.

Insofar as it reflects an institution's ability to secure resources from its environment, size (of the student body, faculty and staff, budget, etc.) is a reasonable proxy for power. (What is happening at the margins, in terms of trends in applications, enrolments, share of government funding, surpluses versus deficits, and the attraction and retention of staff, reflects whether this power is increasing or on the wane.)

It is instructive to look at the Dal/TUNS and OISE/U of T mergers, at both the institutional and the unit levels, in terms of the relative size of the units involved. We do this in Figure 6.1, in terms of numbers of full-time (or, in the cases of OISE and U of T, full-time equivalent tenured and tenure-stream) faculty members.

As we noted in Chapter 5, only the merger of the computer science units was a consolidation from the outset. In the short term, none of the other mergers resulted in a well-integrated new unit or organization. To the extent that one institution or unit was dwarfed by its partner, merger forced the smaller one to change to conform to the larger one's culture and organization, which remained basically unchanged. In other words, of the two institutional-level and three unit-level mergers in our two cases, only where the merging units were of roughly equal size did both change at the outset to form something new.

Observation   Relative size and power matter. Mergers of institutions or units of approximately the same size may create something truly new. Mergers of institutions or units of substantially different size almost always involve the absorption and transformation of the smaller one by the larger.

Obvious as this is, it is often overlooked – with unfortunate consequences.

The consultants we interviewed considered it a 'given' that relative size determines organizational outcome – that mergers of institutions of significantly different size and power are invariably acquisitions. One skeptic doubted that merger ever results in true consolidation (i.e., the melding of the best characteristics of both merger partners) even if the merger partners are equal in size. 'One culture always dominates,' he observed. With respect to the corporate sector, Bengtsson has likewise found that 'even with similar-sized companies, one organisation usually leads because of

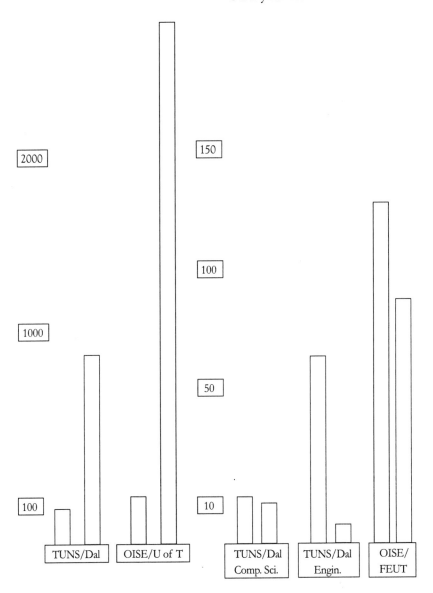

Figure 6.1 Relative sizes of merging institutions and their divisions

financial strength, market potential, company reputation, structure, or a dominant executive management team' (1992, 33).

Gail Chambers, surveying mergers and merger attempts by private American colleges in the 1970s, observed that consolidation was much discussed, 'but most frequently it was acquisition that happened or there was no merger at all' (1984, 10).

Why is this? Organizations dislike uncertainty and seek to minimize it. Large organizations are more successful at this than small ones. The implication for the dynamics of merger is that organizations, faced with uncertainty arising from the prospect of merger, seek to minimize that uncertainty by imposing and implementing their own terms – and the larger and more powerful an organization is, the more readily it can do this.

Chambers found that consolidation, though attractive in theory, was flawed in practice. Specifically, the consolidation model did not specify 'how real differences would be treated within a new institution. Boards needed more assurance before signing over their property and trust. Consequently, when the difficult questions of control, identity, mission, property, and prestige were finally engaged in concrete terms, the concept of equality gave way to perceived dominance by one partner' (1984, 10). In other words, faced with the uncertainty that consolidation entailed, institutions threw 'mutual growth' out the window and sought to dominate each other. Almost invariably, either one institution succeeded and acquired and absorbed the other, or the merger talks broke down. The great majority of mergers in higher education have therefore been acquisitions.

Gillian Rowley's study of higher education merger in England between 1987 and 1994 confirmed the rarity of consolidation, insofar as it equated merger with the integration of B, a 'merged partner,' into A, 'the extant HE institution' – that is, with acquisition. All of the forty-one incidents of merger she identified and studied were of this variety. With respect to size, she found that 'typically, A had 5–10,000 FTE students, while B had fewer than 1,000. Their income ratio was mostly less than 10:1' (1997, 252).

Suggestion   Higher education institutions should go into merger discussions with larger partners with their eyes open to the reality that most mergers are acquisitions, expecially when the parties are of significantly different size.

Does this mean that mergers of institutions of different size inevitably involve the absorption of the smaller institution into the larger one? Do they inevitably require small institutions to change to conform to larger parties' values, processes, and systems? No. First, recall that there are several types of acquisition. Besides pure acquisitions (in which the smaller partner is absorbed into the larger and the latter does not change significantly), transformative acquisitions, semiautonomous arrangements, and subsidiary arrangements are possible.

As was shown in Figure 5.5, the latter entail more change for the large partners than do pure acquisitions. In a transformative acquisition, the larger institution uses merger as an opportunity to take on some of the organizational characteristics of the smaller partner or to develop new ones. Semiautonomous and subsidiary arrangements do not involve as extensive change for the larger partner; that being said, dealing with a new college or managing a subsidiary cannot but involve some change.

Michael Beer observed that 'if there is one thing of which researchers are very certain, it is that organizations do change when they are under pressure and very rarely when they are not' (1980, 47). Resistance to change is particularly great in organizations like universities in which power is dispersed and goals and agendas diverge. As Jaap Tuinman has observed: 'It is not possible to overestimate individual and institutional resistance to change ... The average member of an educational organization does not want to change, does not want more work, does not want to reassess his/her values, does want to be "left alone to do his/her work." In short, many faculty members, when given an unpressured choice opt for the *status quo*' (1995, 44).

Given the tendency of higher education institutions and their members to resist change, what can a small institution do to increase the likelihood that a merger agreement will result in the adoption – or at least toleration – of some of its characteristics by the larger partner? Later in the chapter we offer some suggestions about how to approach merger negotiations. In the final analysis, however, probably the best thing a smaller institution can do is explore whether its larger partner in fact *wants* to change, recognizing that it will not be able to force it to do so. As Tuinman found with respect to collaboration, a merger of institutions of different size is unlikely to change the larger partner unless that partner recognizes the need to re-examine its mission, perceives merger (collaboration) as a means of strengthening its capacity to fulfil its mission, and is prepared to commit the time, energy, and money needed to change itself.

Observation   For the success of acquisitions that entail significant change for the larger as well as the smaller merger partner (i.e., transformative acquisitions, semiautonomous arrangements, subsidiary arrangements):

- *The larger partner must value the strengths of the smaller institution, and be committed to maintaining and/or incorporating those strengths. In other words, it must want to adopt (in the case of a transformative acquisition) or preserve (in the case of a semiautonomous or subsidiary arrangement) characteristics of the acquired institution.*
- *The larger partner must have the leadership, managerial capacity, and resources needed to bring about and manage the resulting internal change, as well as that which takes place within the acquired unit.*

Suggestion   A smaller institution seeking to negotiate a transformative acquisition or to become a semiautonomous unit or subsidiary of a larger institution should therefore make certain of the following:

- *The partner understands the nature of the change involved and is committed to it.*
- *The partner has the leadership, management capacity, and resources necessary to effect and manage the change.*

This is especially important in transformative acquisitions. Because they involve significant change for the acquiring as well as the acquired institution, they greatly increase the uncertainty, anxiety, and resistance that must be managed during the process. A successful transformative acquisition requires political skill and capital, managerial depth, and other resources, which may not be present within the acquiring institution. If, for example, the president of the acquiring university is near the end of her term of office and uncertain of reappointment, she may not have the political authority needed to secure her academic colleagues' participation (or acquiescence) in change. Similarly, if her administrative colleagues don't have a record of success in bringing about organizational change, their capacity to deliver on a commitment to 're-engineering' may be questionable.

It would behoove the leaders of the larger organization to consider all these points just as carefully as their counterparts in the smaller institution. Acquisitions involve an immense amount of work even when any change will be concentrated in the acquired organization. To change one's own organization while acquiring another is a formidable challenge.

Suggestion   *An institution contemplating an acquisition that would transform itself or produce a semiautonomous unit or subsidiary should verify that it has the political, managerial, financial, and other resources necessary to take it on all at once.*

The Perils of Uniqueness

One of the major differences between the OISE/UT and Dal/TUNS mergers is that the combined OISE and FEUT became one of many faculties at the University of Toronto, whereas TUNS became a college within Dalhousie that was to be unique.

In its negotiations with OISE, the university insisted that OISE/UT have 'faculty' status, and this was eventually agreed. In accordance with the merger agreement, OISE/UT is a faculty and enjoys the powers and prerogatives available to the university's other faculties. OISE/UT's place within the university is therefore well understood. By virtue of its size, it is one of the university's 'Big Five' faculties. Several of those we interviewed at OISE/UT commented on this fact, and relish quietly the profile and clout this status bestows.

In accordance with the Dal/TUNS amalgamation agreement, TUNS was to become a 'college/institute of applied science and technology, suitably renamed and amalgamated with Dalhousie.' There was and is one other college at Dalhousie – the College of Arts and Science, composed of the Faculty of Arts and Social Sciences and the Faculty of Science. This college – a vestige of the former Faculty of Arts and Science – meets twice a year to approve the awarding of degrees to students graduating from the two faculties. The two deans take turns serving as provost. Most people at Dalhousie would be hard-pressed to say what purpose the college serves.

The College of Arts and Science was not the type of college that people at TUNS had in mind. They envisioned a college that would be a successor to TUNS in the fullest sense – that would enable them to retain their autonomy, practices, and culture. Some seemed to hope that the change from being a university with a board of governors, a president, and a senate to a college with a board, a principal, and an academic council would be simply one of name, and that operations would carry on much as before.

Most people at TUNS recognized that change was inevitable; but it was not clear what the new reality would be. There was uncertainty about what the new college would actually do. The amalgamation agreement did not require Dalhousie's governing or administrative bodies to delegate substantial authority to the college (with the exception of the authority to allocate budgets to the college's three faculties), and Dalhousie showed no inclination to do so. This being the case, as one of the deans at TUNS pointed out, the only choice for TUNS was whether to have 'a strong college with weak faculties or a weak college with strong faculties.'

From a dean's point of view, one would naturally want strong faculties. Why would one not want all the budgetary powers that other deans at Dalhousie enjoyed? Why would one want to get approval (from the academic council) for new undergraduate courses when other faculties were not required to do so? In their capacity as faculty members, many others would have shared this view. Why would an engineer not want his or her faculty to be as strong as Science or Medicine? The natural desire of former TUNS faculties to assume the powers that other Dalhousie faculties enjoyed tended to undermine the strength of the college.

Other parts of Dalhousie were used to dealing with faculties, not colleges, and this also tended to conspire against the college. At the most mundane level, it meant that in the absence of instructions to the contrary, offices across the university – administrative units, the senate office, the faculty association, and so on – tended to do business with deans and faculty councils rather than with the principal and the College Academic Council. Quite unintentionally, this left the latter 'out of the loop.'

In the event, TUNS did not succeed in carving out a new niche within Dalhousie. Other factors – in particular, the fact that the college lacked strong internal leadership for several months after the merger due to the illness of the principal – no doubt conspired against the college, but the fact that it was unique within Dalhousie undeniably made it vulnerable.

Observation   When an acquired organization becomes a unit that has no equivalent within the acquiring organization, its future is much more uncertain.

For this reason, it behooves the acquiring institution to consider carefully how a potential acquisition will fit into its existing structure. At what levels of both institutions are decisions made? How would the organizations fit together? As Bengtsson observed with respect to the corporate world, all acquisitions have an impact on the acquring company's existing structure, and therefore a company should plan to bring the structure of a newcomer into harmony with the rest of the group (1992, 16).

Suggestion   An institution contemplating acquiring another should ensure that it understands its own structure, that of the potential acquisition, and the changes that would be required – for one or both institutions – to provide good post-merger structural fit.

For example, Dalhousie – as a faculty-centred institution – was not a congenial home for an acquired college. Had it wanted to preserve a college to succeed TUNS, it should have considered making appropriate changes in its own structure – perhaps aggregating some of its other faculties into colleges (e.g., a college of health science faculties) – with the goal of achieving a better fit between TUNS's successor and the rest of the institution.

Structural fit looms even larger as an issue for a small institution that is considering becoming part of another one.

> **Suggestion**   *An institution that is contemplating being acquired should study the organization of its potential acquirer. Are there units within the latter that resemble what it wants or is prepared to become? If so, the unit that succeeds the acquired institution is likely to be more stable than it would be if the successor unit were unique.*

When a successor unit is unique, its prospects are uncertain. It risks being engulfed by forces within the larger institution, as was the college that succeeded TUNS.

> **Suggestion**   *An institution that wants to carve out a unique role within the acquiring institution should attempt to negotiate a form of acquisition that will give it a measure of autonomy (e.g., a semiautonomous or subsidiary arrangement) and to ensure that the leadership, managerial energy, and financial resources committed are sufficient to implement the agreement.*

Understanding the structure of a potential merger partner can inform, not only the form of merger one seeks to negotiate, but also planning and budgeting for the merged institution. In the case of Dalhousie and TUNS, the full extent of the differences in the institutions' administrative practices was not appreciated until after the merger. As a result, faculties and departments at DalTech were swamped with administrative work that they hadn't expected. An *ad hoc* committee established by the Faculty of Engineering opined in its May 1999 'Dalhousie-TUNS Merger Impact Report':

A major difference between TUNS and Dalhousie is that Dalhousie has a quasi-decentralized administration. Dalhousie downloads significant administrative load on the faculties and departments. Therefore, faculties and departments at Dalhousie have parallel services of finance, personnel, student records, etc. At TUNS, these services were all provided from the central administration. At the time of the merger, the central services staff at TUNS were all taken by the central services of Dalhousie rather than being distributed to the departments and the faculty office ... Consequently, the Faculty of Engineering and its departments at DalTech are not properly equipped to operate within the Dalhousie system and are severely burdened and disadvantaged. (Fenton et al, 1999, 17)

Problems like this can be avoided if it is possible to compare the structures and operations of merging institutions early in the process.

Dynamics of Negotiation

Let's assume that an institution knows itself and where it wants to go, has studied a potential merger partner, and has identified objectives for merger that are realistic and appropriate. How should it approach the negotiation process?

It has been said that there are two possible paths to a merger agreement: courtship and combat. The consultants we interviewed agreed with this observation, although they disagreed over which approach was more effective. Those with relatively more public sector experience tended to the view that 'combat' does not work in that sector.

From Courtship to Combat: A Spectrum

Courtship and combat can be envisioned as points on a spectrum of possible approaches to merger negotiations. At one end of the spectrum, there is true harmony. The parties have shared interests and complete trust. Moving across the spectrum, the parties' interests begin to diverge, but initially there is reluctance to acknowledge the differences explicitly and negotiate their resolution. This leads to what Bacharach and Lawler have described as tacit bargaining. It occurs often in intraorganizational and other settings in which parties 'may be hesitant to admit or confront conflict ... and may try to handle issues in a less visible way' (1982, 113).

At the midpoint of the spectrum, parties engage in collaborative bargaining – in other words, they acknowledge their differences, exchange information about their preferences and seek to find mutually acceptable resolutions. There is some trust.

Further yet along the spectrum, each party employs tactics designed to get the other to accept its position, and pays no regard to the other's real interests. The parties do not identify with each other; rather, they perceive each other in terms of 'them' and 'us.' There may not be mistrust, but neither is there trust. According to Raiffa, this negotiating situation, in which the parties are 'cooperative antagonists,' can easily degenerate into one in which they are 'strident antagonists' – that is, into outright conflict (1982, 19).

The Dal/TUNS and OISE/UT cases illustrate nicely the different dynamics and relative merits of courtship and combat. The Dal/TUNS amalgamation agreement was the product of courtship – albeit courtship with a perceived shotgun (in the form of government desire for amalgamation) in the background. The presidents themselves initiated merger talks and drafted the amalgamation agreement. They spoke jointly about the benefits of amalgamation and presented a united front to the government, the community, and their two campuses. There was a very real sense that they were partners in bringing their universities together.

Of course, no partnership is perfect. The parties had their differences. But having agreed to a government announcement of the merger before an agreement had been signed, and having presented the merger to their constituents as a joint enterprise, it would naturally have been awkward for the presidents to acknowledge these publicly. There was a tendency to downplay the differences in the institutions' positions in public – that is, to engage in tacit bargaining and avoid overt conflict.

In contrast, OISE and U of T reached agreement to merge through combat. The government brought them to the negotiating table. OISE did not want to be there. Its initial objective was to avoid merger with U of T; the university's was to select parts of OISE for integration into a new Faculty of Education. The two institutions struck negotiating teams, which met formally to exchange positions. They were unable to make progress. There was much frustration and no trust. Some members of OISE lobbied publicly against the merger. After months of negotiations, the institutions requested a mediator. With his help – and ultimately with the personal involvement of U of T's president – the parties finally hammered out a tentative agreement after several sessions of intensive bargaining.

What, then, are the advantages and disadvantages of courtship and conflict?

Climatic Considerations

In the short run, courtship is associated with a much more collegial, congenial climate. The symbolism of the presidents of Dalhousie and TUNS working closely together was powerful. It created a sense of the universities as partners in an important and exciting joint enterprise. Although there was apprehension, especially at TUNS, members of the two institutions by and large treated each other with cordiality and respect. They perceived amalgamation not as a zero-sum game but rather as a process of mutual gain.

In contrast, the adversarial approach taken by OISE and U of T fed suspicion and mistrust between the parties. Thus, for example, the expert reports commissioned separately by the two institutions in the spring of 1995 were dismissed as ammunition for the other party's position. One former OISE official observed: 'We all knew in advance what the consultants would say. Each side got the views it wanted.' This expert input might have stimulated joint planning had the dynamics of the negotiations been different; instead it was regarded with cynicism and had little or no utility.

By the summer of 1995, communication between the bargaining teams had reportedly broken down.

Observation   *Courtship fosters collegiality and creates a constructive climate for planning and building a new institution. Combat tends to undermine communication, leading to escalating conflict and reducing the likelihood of agreement.*

Courtship and combat also seem to be associated with different psychological climates. The close collaboration between the presidents of Dalhousie and TUNS was reassuring to members and friends of the two universities. It bespoke partnership, collegiality, and mutual respect. Although many at TUNS were apprehensive about amalgamation, they were relatively sanguine.

In contrast, feelings ran very high at OISE. Although some members of the OISE community were quietly supportive of integration, many perceived U of T as opposed to all that OISE stood for. From their perspective, OISE was progressive, feminist, and democratic, while U of T was arrogant, authoritarian and right wing. The statements of U of T's president and provost, as reported in the *Bulletin* (4 February 1994), that OISE would become part of an expanded U of T Faculty of Education, but that not all OISE faculty would be offered jobs by the university, were interpreted as evidence of the university's supreme arrogance and complete lack of respect for OISE. Faculty and staff at OISE felt much more threatened by the prospect of merger than did those at TUNS, and experienced correspondingly greater levels of anxiety and emotion.

Observation   In the short run, courtship minimizes conflict and damage to the morale of members and friends of the smaller institution. In contrast, combat tends to reinforce divisions, create perceptions of winners and losers, alienate members and friends of the smaller institution, and cause high levels of anxiety and emotion for the latter during negotiations.

The Costs and Benefits of Ambiguity

Combat is associated with short-term damage to relationships and morale. However, it does have advantages. Precisely because the parties do not trust each other, they tend to want to spell everything out in detail. The result is clearer, more comprehensive agreements. According to Bacharach and Lawler:

> Explicit bargaining is a more effective mode of conflict resolution than tacit bargaining – Agreements established through explicit rather than tacit bargaining are likely to be more stable. Tacit agreements are likely to be more ambiguous, nonbinding and unenforceable in a strict sense. Such agreements can be broken with relative impunity and typically require more trust than is likely to be present under conditions of tacit bargaining. On the other hand, agreements from explicit bargaining tend to be more specific and unambiguous. Unlike tacit agreements, explicit ones are likely to include some safeguards against a breach by either party. (1982, 116)

In a paper on a possible model for the DalTech college, Orest Cochkanoff, Dean of Engineering at NSTC during the attempted merger with Dalhousie in the 1970s, alluded to the relationship between conflict, clarity, and comprehensiveness. He noted that the 1997 merger 'did not include detailed planning. This is in contra-distinction to the previous effort wherein very vigorous anti-amalgamation forces required that meticulous, detailed development of academic, administrative, physical plant and financial planning be carried out' (1998, 2).

Observation   Courtship may be associated with issue avoidance and ambiguity, if lead negotiators are intent on preserving a harmonious facade.

On the other hand,

Observation   *Combat tends to produce clarity and comprehensiveness in any resulting agreement.*

The Dal/TUNS case illustrates clearly the advantages and disadvantages of ambiguity. In contrast to the OISE/U of T merger agreement, the Dal/TUNS amalgamation agreement and subsequent legislation were susceptible to differing interpretations. They could be read as providing for a true consolidation of Dalhousie and TUNS ('an amalgamated university'), for the acquisition of TUNS by Dalhousie ('the amalgamation of Dalhousie and TUNS shall be known as Dalhousie University'), or for a semi-autonomous successor to TUNS within Dalhousie ('a strong college/institute of applied science and technology').

This lack of clarity was not lost on people. Throughout the fall of 1996, the TUNS Senate and its committees considered many motions that addressed the amount of autonomy the successor to TUNS would enjoy. For example, on 18 September 1996 it considered a motion that:

> Whereas Her Majesty the Queen, in right of the Province of Nova Scotia considers that, as a matter of strategic public policy ... a strong college/institute of applied science and technology are fundamental cornerstones of the economy and future of Nova Scotia, and
> Whereas the amalgamation with Dalhousie was voted upon in the spirit of TUNS remaining an autonomous college within the merged University, and
> Whereas the autonomy of TUNS is an essential ingredient to fulfill the considerations of Her Majesty the Queen ...
> IT IS MOVED that the amalgamation with Dalhousie must be effected in such a way as to retain the financial, academic and research autonomy of TUNS and that the amalgamation should only proceed if these are enshrined in the operating procedures and constitution of the new university. (TUNS Senate, 18 September 1996)

TUNS's president commented that 'the spirit of the motion is what we all want to happen.' The motion was referred to the Senate's steering and planning committees, which were to propose a list of 'needs' arising from the motion.

At the meeting of the TUNS Senate on 16 October 1996, the chair of the steering committee (who had been engaged in discussions with the steering committee of the Dalhousie Senate) distributed a sheet showing three models for amalgamation: (1) 'full amalgamation'; (2) 'amalgamated but autonomous'; and (3) 'an affiliated university.' As reported in the Senate minutes, 'he noted that in his view Dalhousie sees the pending amalgamation in terms of Model (1), while TUNS generally expects to work towards Model (2) ... He felt that Dalhousie would, in the long run, work toward a full amalgamation; ... [whereas] the desire [of the TUNS faculty] is to retain autonomy and approach the status of an affiliated unit' (TUNS Senate, 16 October 1996). The different conceptions of what amalgamation was about were also apparent to those on the Dalhousie side of the Senate-level discussions. The presidents of Dalhousie and TUNS were, of course, aware that there were different conceptions of the outcome of amalgamation on the two campuses, but they did not confront the issue.

The ambiguity surrounding the proposed merger did not escape at least one Nova Scotia MLA. Whereas most who spoke at the second reading of Bill 44 applauded amalgamation as a step forward, John Leefe, the MLA for Queen's County, proposed a wait-and-see approach:

Dalhousie has a reputation over the past century and one-half of a kind of academic imperialism, seeking from time to time, from the middle of the 1800s forward to very recent times, to gobble up other academic institutions in Nova Scotia ... Dalhousie is now involved by this bill, if it passes, in a merger of the Technical University of Nova Scotia and Dalhousie. We will all be watching very carefully to try to determine whether in fact this is a marriage of two equal partners who will share the matrimonial property each of them brings with them on an equal basis, to see if TUNS is an equal partner with Dalhousie in this new arrangement, or if, as one would hope would not be the case, TUNS comes to be swallowed up in what some would call the black hole of Dalhousie ...

We will be interested to see what the reaction to this is as time passes by and, indeed, I am sure that other institutions in Nova Scotia, in particular, will watch this merger to determine what the relationship is between those who enter into it and to determine how, at a future date, mergers are suggested between the now larger Dalhousie and those other universities, just whether those mergers do, in fact, result in partnerships, or something less than that, which would not, in the view of many, be desirable for post-secondary education here in Nova Scotia. (Nova Scotia Assembly Debates, 29 November 1996, 2625)

Ambiguity is by no means unusual at the outset of merger negotiations. The very term 'merger' is often used imprecisely. It is frequently used to denote formal forms of cooperative endeavour among institutions that are less than true mergers, in which one or both participants forego an independent and separate identity. 'Merger' is often confused with other forms of organizational behaviour; also, it itself takes many forms, as noted in Chapter 5. To describe a particular venture simply as a 'merger' may shroud its actual nature.

Thus imprecision is common. So is obscuration. A study of corporate mergers and acquisitions found that when talking with representatives of the target firm, representatives of the acquiring company invariably referred to a "merger" of the two firms, whereas among themselves they described the same combination as an "acquisition." The researchers concluded that 'there is an inoffensive quality in the word "merge" not found in the word "acquire"' (Buono and Bowditch, 1989, 60).

Voluntary mergers of universities and other institutions of higher education usually require faculty members' implicit (and in some cases explicit) approval, so the tendency to obfuscate is even greater. Both sets of institutions we studied avoided 'hard,' corporate terms such as 'acquisition' and indeed 'merger,' in favour of more amorphous terms such as 'integration' and 'amalgamation.'

The exceptional thing about the Dal/TUNS merger is that the ambiguity was never confronted. Right up to the time it was implemented, people continued to have very different conceptions of what amalgamation would mean. This had both costs and benefits.

The major benefit was that amalgamation could be 'sold' to different constituencies with different interests. The terms in which Dal/TUNS amalgamation was couched were sufficiently reassuring to people at TUNS about their continued identity and autonomy ('a strong College') and about change at Dalhousie ('the amalgamated new university') to secure their approval. By the same token, they were sufficiently vague that they did not alarm people at Dalhousie by promising real change on their campus.

Observation   *Ambiguity can facilitate agreement.*

This aspect of ambiguity is well known to experienced negotiators. As Willam Zartman and Maureen Berman have noted:

Calculated – or, as Kissinger termed it, 'constructive' – ambiguity is often very useful. Careful sidestepping of a delicate issue on which no agreement is possible, and deliberately equivocal wording, have each saved the day on more than one occasion ... If the rest of the details all fall into place, one point of disagreement should not be allowed to hold up the accord ... However, precise agreement is important; only in exceptional cases should ambiguity be used, and then only consciously. (1982, 182)

The costs of ambiguous agreements (as distinct from agreements that contain some ambiguity) are illustrated by the Dal/TUNS case. Very simply, when there are two different interpretations of an agreement, at least one will be proven wrong. And it is most likely to be that of the smaller and less powerful partner to the agreement. Ambiguity gives the acquiring institution – or the larger partner in a consolidation – freer rein.

Ambiguous merger agreements between partners of different sizes have several characteristics typically associated with implementation problems. Besides lacking clarity and definition, they require sustained action by 'the other side' (Lebow, 1996). Since an acquired institution ceases to exist as a separate legal entity after a merger, implementation of the agreement is up to the acquirer. Also, the cost of non-compliance with the agreement is low, and there is little effective recourse for former members of the acquired institution. For these reasons, an ambiguous merger agreement between partners of different sizes is fraught with risk for the small institution.

Observation   Ambiguity tends to serve the interests of the larger, more powerful merger partner.

Suggestion   An institution negotiating with a larger merger partner should be clear about its desired model and its operational requirements, and should seek a clear, reasonably detailed agreement.

If a clear, comprehensive agreement is in the interests of the smaller partner, is a sketchy, ambiguous agreement in the interests of the larger one? Should a larger partner ignore, tolerate, or even foster ambiguity? Quite apart from ethical considerations, not necessarily.

The advantage of an ambiguous agreement is that it tends to give the larger party a freer hand in implementing the merger or acquisition. Such flexibility is desirable because it makes possible an incremental approach to organizational design, the advantages of which are explored in Chapter 10 below.

The disadvantages are twofold. First, an ambiguous agreement entails

risk – even for an acquiring institution or the larger partner in a consolidation – that another outcome will unfold. The extent of the risk tends to
depend on the relative size of the parties. The more equal the size and
power of the two parties, the more risk there is that the outcome of a vague
or ambiguous agreement may not reflect the larger party's objectives. Had
TUNS approximated Dalhousie more closely in size and power, their
amalgamation might have produced a more semiautonomous structure –
or even two institutions in one – rather than an acquisition.

The personalities of the institutions' leaders are also a factor. Their
respective determination, energy, and toughness – their willingness to
mobilize political, financial, and other resources to bend the merger to
their objectives – also affects how the product of a sketchy agreement turns
out.

*Observation   The extent of the risk an ambiguous agreement poses
for a larger partner is inverse to the difference in size and power
between the partners.*

Suggestion   *Seek greater definition if your merger partner approxi-
mates your institution in size and power, especially if your partner's
leadership is determined.*

The second disadvantage of ambiguity is that those whose expectations
are disappointed are likely to feel betrayed, both by their former leaders
and by the institution of which they have become part. Most people
associated with TUNS – alumni and donors as well as faculty, staff, and
students – interpreted the amalgamation agreement as providing for the
continued existence of a relatively autonomous successor to TUNS within
Dalhousie. As the structure associated with the college (i.e., a full-time
principal, a DalTech Board, a functioning academic council) fell away,
many TUNS loyalists – especially in the Faculty of Engineering, which
had dominated TUNS – felt betrayed.

*Observation   The implementation of an ambiguous agreement is
likely to lead to loss of trust in the successor institution on the part of
those whose expectations are not fulfilled.*

This is in turn likely to have a negative impact on performance and
morale. Research on corporate mergers and acquisitions has found that
unfulfilled expectations are common and that they erode trust and com-

mitment, create dissatisfaction and disenchantment, and lead to performance declines (Buono and Bowditch, 1989, 121).

This is not to suggest that fulfilment of negative expectations produces
happy campers! Low morale appears to be the norm following mergers.
According to Buono and Bowditch:

> The period following an organizational consolidation is often characterized
> by 'we–they' tensions, power struggles, turnover and absenteeism, and de-
> clines in job-related attitudes and performance in the acquired or merged
> firm that typically require at least one to two years to resolve ... This type of
> 'postmerger drift' – performance declines, a slow learning process, and gen-
> eral dissatisfaction with the organization – appears to be a basic attribute of
> virtually all organizational consolidations. (1989, 193)

There is, however, evidence that the extent of the decline in morale and
performance is proportional to the gap between expectations and reality.
The Dal/TUNS case bears this out: the postmerger morale of members of
the Faculty of Engineering (who had been relatively well disposed to
amalgamation) was worse than that of members of the former School of
Computer Science (who had been more strongly opposed).

The state of morale in Engineering was described in the preamble to a
motion passed by the Faculty of Engineering in March 1998 to cede from
DalTech and recover its share of the administrative resources of the college. The first four clauses of the motion were as follows:

> Whereas morale and productivity among the faculty and staff of the Faculty
> of Engineering have been declining steadily to the detriment of our pro-
> grams, external relationships and ongoing projects;
>
> And whereas the continuing uncertainties and split loyalties within DalTech,
> the ambiguity and lack of authority in its governing structures, and a lack of
> internal communication and purpose are a major source of this malaise;
>
> And whereas the individual Deans and Faculties within DalTech, the
> Principal of the College, the DalTech Academic Council, and the DalTech
> Board have been unable to ameliorate this confusion with a vision and
> mission that merges our interests or excites our collegial loyalty;
>
> And whereas the recently required reorganization of the College govern-
> ance has led to disagreement and another year's delay in defining how the
> College might work ...

The outcome of amalgamation was not what the engineers had expected, and this damaged their morale. To the extent that their energy was diverted from teaching and research to agonizing over DalTech's future, amalgamation also damaged their productivity.

Given the autonomy enjoyed by faculty members, and the correspondingly strong relationship between internal motivation and performance, disenchantment can have a major impact on academic productivity and students' experience.

Suggestion   *If it is important to the acquiring institution to retain the trust and commitment of members and friends of the institution that is being acquired, the former should attempt to ensure that both parties have the same basic understanding of what the merger agreement means.*

Collaborative and Competitive Approaches

In light of the different ways in which courtship and combat shape the climate of negotiations and the contents of any resulting agreement, which approach to negotiations is most effective? The answer depends fundamentally on the distance between the two institutions' positions.

Collaborative bargaining, in which (following Lebow's description of the strategy of coordination) the parties exchange information about their preferences and seek to accommodate them, is effective only when the parties' positions are compatible – that is, when a mutually satisfactory solution can be found. It is particularly effective if the issues are linked and have asymmetrical utilities (because 'if the benefit of receiving a concession is greater than the cost of making it, the principal demands of one or both sides may be met at little cost to the other'), and if there is mutual trust between the parties (Lebow, 1996, 62).

Lebow further suggests:

If preferences appear close enough to make the strategy of coordination feasible, there are two ways to proceed. The bargainers can enumerate all the issues on the table with the aim of identifying those on which agreement is possible without any, or with very little, bargaining ... By identifying issues on which agreement is easy, the bargainers emphasize their common interests, encourage expectations that coordination will advance those interests, and provide stronger incentives to find solutions to the contentious issues that remain ...

An alternative approach also begins with a discussion of issues and prefer-

ences, but it then makes use of offers and counters to find possible accommo-
dations . . . The purpose of the offers and counteroffers is not to get a good
deal at the other side's expense, but to elicit new information that will allow
the side making the offers to fashion a more attractive offer. (1996, 67)

If this approach to merger negotiations is possible, an agreement can be
reached without the damage to morale and relationships associated with
competitive or adversarial bargaining.

*Suggestion   If the institutions' interests are reasonably compatible,
they should attempt collaborative bargaining, particularly if the continued allegiance of the faculty, staff, students, alumni and friends of
the smaller institution is important for the future success of the merged
institution.*

If the positions of the negotiating parties are at odds – if, in other words,
no mutually satisfactory outcome is possible – a collaborative approach
will not be effective. Adversarial bargaining – in which parties use rewards
(e.g., low-cost concessions, side payments, linkages) and punishments
(e.g., threats of withdrawal from existing partnerships or non-settlement)
to change the other party's assessment of the costs and benefits associated
with the offered terms (Lebow, 1996) – is appropriate, indeed, unavoidable, when the parties want different things and are unwilling to change
their positions.

In separate interviews, we asked the president of U of T and the executive director of OISE, and the leaders of their respective bargaining teams,
whether they had considered in advance any alternatives to negotiation by
teams, or would recomend any in retrospect. None of them felt that a less
divisive alternative had been available, given the differences in the institutions' positions.

*Suggestion   If merger discussions begin in a context in which the
parties' interests are substantially different, adversarial bargaining is
inevitable, but efforts should be made to ensure that relations between
the parties do not deteriorate into distrust and conflict.*

In this situation, the institutions will establish negotiating teams, exchange positions, and enter into formal negotiations. Generally, it is inadvisable for presidents – and especially for presidents who might wind up at
the head of the merged institution, should negotiations succeed – to

participate directly in the negotiations, unless possible agreement is in sight. If negotiations deteriorate into conflict, attempts can be made to re-establish communication by introducing a trusted third party into the process as a mediator. This was done by OISE and U of T. According to interviewees who participated in the negotiations between those two insti-tutions, the involvement of legal counsel for both parties in the final stages of the negotiations also helped facilitate effective communication.

Size and Negotiating Strategy

Thus far, the topic of negotiations has been addressed as if the positions and interests of the negotiating partners were similar. But as noted earlier, that is not usually the case. The parties are typically institutions of differ-ent size and power. This calls for a different approach to negotiations.

With respect to the general topic of negotiations between parties with unequal power, Bacharach and Lawler wrote that 'nonconvergent [in other words, unequal] power not only reduces the likelihood of agreement, but also engenders greater departures from equality when agreements do oc-cur' (1981, 201). For this reason, institutions negotiating with larger part-ners are well advised to approach negotiations in such a way as to minimize the effects of the other party's greater power.

First, it is important to recognize two things: ambiguity is not in the interests of the smaller partner, and some conflict is usually necessary to secure a good agreement. As Dean Priutt noted: 'Social conflict is often necessary for the emergence of high joint benefit ... Failure to be stubborn about one's goals often results from a desire to avoid conflict ... Such desire can undermine both one's own benefit and the joint benefit' (1981, p.191).

Suggestion   Smaller parties should ensure that bargaining is explicit rather than tacit – that is, that differences are formally articulated and acknowledged.

Second, it is advisable for smaller negotiating partners to take a formal, structured approach to negotiations. Robert Michels observed in 1911: 'Organization is the weapon of the weak in their struggle with the strong' (in Zartman and Berman, 1982, 205). Zartman and Berman saw evidence of this in international negotiations: 'Weaker parties tend to seek more formal negotiating forums and to strengthen their hand through organization' (205).

Suggestion   It is in the interest of the smaller party – and of those negotiating on behalf of the smaller party, in particular – that negotiations be formal and structured (e.g., that mandates be established for negotiating teams, that there be formal exchange of positions, that there be a ratification process). This constrains the capacity of the larger party to extract concessions.

What advice can be offered to larger parties about how to conduct themselves during merger negotiations?

If engaged in collaborative negotiations, such parties should recognize the costs of creating – or failing to correct – expectations they can't or won't fulfil. The tendency to foster unrealistic expectations is by no means limited to potential merger partners in the higher education sector. In *Mergers and Acquisitions of Privately-held Businesses* (1987), Albo and Henderson observed:

> A major mistake purchasers continually make in acquisitions is overselling themselves. That is, the purchaser raises expectations which cannot be fulfilled. Throughout the process, the purchaser will extoll the virtues of its corporation, including how they treat their employees, what they can bring to the table, how they are going to help the combined entities, how they are going to transfer the strengths of their organization to the vendor organization, and so on. It is virtually impossible for the purchaser to live up to all the promises that it makes.

The temptation to oversell is even greater in higher education, where power is decentralized and faculty approval or acquiescence is usually a prerequisite for merger. But if members of acquisition targets come to expect that merger will bring improvements in quality, resources, and reputation with minimal disruption and little loss of identity, they are bound to be disappointed. And their disappointment will result in alienation and loss of academic effectiveness and productivity.

At the same time – and as illustrated by the OISE/U of T case – a larger, more powerful institution engaged in negotiations should recognize that a smaller potential partner may be quick to perceive its statements or behaviour as threatening. Negotiations in which there are genuine or perceived differences in power between the partners, or into which feelings of superiority or inferiority enter, are especially difficult (Tuinman, 1995). Even mild attempts to coerce a smaller partner can prompt a disproportionate reaction from the latter, and quickly transform a collaborative bargaining relationship into an adversarial one. And some of the dynamics associated with adversarial bargaining, such as the growth of distrust and suspicion, militate against agreement. Representatives of a small institution, mistrustful of a larger negotiating partner and feeling that 'their backs are against a wall,' are unlikely to recognize an agreement. According to the last chair of the OISE board, one of the reasons that mediation led to an agreement was that it empowered OISE's negotiating team. The mediator, who had been suggested by OISE, validated some of their positions and in doing so increased their sense of power. This, in turn, helped them reach an agreement with U of T.

Observation   Smaller parties to merger negotiations tend to be inclined to perceive the statements and actions of their potential partners as threatening.

Suggestion   Larger partners should take care to avoid statements and actions that might be perceived as threatening or coercive, if they wish to establish and sustain a collaborative bargaining relationship.

Those who negotiated integration on behalf of OISE expressed the view that U of T had implemented the agreement more than fully. In contrast, immediately after amalgamation, there was a disagreement between the president and administrative vice-president of Dalhousie and the principal of DalTech (formerly the president of TUNS) over the amount of government funding that would be available to DalTech in the 1997–98 budget year. The position of the former was that to accede to the principal's demands would be fiscally irresponsible, given the university's financial situation and funding prospects. The word on the DalTech campus was that now that Dalhousie was in control, it was not living up to the agreement. The university eventually conceded to the principal. In spite of this – and even though Dalhousie assumed a portion of TUNS's accumulated deficit and the consequences of the loss of a substantial endowment – people at DalTech perceived that Dalhousie was not delivering on its commitments. This did not foster identification with the university.

Observation   Generous implementation of merger agreements promotes good relationships after the merger and facilitates identification with the merged institution.

Suggestion   *An acquiring institution that signs an agreement it cannot afford to implement generously – or an agreement too ambiguous to be seen to be fulfilled – should anticipate that implementation will lead to complaints and disaffection on the part of members of the acquired institution.*

Fit between Mission, Structure, and Resources

The Mission of DalTech

The establishment of a college to succeed TUNS was a key feature of the Dal/TUNS amalgamation agreement, and was of utmost importance to people at TUNS. It is possible that they needed and wanted a successor college so much – that the need was so self-evident to them – that few considered seriously what the purpose of the college was, beyond carrying on TUNS's identity.

Early in 1998, DalTech's academic council attempted to come to grips with this question. It was struggling to define a role and structure for itself within the college and the university. Its meetings were poorly attended. It often failed to achieve a quorum. Council members questioned 'whether DalTech has the will to continue' (DalTech Academic Council, 21 January 1998, 4). Finally, they addressed themselves to the fundamental question: What is the college for? In response, individuals identified a number of characteristics shared by the three faculties: that they were design-based, that they had professional programs, that they had co-op programs, that they conducted applied research, and that they shared the history and culture of TUNS. The implicit suggestion was that the existence of these common characteristics justified the existence of the college.

The problem with this argument was that most of these characteristics were shared by other faculties of the university. Most Dalhousie faculties offered professional programs. Most were conducting applied research. Several had co-op programs. Membership in a college was not necessary to enable a faculty to sustain these.

What about the characteristics that *were* unique, such as the common emphasis on design? Did they not necessitate and justify the.existence of DalTech? Even that was not clear. The Faculties of Medicine, Dentistry and Health Professions were all health science faculties, but they did not form a college, nor was it evident that they would be stronger if they did.

Only one of the people we interviewed put forward a strong functional argument for the existence and autonomy of DalTech. The former chairman of the TUNS board reminded us that TUNS's mission included contributing to the development of industry in Nova Scotia. Noting that Dalhousie's faculties did not serve provincial needs in this direct way, he argued that DalTech required autonomy so that its faculties could continue to focus on meeting the needs of industry in Nova Scotia. Cogent as this argument may have been, it was not prominent among those made by the faculty. It was not clear that it would have been universally accepted by them.

And what about the role of perpetuating the identity and culture of TUNS and its predecessor, NSTC? Was that not enough to sustain a college? If plentiful resources had been available or if strong and charismatic leadership had been present, it might have been. But when there is a lack of continuous leadership and when human and budgetary resources are scarce, as was the situation at DalTech, people may be unwilling to pay for an entity that serves no compelling purpose.

Observation   However emotionally attached people are to what it symbolizes, an internal structure without a widely accepted functional mission is – in a climate of scarce resources – unlikely to last.

The Matrix Structure at OISE/UT

The July 1995 report of the Academic Integration Task Force proposed a matrix structure for OISE/UT, in which seven academic departments would contribute to the three major functions: (1) graduate studies; (2) preservice programs and laboratory schools; and (3) research and field activities (see Figure 6.2). Each of the three functions would be led by an associate dean.

The report stated that 'the Associate Dean, Preservice Programs and Lab Schools, will be responsible for the maintenance and support of all preservice teacher education programs and laboratory schools and for all matters relating to recruitment, admission and financial support of preservice students' (Academic Integration Task Force Report, 1995, 19).

The proposed matrix structure was eventually approved, albeit with fewer departments. A year and a half after integration took place, the associate dean in charge of preservice programs told us that it was not working as planned. Having identified a number of positive outcomes of the merger, she observed: 'What has not been achieved – and may even be going backward – is closer integration of preservice and graduate educa-

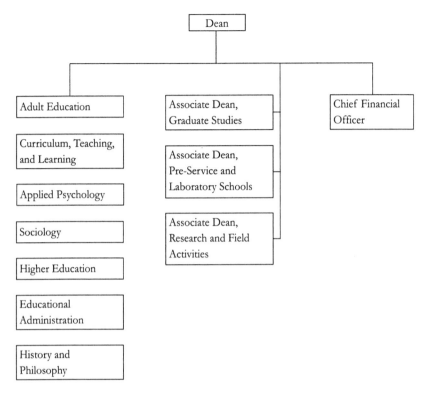

Figure 6.2 Proposed organizational chart for OISE/UT

tion.' The preservice and the graduate programs were not more closely linked, and serious problems were engulfing the former programs' delivery.

What had happened? For one thing, the task force's proposal that 'as part of the final Academic Plan, approximate budgets (FTE's and other resources) will be allocated by function' had not been accepted. The provost decided that, consistent with the university's academic administrative policy and practices, budgets would be assigned to departments. The result, as described by the incumbent, was that the associate dean for preservice programs 'had responsibility for programs and students, but no faculty.' In other words, she did not have sufficient control over the faculty's human and financial resources to ensure fulfilment of its preservice mission.

And what of the departments in which the real power lay? They had not turned out quite as had been hoped and expected by OISE/UT's architects. The organizational plan for OISE/UT, which had been approved early in 1996, called for five departments (replacing the seven departments at OISE and the four at FEUT). The hope and expectation was that the new departments would be of similar size and would be comprised of similar proportions of FEUT and OISE faculty. Faculty members were invited to indicate which department(s) they wished to belong to. The unexpected – and rather unfortunate – outcome of this process was that 62 per cent of the faculty from FEUT who became part of OISE/UT (i.e., who did not retire, resign, or reach the end of their contracts) joined one department: Curriculum, Teaching and Learning. This meant that preservice education – which was to have been every department's responsibility – became identified with one of them and that the great majority of faculty members taught either in the graduate program or in the preservice program, rather than in both. In the words of the associate dean, the initial result of the merger was 'powerful departments which see themselves as graduate departments. Everyone and no one is responsible for preservice education.'

Since that time (winter 1997–98), the task of integrating preservice and graduate education has received a great deal of attention at OISE/UT, and much has been achieved, as we noted in Chapter 4.

Observation   Structures without human and financial resources are unlikely to succeed in fulfilling their missions.

Suggestion   Ensure that institutional mission(s), structures, human resources, and budgets are well aligned from the outset.

Unit-Level Transition Planning

Mergers require active and coordinated transition management and planning at multiple levels of the institutions involved. The following pages list the issues and steps involved in a typical merger of faculties or equivalent units. Some of the steps involved in mergers of faculties are performed at the institutional level, others by members of the faculties themselves. Typically, institutional-level actors perform those steps which provide the framework (e.g., leadership, governance, and budget) within which members of a faculty-to-be plan their post-merger programs and activities.

The precise nature of the issues and steps, and who addresses or performs them, will vary from institution to institution, depending on goverance, culture, and circumstances. Nevertheless, Table 6.1 may provide a useful checklist.

TABLE 6.1
Typical issues and steps in faculty merger

Leadership
Determine and clarify the status of existing dean(s) or equivalent, bring their appointments to conclusion, and establish their positions in any searches. (If new leadership will not be sought, transfer appointment(s) to the merged institution, as appropriate.)
Establish terms of reference for the dean of the merged faculty (if not specified in the agreement).
Define the decanal search process (if not specified).
Define the dean's terms of employment.
Search for and appoint the dean (who will in turn conduct searches to fill the next level of administrative position).

Administrative structure, positions, and personnel
Determine and clarify the status of other existing administrators (e.g., associate deans, department heads), bring their appointments to conclusion, and establish their positions in any searches. (If new leadership will not be sought, transfer appointments to the merged institution, as appropriate.)
Design new administrative structures and positions (if not specified in agreement) by means specified in the agreement or determined by relevant authorities.
Secure approval for new structures.
Determine and implement processes by which faculty and staff members will move into new units.
Establish terms of employment for administrative positions, conduct searches and make appointments.
Once new structures and people are in place, provide orientation and training.

Governance
Design new governance structures and positions (if not specified in agreement) by means specified in the agreement or determined by relevant authorities.
Secure approval for new structures.
Initiate election and appointment processes.
Provide orientation for members of new bodies.

Education
Maintain existing programs during the transition period:
– Determine whether existing programs will continue or be discontinued (e.g., phased out, transferred) after merger.
– Decide whether to continue or suspend admissions.
– Determine how best to maintain existing programs during the transition period.
– Teach existing students in existing programs.

Plan/prepare for post-merger continuation of existing programs (as required and/or appropriate):
– Ensure continued accreditation following merger (if applicable).
– Plan and schedule post-merger continuation of existing offerings (degree, non-degree) and associated services (e.g., co-op placements).

TABLE 6.1–(*Continued*)
Typical issues and steps in faculty merger

- Assign faculty and other resources (see Resources, below).
- Recruit new students (if applicable).

Plan new programs (NOTE: There may be advantages to deferring planning for new programs until after merger).
- Assess need and market demand for potential offerings.
- Plan new offerings.
- Assess feasibility.
- Secure approval.
- Secure and assign resources.
- Recruit students.
- Teach new programs.

Research and professional services
Inventory research and service obligations of pre-existing units.
Inventory research and service capabilities of pre-existing units.
Determine adequacy of existing and planned capacities to fulfil obligations.
Assign resources to the fulfilment of, and/or renegotiate the terms of, contracts and agreements.
Carry out projects and contracts.
Facilitate consideration of new opportunities and areas of concentration.

Resource allocation

Within budget for merged unit:

Faculty and Staff
Inventory existing faculty and staff resources. (This should include the development of a faculty age/salary profile).
Identify post-merger staffing requirements.
Develop a complement plan for review and approval at the appropriate level, taking into account staffing requirements and the costs and benefits of alternative staffing strategies.
Reassign/redeploy/sever (voluntarily or involuntarily) faculty and/or staff upon merger in accordance with applicable legislation, contracts, agreements, complement plan, etc.
Appoint new faculty and/or staff, if and as called for by the plan.

Facilities and Equipment
Inventory existing facilities and equipment.
Identify post-merger requirements for teaching, research, and administrative space and equipment.
Ascertain the adequacy of existing facilities and equipment in light of requirements and standards applicable at the merged institution.
Assess alternatives in conjunction with appropriate institutional offices.
Secure and assign space and equipment, by means of appropriate processes.

TABLE 6.1–*(Concluded)*
Typical issues and steps in faculty merger

Budget

Plan to allocate budgetary resources to subunits/expenditure categories, in conjunction with the approved structure and programs and relevant policies. (Note: There may be a case for a relatively centralized budget in the early stages of merger.)

Financial planning

Inventory internal and external sources of revenue for the merged faculty.
Project revenues and expenditures.
Identify and pursue new fund-raising opportunities.

Policies

Inventory pre-existing faculty-level policies.
Establish processes for identifying the merged faculty's policy requirements and determining new policies.

External relations

Implement any new advisory bodies specified in the merger agreement.
Identify the bodies (within and outside the merging institutions) and the associations on which the pre-existing units were represented, and arrange representation for the merged faculty, as appropriate.
Identify the merged faculty's key external stakeholders, e.g.:
– accreditation bodies
– professional bodies and associations
– alumni
– industry (as applicable)
– government agencies (as applicable)
– current and potential funders and donors
– research and educational agencies
– other parts of the merged institutions
– other universities and schools (e.g., sources or recipients of students)
– other stakeholders
Ensure that relationships with key stakeholders are sustained.

According to the consultants we interviewed, the structure most commonly used for planning the merger of units (e.g., faculties or administrative units) or functions is the joint planning team. Usually reporting to a joint oversight body, it brings together a small number of representatives of an academic or administrative function duplicated at each institution (e.g., two faculty, one staff member, and one student representative from each of two merging academic units). The Academic Integration Task Force of OISE and U of T and the Dal/TUNS Joint Transition Committee for Computer Science represent variations on this, reflecting the vastly different scales of the two operations.

Regarding planning and new stuctures for the merging academic units, the two sets of institutions took a similar approach; regarding transition planning for administrative fractions, they took different approaches. Dalhousie and TUNS entrusted the preparation of operational plans for merging units to those who were to head the units. (These appointments were announced in November 1996. The new heads had been selected from among the heads of the existing units. The latter had been asked early in the fall whether they wished to be considered to head the merged unit, or whether they would prefer another option – for example, another position within the same unit, or a position elsewhere in the university, or a voluntary separation. In the event, the TUNS directors all chose other options, so there were no competitions for positions at the director level. Dalhousie's administrative directors took responsibility for the merged functions.) They were given until the end of January 1997 to prepare operational plans for their units – plans that were to address changes in functions and services, organizational charts, staffing, budgets, space, computing systems, and so on. The extent of consultation with staff and clients at both institutions was left up to each director. In spite of the very short time frame, the resulting plans were quite detailed. They were approved by the responsible vice-presidents at both institutions and by the two presidents. There was no formal process for sharing information and ensuring consistency of plans across portfolios, or for assessing the cumulative impact of combined changes on students, faculty, and staff at TUNS.

The approach taken by Dalhousie and TUNS had two main strengths: plans for the merging of administrative units were developed by individuals who had expert knowledge of the functions and who would have to make the plans work; and plans and decisions were made quickly. The approach had one main weakness: there was little consideration of crosscutting issues and of the cumulative impact of departmental actions on individuals at TUNS.

Actions were sometimes at cross-purposes, because units lacked information about each other's plans. For example, the phone numbers for DalTech were changed shortly after new stationery was printed for a number of departments. Lack of interunit coordination also meant that there was no one source of assistance, advice, and information on Dalhousie: administrators, faculty, and staff at DalTech trying to get things done within the university all too often found themselves 'bounced around from department to department.'

OISE and U of T took a different approach to planning the merger of administrative functions, as required by the integration agreement. As noted earlier, they struck an Administrative Integration Task Force composed of two management representatives from each institution. The task force members were the director of OISE, the associate dean of FEUT, the administrative vice-president of U of T, and OISE's chief financial officer. Both OISE's chief financial officer and its director of human resource services were scheduled to leave. Even so, they were made responsible for managing the transition in their functional areas, besides being expected to contribute to the work of the task force. Searches for managers at OISE/UT (for example, the registrar, librarian, and chief financial and administrative officers) could not begin until the academic plan and organizational model were approved, so these individuals were not yet in place. The co-chairs of the task force identified administrative staffing requirements, relying on statistics about comparable units. Experience subsequently showed that staffing requirements in a number of areas were underestimated.

OISE/UT's new financial officer took office in July 1996, and its human resource manager in August 1997. Some in the dean's office wished, in retrospect, that these individuals had been appointed much earlier.

Observation The best input into plans for merged administrative functions is likely to come from those who will be responsible for making them work. These people are also best equipped to manage the transition.

Suggestion *Appoint the heads of the merging functions and units as early as possible, consistent with a sound selection process.*

Conditions for Constructive Grassroots Participation

The Case of Applied Mathematics

There was a history of competition and animosity between the School of Computer Science at TUNS and the Division of Computing Science at Dalhousie. Even so, the two units came together quickly as a new faculty after amalgamation was announced. According to the faculty members we interviewed, two factors – besides the relatively equal size of the pre-existing units – made this possible. *First*, members of both units recognized that amalgamation was an opportunity to secure badly needed resources for Computer Science, but that they would have to work vigourously together to seize it. If they didn't, others would grab whatever resources might be available. *Second*, the administrations permitted a few individuals who had been prominent in the old order and who had opposed amalgamation to move gracefully into other units (leaving their positions behind). To have forced these individuals to become part of the new faculty would have hindered integration and the adoption of new ways. In the event, the computer scientists came together quickly as a group and began to integrate their offerings.

Events unfolded differently in Applied Mathematics. Thanks to the publicity surrounding the Nova Scotia Council on Higher Education's review of Computer Science in Nova Scotia, there was a high level of governmental, public, and institutional awareness in the mid-1990s that programs in Computer Science were being 'duplicated' at Dalhousie and TUNS. Yet few noticed that both institutions also had programs in Applied Mathematics. The issue was brought to the fore by members of Dalhousie's Department of Mathematics, Statistics and Computing Science around the time the amalgamation agreement was signed.

The twenty-five mathematicians and statisticians within the Department of Mathematics, Statistics and Computing Science (MSCS) of Dalhousie's Faculty of Science offered degree programs from the bachelor's to the doctoral level; in addition they provided a great deal of service teaching to other units of the university. The five-person Department of Applied Mathematics at TUNS provided service teaching to other departments within the Faculty of Engineering and offered MSc and PhD programs in Engineering Mathematics.

Members of the Dalhousie department, stung by the impending 'loss' of Computing Science, argued that the continued existence of two math departments after the merger would make a mockery of amalgamation and of the university. ('Who's ever heard of a university with two math departments?!') They also argued that the result of combining the two units would be a stronger department.

Meanwhile, the Faculty of Engineering at TUNS was bound and determined not to lose its applied mathematicians. No progress was made on the issue in the months leading up to amalgamation. At one of its last meetings, the TUNS Senate voted to change the name of the TUNS unit to the 'Department of Engineering Mathematics.' Immediately after amalgamation, Dalhousie's academic vice-president and Engineering dean wrote jointly to the heads of the two departments to indicate that the university Senate would be asked to strike a task force, with external representation, to advise on the structure of mathematics at the university and to ask, in the meantime, that the two departments strike a joint committee to compare their offerings and identify opportunities for consolidating courses. The dean subsequently disavowed the memo. Tensions between the departments were heightened when members of the DalTech department 'appropriated' the teaching of a number of mathematics courses in the new Bachelor of Engineering curriculum.

Negotiations between the two departments and their respective deans continued through 1997 and most of 1998. Proposals and counterproposals went back and forth. The Department of MSCS refused to drop 'Computing Science' from its name until the applied mathematics issue was resolved. This did not happen until the fall of 1998. In December of that year, the Department of MSCS recommended to the Senate that its name be changed to the Department of Mathematics and Statistics.

Why, when it took the computer scientists a matter of weeks to begin to work together, were the mathematicians – who had much less 'history' – unable to do so? Why was the announcement of amalgamation followed by a rapid mending of relations among the former but by two-and-a-half years of controversy and bad blood among the latter? In the case of Computer Science, the fundamental structural decision was made at the outset. In the case of Applied Mathematics, it was not.

Observation   *Grassroots faculty and staff participation in planning is desirable and necessary, but can only be effective if the organizational structure has been decided.*

Suggestion   *As recommended by Herman Bakvis (1995) in his study of the formation through merger of Human Resources Development Canada:*

- *Use a top-down approach for setting down the basic parameters of the new organization and for putting into place those components which are crucial or immediately necessary to making the new organization function.*
- *Use a bottom-up and broadly based participatory framework in creating and implementing the more detailed design of the new organization and in helping to articulate the longer term goals of the organization; at the same time, retain a capacity to give direction and to intervene if the process becomes stalemated.*

'Rethinking Administration' at OISE/UT

The job of the Administrative Integration Task Force that was established in accordance with the integration agreement was to propose a plan and schedule for integrating administrative support services at OISE and FEUT, consistent with available resources. OISE's director, who co-chaired the task force, took the initial view that the necessary budget reductions could and should be achieved with relatively little disruption, by eliminating a couple of central administrative units at OISE (e.g., human resources) and relying on central university services. By the fall of 1995, university officials, perceiving OISE as overstaffed, were not in favour of allowing the *status quo* to continue. They proposed a re-engineering of administrative support services for OISE/UT.

When it became apparent that due to a 15 per cent cut in government funding to universities, OISE/UT was going to have to reduce its budget by roughly 20 per cent, OISE's director accepted that re-engineering was necessary to achieve greater administrative efficiency. 'Rethinking Administration' – an initiative launched in 1993 to re-engineer administrative services at U of T – would be applied to OISE/UT.

According to one individual associated with the process: 'The FEUT people were secure [because they had been given assurances of continuing university employment] but the OISE people knew a lot of their jobs were going to disappear. As they saw it, they were being asked to plan to cut their own jobs. They were angry. The process fell apart before any useful recommendations emerged.' Specifically, OISE's staff unions refused to have anything to do with any recommendations that would affect staffing levels. The identification of OISE/UT's administrative staffing requirements fell behind schedule, and this contributed to the disarray surrounding staff departures in OISE's final days.

The co-chairs of the task force and others associated with the process described 'Rethinking Administration' as a failure. One observed: 'It was the worst thing we could have done.' It did not produce the desired results; even worse, it caused people to feel manipulated, and it exacerbated labour strife.

Observation   Exercises that require participants to contribute to or endorse plans potentially resulting in the loss of their jobs or those of their co-workers – or otherwise adversely affecting their interests – are unlikely to be effective.

Suggestion   Do not structure integration planning processes so that their progress depends on the continuing participation of people whose employment or other interests are threatened by merger.

This is not to suggest that one shouldn't involve staff members in planning if their jobs are insecure. To ignore their knowledge and expertise would be worse. And as one consultant observed: 'What alternative [to involving the people who actually do the work] is there?' However, one should solicit the input of people whose jobs may be threatened; one should not expect their ongoing participation in planning.

On Organizational Redesign and Staff Redeployment

There must be a better way of handling downsizing and severance and of helping the survivors. I don't know how it should be done, but there must be a better way. It was incredibly painful.

A. Hildyard, Executive Director, OISE

The Dal/TUNS and OISE/U of T mergers made staff members in units that were to be merged very anxious about their jobs. At Dalhousie and TUNS, the anxiety was shared by central administrative staff in both institutions, because the amalgamation agreement stated: 'To the extent that amalgamation of the two institutions leads to fewer administrative and staff jobs, the employees of the two institutions will be entitled to compete for available positions on a fair, open and equal basis consistent with applicable collective agreements.'

In other words, staff at both institutions faced the possibility of being laid off. Some staff at Dalhousie saw this as unfair. They were upset that after long service to Dalhousie, they might be cast aside to make way for someone from TUNS.

In the OISE/U of T case, the view that merger should not threaten the jobs of people at an acquiring institution was shared by the university's administration: staff at FEUT were assured that they would not lose their jobs at the university as a direct result of the merger. In contrast, staff at OISE were already anticipating job losses because of the institute's financial predicament, and so felt very threatened by the prospect of integration.

In the 'Q & A' section of a November 1996 *Amalgamation Bulletin*, Dalhousie and TUNS explained the processes by which staffing requirements would be determined and redeployment effected:

Q: I'm a staff member in one of the units being merged with its counterpart. How will all of this affect me, my job, my reporting relationship, my overall responsibilities?

A: At this point in time, staff members at both universities will continue in their current positions, with no immediate changes in responsibilities, duties, hours of work, salary/wages, pension or insured benefits. Furthermore, there will be no changes to reporting relationships at this stage of the amalgamation process.

Q: *What are the next steps in the process?*

A: Now that we have determined the basic organizational structure for the university as a whole, we can begin the process of planning for individual departments and operations. This step is key to determining the actual staffing requirements for each department ...

Q: *What will be the process for developing operational plans?*

A: The planning process will vary from unit to unit, reflecting the nature of the unit's clients, programs/services and operations. The process will be led by the designated head of the new unit.

Q: *I am a staff member in an administrative unit. Is my job at risk?*

A: One of the objectives of amalgamation is to maintain or improve administrative services while eliminating unnecessary duplication and reducing costs. Over time, there will be some overall reduction in staff numbers. We hope that much of this reduction will be achieved through natural attrition, by taking advantage of current vacancies and by use of the early retirement incentive programs now available at both institutions.

Q: *Will there be layoffs or terminations of staff members in either administrative or academic units?*

A: If, at the end of the day, some layoffs/terminations are unavoidable, we will follow the applicable provisions (organizational change, re-deployment, layoff and severance) of the relevant union contracts. Where non-union positions are combined, the incumbents will be given the opportunity to compete for the new position. Every reasonable effort will be made through redeployment to find alternative employment for the unsuccessful applicant. If a layoff/termination of a non-unionized administrative employee is unavoidable, notice/compensation will be provided in accordance with terms agreed to by the Dalhousie University Administrative Group, which will be extended to comparable TUNS employees.

The process took place essentially as described. Operational plans were prepared. Not surprisingly, given that immediate achievement of major savings was not an objective of amalgamation, the plans revealed that job loss would be minimal. The 25 February 1997 *Amalgamation Bulletin* reported:

Employee groups have already been advised informally that, based on the draft business plans, it is anticipated that the integration of staff will result in minimal job loss and that redeployment opportunities will offset this where possible ... As unit operational plans are approved, staff members will be advised of any changes that affect them personally, as soon as possible in accordance with the provisions of any applicable agreements with employee groups.

The news that few jobs would be lost facilitated agreements with the unions on a new bargaining unit structure and bridging provisions. These agreements were reached in March, and made it possible to redeploy staff in accordance with the plans. A small number of competitions were held for duplicated administrative positions.

The result of all this was that most staff in the central administrative units at TUNS that were being merged with their Dalhousie counterparts were able to find comparable positions in the latter units, without the need to compete. The additional person-power enabled the Dalhousie departments to extend their services to the new campus. There was a modest reduction in the combined staff complement, achieved mainly through voluntary departures and the 'cancelling' of vacancies. The jobs of most central administrative staff at Dalhousie did not change. Only three people whose jobs disappeared were not redeployed within their merged units. One of these elected voluntary separation, and another was redeployed to another unit of the university. The process worked relatively smoothly – although undoubtedly not entirely happily for those involved.

The situation at OISE and U of T was much more difficult, mainly because budget cuts necessitated a deep cut in the number of staff jobs. Anticipating this, the university and OISE had negotiated with the provincial government, as part of the integration agreement, a transition fund that could be used to pay severance costs.

Layoffs are always painful and difficult. The need to cut jobs at OISE/UT would in itself have made the human resource transition associated with merger very difficult. The full enormity of the management challenge became apparent when close examination of OISE's collective agreements revealed that for all practical purposes, it was impossible to lay off staff at OISE. How were OISE and U of T to achieve the necessary job reductions, given that those staff (at FEUT) who could be laid off had been given employment assurances, and those (at OISE) who hadn't been given such assurances couldn't be laid off?

Although there were apparently different schools of thought within the

Administrative Integration Task Force about how to proceed, the initial plan was to encourage staff to leave voluntarily by offering generous severance packages. The organizational and staffing plans were to be developed later, based on the skills of those who were left. The goal was to achieve the necessary job reductions and to establish a sound administrative structure for OISE/UT.

Enhanced severance packages were to be offered to staff at both OISE and FEUT, so as to achieve the greatest possible number of voluntary departures. The process of negotiating the terms of severance was prolonged because OISE's unions expected – and OISE was prepared to offer – packages that the university feared would set an unaffordable precedent. Severance packages were offered to staff early in 1996. The deadline for applications was extended several times.

Before deciding whether to apply for severance, staff members – especially at OISE – wanted to know what the future would hold for them at OISE/UT. As one task force member recounted: 'People were saying, "How can we possibly decide whether to go or not if we don't know what jobs there will be?!" The administration was saying, "We can't say what jobs there will be until we know how many people are leaving." There was a lot of to-ing and fro-ing on this. Eventually, a list of jobs was posted.'

On 24 April 1996 a memorandum was sent to unit heads describing the 'Proposed OISE/UT Administrative Structure.' It listed the types and numbers of administrative and staff positions there would be in each unit of OISE/UT. The covering memo indicated that 'while we think that the proposed structure is a fairly close approximation of the final structure, further study, analysis and consultation will no doubt result in some changes.'

Of great import for staff seeking to read the tea leaves was the note that 'the right hand column designates the current affiliation of individuals who are likely to fill the positions.' The designation next to the vast majority of positions was 'OISE' or 'FEUT.' The symbol '**' indicated that 'it is not clear at the present time whether the position will be filled by an OISE or a FEUT employee but it is not anticipated that the position will be searched.' Also: 'The designation OISE/UT means that it is a new position and will be classified, posted and searched according to U of T administrative staff policies.' The new positions were mostly senior ones (e.g., chief financial and administrative officers, institutional researcher, departmental administrator). The overall breakdown was as shown in Table 6.2.

The decision to post the new positions as university positions was

TABLE 6.2
Distribution of administrative staff positions at OISE/UT*

	FEUT	OISE	OISE/UT	Internally filled**	Total
Deans' offices	3.0	2.5	2.0	1.0	8.5
Central services	2.0	4.0	4.0	2.0	12.0
Registrar	16.0	3.0	2.0	0	21.0
Student services	1.0	0	1.0	0	2.0
Academic units	18.05	15.5	5.5	14.0	53.05
UTS	3.0	0	0	0	3.0
Educations Commons					
Library	8.5	17.6	1.0	0	27.1
Technology	3.0	11.0	6.0	0	20.0
Field centres	0	6.05	0	0	6.05
Print shop	0	4.0	0	0	4.0
Building management	0	5.0	0	0	5.0
Communications	0	5.0	0	0	5.0
Journals	0	3.35	0	0	3.35
Totals	54.55	74.0	21.5	17.0	167.05
1995 Totals	68.4	159.19			227.59

*Excluding sponsored research
**Positions filled without searches by persons formerly at either FEUT or OISE
Positions eliminated: 49.54. The balance – 11.0 positions – was transferred to other
U of T departments.

controversial. Although U of T had indicated its intention to apply for decertification of OISE's unions, it had not yet done so: the unions were still in place, and there was no agreed process for posting and staffing new positions. OISE staff could apply for the new university positions, but they would have to leave their unions to do so. Although the task force members knew that posting the new jobs as university positions would produce an outcry, they felt that they had no choice, given the urgent need to staff these key positions and the university's desire to achieve consistent terms and conditions of employment across the institution. Grievances were filed, but searches for the new positions were conducted and concluded.

How did staff at OISE and FEUT get from their pre-existing positions into positions at OISE/UT? Interviewees' answers to this question varied:

People had to compete for the senior positions, but for the junior ones, it was varied.

The idea was that if you wanted a new job, you had to compete. If you wanted to stay in the same job, you didn't.

It was a terrible mess. Some people had to compete for jobs; others didn't. No one knew what was going to happen to them.

In the event, those staff members who stayed carried on more or less as before, until told to do otherwise.

The process of moving former OISE staff formally into university positions could not begin until their unions had been decertified. The university and the General Support Staff Association (GSSA) negotiated the latter's decertification, which took place in 1997. The Professional Staff Association was decertified, again voluntarily, later the same year.

Before the GSSA was decertified, the university identified for the union where each of its members was expected to fit within the university's classification structure. Although this list was intended to be preliminary, the union distributed it to its members, who regarded it as definitive. Unfortunately, the preliminary classification was based in part on job titles and salaries, which had been inflated at OISE relative to FEUT. Former OISE staff positions were tentatively classified higher than positions with the same content held by former FEUT staff. The latter were devastated.

By the spring of 1997, it was apparent that OISE/UT needed not only a human resource coordinator, but also a more senior human resource manager. A search was held, and a new manager took office that summer. One of her major tasks was to conduct an institutional job review – that is, a review to ensure that all staff jobs were appropriately described, titled, and classified. By all accounts (in late 1997 and early 1998), the process was fraught. Former OISE staff, feeling that they – in contrast to the faculty – had been treated like garbage, sought (in the words of one interviewee) '(a) justice and (b) upgrades.' Former FEUT staff looked for parity with their colleagues from OISE. Expectations were bound to be disappointed.

Another outstanding human resource task was the transfer of ten former FEUT staff, still working in the former FEUT building, to new positions at OISE/UT. The ten new positions had been identified. When it was suggested that FEUT staff compete for them, the latter were aghast: Why should they have to compete for jobs when others hadn't?

Neither at Dal/TUNS nor at OISE/U of T did the majority of staff in merged units have to compete for jobs. In the Dal/TUNS case this worked satisfactorily, because the scale of Dalhousie's administrative units was much greater than that of their TUNS counterparts, which they absorbed.

Unit-level 'merger' in fact involved the former units acquiring additional human and other resources from the latter, as well as the extension of Dalhousie services to the merged campus. It was not necessary – and would not have been appropriate – to eliminate the jobs of, say, thirty people in a major central administrative department at Dalhousie and four or five people in the equivalent unit at TUNS and to require them to apply for new jobs, in order to end up with a merged department, virtually identical to the former Dalhousie unit, with a combined staff of thirty-three or thirty-four.

The same basic approach – leaving most people in existing or modified jobs and building organizational and staffing structures around them – was necessary at OISE/UT, because OISE's collective agreements made layoffs and restructuring virtually impossible. But the approach proved to be much more problematic for OISE/UT. 'Merger' of administrative functions at Dalhousie and TUNS in fact involved the extension of Dalhousie's services to the former TUNS. In contrast, real change was sought – and required – at OISE/UT. OISE's administrative units were merged, not with their institutional counterparts at U of T, but rather with their counterparts at FEUT. (For example, OISE's admissions office merged with FEUT's admissions office, rather than with a university-wide operation.) The greater similarity in size of the units and their staffs meant that one could not as easily absorb the other. Genuine organizational and job redesign was needed.

Observation   *The implementation of merger plans that entail real change in functions and structures requires corresponding human resource changes.*

Suggestion   *When merger of duplicated administrative functions or units will involve significant restructuring of jobs (e.g., when significant change is sought or when merging units are of comparable scale), all jobs should be re-designed, -titled, -classified, and -staffed.*

Several former members of OISE commented to us on how painful the downsizing process had been. Even if the approach we suggest had been possible at OISE/UT, and even if the institute and the university had chosen to adopt it, the pain would not have been substantially less. When merger involves job loss, pain and anger are inevitable.

That said, a well-defined process of administrative and job redesign and restaffing might provide greater clarity. Research on corporate mergers suggests that people find clarity and structure helpful in situations of uncertainty and distress. According to McCann and Gilkey, 'in a transition environment, the only thing worse than bad news is uncertainty' (1988, 159).

Whether or not a merger involves substantial job loss, it places immense demands on human resource services.

Observation   *Strong human resource services, involved in merger negotiations and planning from the outset, are crucial for effective transition management.*

If human resource services are themselves to be merged, it may be advisable to do this first, so that they themselves are not in the throes of change at the point of greatest need for their services.

SEVEN

On Roles and Behaviour

The Players

Higher education mergers are complex, far-reaching events involving many stakeholders. Which stakeholders are actively involved depends on the specifics of the case – in particular, it depends on the cultures of the merging institutions, the internal and external governance arrangements in place (e.g., on who can grant or withhold necessary approvals), the location of needed expertise within and outside the institutions, and the identity of the constituencies whose support is vital for institutional well-being and survival.

That said, a comparison of the Dal/TUNS and OISE/U of T cases and a review of accounts of other higher education mergers reveal common patterns.

Negotiators, Advisers, and Governors

In the first part of the negotiation phase, active participation is generally limited to those whose authority, expertise, or legitimacy is required to develop the merger agreement. At the outset, the presidents or heads of the institutions are typically at the centre of events. In cases of publicly funded institutions such as those we studied, government officials (in particular, ministers and deputy ministers responsible for post-secondary education and other senior officials) are also key. Although in neither of the cases at hand did the provincial intermediary body – the Nova Scotia Council on Higher Education and the Ontario Council on University Affairs – play a significant role in the negotiations, that is certainly a possibility.

Other key participants in this phase typically include executive members of the board, whose approval is needed for negotiations to take place. The nature of consultations with the university Senate depends on the governance arrangements in place.

Commonly involved as participants in the negotiations or as advisers to the negotiators are vice-presidents, representatives of potentially merging units, key functional managers (e.g., human resources, finance), and key staff (e.g., legal counsel). As noted earlier, the identity of the participants in negotiations varies from case to case according to institutional culture, governance arrangements, and other factors. The OISE/U of T negotiations provided a fascinating example of this. OISE being a highly 'democratic' institution, its negotiating team included representatives of its major 'constituencies' – its board, administration, chairs' council, faculty, staff, student body, and alumni. The team comprised four women – one of whom was team leader – and three men. Ranged across the table from them – and no doubt confirming OISE's worst fears about the U of T – were five representatives of the university (four men and one woman) appointed by the provost. They included the administrative vice-president, the associate dean of FEUT, the vice-provost and assistant vice-president for planning and budget, and the associate dean of Graduate Studies. The team was chaired by a professor of Political Science. The asymmetry of the teams at the bargaining table reflected the great differences between the two institutions' cultures and structures – differences that made it so hard to reach agreement.

When negotiations are conducted by teams, mechanisms are often established for the teams to consult with and receive feedback from their constituencies. For example, U of T's team had a 'reference group' composed mainly of administrators. OISE's team held a series of consultations with students, staff, faculty, alumni, and others.

In addition to or in lieu of formal consultative/advisory mechanisms, those who are involved in discussions with a potential merger partner invariably consult informally within their institution. Whom they consult depends heavily on the politics of the situation.

Also, potential merger partners often draw upon outside expertise during the negotiation phase – particularly legal expertise. Of the four institutions involved in the two cases, U of T was the first to do so; from the outset, it involved outside labour relations counsel in the development of its negotiating strategy and position.

If and when a merger agreement is reached, it is brought forward for approval by the relevant authorities of both institutions (and, in the case of tripartite agreements such as those we studied, government). In the OISE/U of T case, the university's Governing Council and the institute's Board of Governors approved the tentative integration agreement before it was signed. In the Dal/TUNS case, there was no ratification of the agreement. The senates and boards of both institutions approved terms of agreement before the document was drafted and approved the agreement after it had been signed.

Planners, Decision Makers, and Managers

During the transition period, the focus shifts from those empowered to make and approve a deal on behalf of the institutions to those with the expertise and legitimacy needed to make plans for the merged institution, those with the authority to approve those plans, and those who must attempt to manage the transition. (In the Dal/TUNS case, the shift was much less pronounced than in the OISE/U of T case. Owing to the smaller size of the institutions, the level at which amalgamation took place, and the non-binding nature of the agreement, the presidents remained at the centre of the process.)

Planning for the merger of academic units typically involves the heads of those units, representatives of the faculty, and selected staff and students. The vehicle for planning is often joint committees or task forces. The Joint Transition Committee for Computer Science at Dalhousie and TUNS and the Academic Integration Task Force established by OISE and U of T were variants on this.

Being outside the realm of academic self-governance, administrative issues are typically resolved by less democratic means. In the Dal/TUNS case, the operating plans for the merging administrative units were developed by those selected to head the units. In the OISE/U of T case, this was the job of the Administrative Integration Task Force, to which OISE and U of T appointed management representatives. Another common approach is to appoint functional planning teams, each team being composed of a small number of people from each merging institution (e.g., a library services integration planning team composed of the head librarians, one or two other members of each library, and the heads of the Senate library committees).

Managers of institutional functions such as human resources, finance, facilities management, and computing are deeply involved in transition planning because their responsibilities touch every corner of the merging institutions, and because the facilities and services they provide are so broad in scope.

In a unionized environment, the institutions, their unions, and the body that approves the creation, scope, and termination of bargaining units in the jurisdiction (e.g., the Nova Scotia Labour Relations Board and the Ontario Labour Relations Board) typically determine during the transition period what the new bargaining unit structure will be, as well as how employees will move from the old structure to the new.

As the transition continues, plans for the merged institution are brought forward for approval by the individuals or bodies with the necessary authority. At the same time, appointments are made to positions in the merged institution. Although officials of the pre-existing institutions may continue to carry out their roles until the date of merger, the momentum generally shifts toward those appointed to positions of leadership in the new organization. As they begin to appoint other administrators and staff and to build the new organization, they carry the transition forward. A certain amount of chaos is normal.

Implementers

Typically, participation in the merger process is restricted to a small number of key players in the early phases of the process and broadens out as internal and external approvals and buy-ins are sought (see Figure 7.1). Once the merger has taken place, participation expands to encompass all the employees of the merged organization, who contribute to – or hinder – its operation as they carry out their various roles.

The capacity of managers, faculty, and staff to contribute positively is a function of variables such as the following:

- the degree to which they accept the changes that have taken place
- their attitudes toward the merged organization
- the effectiveness of the new structures, systems, and resources
- the effectiveness of the orientation they have received to the new organization and their roles within it

At this stage, other stakeholder groups – students, alumni, donors, community leaders – also become participants in the merger, insofar as they provide or withhold support for the merged organization. Do students return or go elsewhere? Do alumni participate in activities sponsored by the new institution, or do they withdraw? Do donors increase, decrease, or cease their financial contributions?

Human Factors

How people cope with and respond to merger has a direct impact on institutional performance in the short to medium term – on the educational

	INTERNAL PLAYERS	EXTERNAL PLAYERS
KEY PLAYERS AND	President Key vice-presidents Key managers – e.g. • human resources • planning • budget Legal counsel Heads and members of merging units Board of Governors Senate Unions Student government	Government Legal Counsel Consultants Government regulatory agency Labour relations board Accreditation agencies Alumni association Corporate and institutional partners
OTHER PLAYERS	Other administrators, faculty, students, and staff	Major donors Other universities Alumni Local community

Figure 7.1 Typical players in public sector higher education mergers

experience students receive, on research productivity, on the quality of administrative and other services, and so on.

Even in the corporate world, the human side of merger is immensely important. The anxiety, disruption, and upheaval experienced by employees undermines organizational performance. Merger is often followed by 'general declines in post-combination employee performance and what has been referred to as "post-merger slump,"' characterized by losses in productivity, revenues, opportunities and human resources' (Buono and

Bowditch, 1989, 231). In academe, human factors are arguably even more important. Notwithstanding the commercialization of higher education, the use of new technologies, and increasing student/faculty ratios, teaching and learning of all kinds remain personal activities. The fact that people – intelligent, articulate, individualistic people – are at the centre of the academic 'enterprise' defines the culture of higher education, drives its cost structure, and distinguishes higher education mergers from other types of mergers. Institutional strategy, management, technology, marketing, and so on all contribute in important ways to institutional success; but the contribution of human resources is even larger. For that reason, the effect on institutional outcomes of a post-merger decline in motivation and commitment on the part of faculty and staff is even more dramatic and direct than in the corporate sector.

A second reason why human factors loom especially large in higher education mergers is that professors have great collective power within these institutions. Thus, for example, the Dal/TUNS merger required the approval of the Senates of Dalhousie and TUNS, which were composed mainly of faculty members, and the OISE/U of T merger required the approval of the Governing Council of the University of Toronto, on which its faculty is represented. The collective power of the faculty no doubt explains why voluntary higher education mergers rarely involve faculty job loss. A third and final reason why human factors are relatively important in higher education mergers is that faculty members enjoy a great deal of autonomy. It is difficult to discipline or fire them. They can get away with a lot if they are so inclined, so their motivation to do well and their commitment to their students and their institution are very important.

Suggestion   Given the collective power and the individual autonomy enjoyed by faculty members, and the extent to which institutional success depends on their performance and achievement, it is especially important to attend to the human side of higher education mergers.

The following are illustrations, drawn from the Dal/TUNS and OISE/ U of T mergers, of how human factors play out in higher education mergers. Associated observations and suggestions are provided.

Symbolism and the Search for Meaning

Mergers give rise to uncertainty for faculty members and students, but especially for staff, who are relatively powerless in institutions of higher education. Whereas faculty members are rarely let go in the course of mergers, staff layoffs are not infrequent.

OISE and U of T estimated that sixty-five staff jobs would have to be cut in order for OISE/UT to meet its budget target. Voluntary separation packages were offered to staff at both OISE and FEUT. During early 1996, staff wrestled with whether to take separation packages or stay on. Uncertain about what the future would hold for them at OISE/UT, most OISE staff hedged their bets. The deadline for applications for severance packages was extended twice. By 14 May, OISE's director was able to report to its board that 'the proposed administrative structure called for a reduction of approximately 60 positions and the number of requests for early retirement and enhanced severance were almost at that number' (OISE Board of Governors, 14 May, 1996). Nevertheless, at the urging of union representatives, the board voted to 'direct the Administration to postpone the May 17th deadline for early retirement and severance packages to May 24, 1996.'

Some time earlier a respected member of OISE's staff with many years of seniority had decided to apply for a position at the university for which he seemed to be eminently qualified. He was among the first staff at OISE to do so. Everyone concerned assumed that he would get the position. The relevant university department went through the motions of interviewing him before offering him the position. But the interview revealed unexpected gaps in his qualifications, and he did not get the job. Word went around OISE like wildfire. Staff at OISE got the message. A flood of severance applications came before the third and final deadline. Eventually, between 105 and 115 staff members – the vast majority from OISE – left.

The effect of the OISE staff member's story on the behaviour of his colleagues was regarded as pivotal by those involved in managing the transition. Although the latter bent over backwards to ensure that the individual in question got another job at the university, the psychological damage was done – staff at OISE knew what U of T thought of them. The fact that other OISE staff did get U of T positions immediately afterwards changed very few minds.

No doubt every merger has such stories. The incidents that give rise to them cannot be avoided completely, even if one is willing and able to micromanage. It is often their timing that accounts for their impact. The lessons people draw from them can be positive ('they respect our traditions') or negative ('our people don't have a chance'), accurate or not.

Observation   In the uncertainty created by a pending merger, people look for signs of what the future will be like in the merged organiza-

tion. They tend to interpret events symbolically and to act on what they infer.

Suggestion   *Although the emergence of 'stories' cannot be controlled, those involved in negotiating and managing mergers should consider how potential decisions and actions may be perceived and to what stories about the new organization they may give rise.*

The Prestige Factor

The name for the college that would succeed TUNS was unveiled at a well-attended meeting on the TUNS campus on 6 March 1997, at which the lieutenant-governor, the university presidents, the TUNS student union president, and others spoke. The chosen name was 'Dalhousie University Polytechnic.'

Although the name did not receive an especially critical reception on that day – just a few muted boo's from students at the back of the room, who were opposed to amalgamation in any case – opposition to it grew rapidly, particularly within the faculty. At the meeting of the TUNS Senate on 19 March 1997, a senator 'objected strenuously to the new name for TUNS and said that the use of the word "Polytechnic" was insulting.' He moved 'that the Senate of TUNS record its objection to the choice of the name Polytechnic' (TUNS Senate, 19 March 1997). The motion was carried.

The Senate met again on 26 March. Clarifying its intentions of the previous week, it directed its secretary to convey to the chairman of the TUNS board that 'the Senate of TUNS rejects the choice of the name Polytechnic' (TUNS Senate, 26 March 1997). Its members voted to recommend to the boards of TUNS and Dalhousie that 'the name of the amalgamated college/institute be Dalhousie University Institute of Applied Science and Technology.' Few would have predicted a year – or even a month – earlier that TUNS senators would vote for a name beginning with 'Dalhousie University.' Although some would have preferred not to give Dalhousie top billing, it was the use of 'Polytechnic' to describe their institution that was really galling. To many faculty members – especially those of British or Commonwealth origin – it was most demeaning. One young faculty member from another Commonwealth country quipped: 'I'm afraid to tell my parents I'm now at Dalhousie University Polytechnic. They'll think I've been demoted!'

The TUNS board agreed to the presidents' suggestion that it reconsider the choice of name. Meanwhile, the informal name 'DalTech' was used to refer to the college/institute – not only in speech, but also on letterhead, in announcements, and so on. The DalTech board polled faculty, students, staff, and alumni late in the spring on whether they preferred 'Dalhousie University Polytechnic' or 'Dalhousie University Institute of Applied Science and Technology.' Finding that neither option won people's hearts, it confirmed 'DalTech' as the name of the successor to TUNS, leaving unresolved the question of whether the new entity was a college, an institute, or a polytechnic.

A possible explanation for the faculty's rejection of 'Polytechnic' and for the collective failure to adopt a formal name for DalTech is that none of the possible names for a multifaculty unit within a university – college, institute, polytechnic – are as prestigious as 'university.' To adopt any of them would imply a drop in status. Rather than risk perceived loss of status, the TUNS community effectively forwent a formal new identity.

Observation   *Changes that give people additional status or prestige are likely to be accepted much more readily than changes that deprive them of it.*

Suggestion   *In formulating their negotiating positions and subsequent transition plans, participants in higher education mergers should bear in mind the likelihood that changes which involve an increase in status or prestige will unfold much more smoothly than changes which are perceived to involve a loss.*

The Trust Factor

At numerous junctures in the Dal/TUNS and OISE/U of T mergers, trust made forward movement possible.

For instance, trust enabled U of T to get to the negotiating table. With the powerful exceptions of the president of U of T and the dean of FEUT, the members of the university's administration were arrayed against integration. To bring them on board, U of T's president, Robert Prichard, appointed a senior professor for whom they had the greatest respect to lead the university's negotiating team. In Prichard's words, 'because they all trusted [Stefan] Dupré so much, they could accept the process.'

Observation   *In mergers of higher education institutions and other organizations in which central authority is relatively weak and units and individuals enjoy extensive autonomy, trust is important to elicit agreement and cooperation.*

Suggestion   *It is important that those appointed to leadership roles in the negotiation and transition processes enjoy the trust of administrators, faculty members, staff, and students at their institution.*

The importance of trust – this time between rather than within institutions – was again demonstrated several months later. Talks between U of T and OISE had gotten nowhere. In the words of one member of OISE's team: 'There was such mistrust at the bargaining table that it really didn't matter what U of T said. No one believed them.'

Observation   *Distrust works against effective communication and, hence, collaboration.*

At the institutions' request, the Education minister appointed John Stubbs, then president of Simon Fraser University, to mediate in the fall of 1994. Most of those close to the negotiations described his role as crucial. He was able to play a crucial role largely because OISE's representatives trusted him. He had been president of Trent – a small, 'democratic' university. He was known as a fine individual. Last but not least, OISE had proposed his name to the minister. Its representatives perceived him as their man. Because they trusted him, he could persuade them to listen to what the university was saying. One person close to the negotiations described Stubbs's role as follows: 'He talked sense to both sides. He listened and understood and helped us communicate. We [at OISE] got the message that if we [the parties] didn't reach agreement, the government would force the issue. We began to see this as an opportunity to negotiate our future. Stubbs told us that we were being offered a good financial deal and urged us to look seriously at the advantages of what was being proposed.' Asked what had made agreement possible, a member of the university's negotiating team replied: 'The university and the government made OISE a good offer. More importantly, OISE's people awoke to the realization that the alternatives were all worse.' Because he was trusted, John Stubbs was able to help OISE to this realization.

Suggestion   *Impasses resulting from lack of trust and communication may be overcome by injecting into the process a new player who is trusted by the parties.*

In our interview with Stubbs, we asked what (if any) role trust plays in higher education merger. 'Trust is central,' he replied. 'The academic community is, in many ways, built on a series of trusts. The collegial model we talk so much about is based on trust between colleagues to do what is best for the collective. In merger situations, that expectation is particularly acute.' A corollary is, of course, that the consequences of loss of trust are serious. Many former members of TUNS, having expected that TUNS would carry on, in modified form, as a college within Dalhousie, reacted to the dismantling of the college as a betrayal. This was particularly true of engineering professors, whose faculty had dominated TUNS. One computer scientist observed: 'You have to understand: Engineering wasn't just a faculty of TUNS – Engineering *was* TUNS.' Having dominated a university, many engineers were angry and bitter to discover that they were destined to become 'just a faculty' of Dalhousie. The result was a bad case of post-merger drift. The Faculty of Engineering was beset by internal tensions and malaise and had great difficulty moving forward.

To avoid or minimize post-merger drift, McCann and Gilkey suggest that top managers provide 'an intermediate vision that links the past with the present and the present with the future' (1988, 167). The Dean of Engineering attempted to do just that. Recognizing early in 1998 that a college to succeed TUNS had not and would not become a reality, he suggested to his colleagues an alternative vision of their collective future. He proposed that the faculty secede from the faltering DalTech college and strike out on its own as a strong and relatively autonomous professional faculty. At a faculty meeting in March 1998, he proposed that his faculty cede from DalTech. The first four clauses of his motion were quoted in Chapter 6. Other parts of the motion read as follows:

And whereas the culture of Dalhousie is structured to deal with Faculties as semi-independent entities and the college concept simply confuses our communications and lines of authority; ...

We therefore resolve that the Faculty of Engineering undertake to separate from DalTech and recover its share of the administrative resources of the College; that it function independently of the College and directly through the Senate, Board of Governors, and Administration of Dalhousie University in all matters; and that it become a full member of the University's 'family' of Faculties without reference to a College Board, an Academic Council, or a Principal.

The dean's motion was approved in the first instance, but rescinded shortly afterwards. Its opponents were not ready to let go of the idea of a strong college within Dalhousie to succeed TUNS. So the dean's attempt to provide an alternative vision that would enable his faculty to move forward did not succeed at that time.

When people have taken to heart a vision of the future that has not been fulfilled, they tend to be reluctant or unable to embrace another vision.

Observation   If the outcome of merger is significantly different from what was expected by members of the acquired institution, loss of morale and productivity and feelings of betrayal will probably result, and make it difficult to move forward.

By the spring of 1999, there were signs that the Faculty of Engineering was beginning to come to terms with the reality of amalgamation. An *ad hoc* committee of the faculty, established to study the impact of amalgamation on its operations, consulted extensively with faculty members, students, administrators, and staff and reflected as follows:

> It is clear that the Faculty of Engineering entered this merger somewhat naively. There are many things that, in hindsight, would have been extremely useful to have known about Dalhousie prior to making any decisions. A detailed business analysis and strategic plan should have been carried [out] long before the merger to avoid loss of effectiveness on the part of all parties to the merger. However, it is now two years after the merger, and the new reality is that TUNS is a part of Dalhousie. As such, we must strive to function effectively and efficiently within Dalhousie's framework ...
>
> The concept of 'DalTech' needs to be given some careful thought ... It is possible that the Faculty of Engineering would be better off on its own two feet. Granted, the loss of our unity and background would be unfortunate. The issue needs further consideration by the Faculty. (Fenton et al., 1999, 34)

Two years after amalgamation, it was possible for the faculty to consider relinquishing the concept of the college and pursuing an alternative vision of its own future.

A Question of Identity

The highest level of change in a merger or acquisition is in the individual manager or employee, who will ideally internalize the values, beliefs and assumptions – that is, the 'culture' – of the acquiring organization ... The simple adoption of change does not necessarily mean that true internalization of the change occurs. Adoption may mean compliance while internalization yields commitment.

McCann and Gilkey, 1988, 133

Alceste Pappas has described the process of achieving commitment to organizational change as an eight-stage process that begins with 'Contact' and 'Awareness of Change' and ends with 'Adoption,' 'Institutionalization,' and, finally, 'Internalization' (in Hughes and Conner, 1989). Once the seventh stage of the process, institutionalization, is achieved, the change is no longer experimental: it is part of the institution. In the eighth and final stage, individual members of the institution have internalized the change: 'The targets of change become advocates or even sponsors, displaying enthusiasm, persistence and a high personal and professional investment' (1989, 45).

As of early 1999, the Dal/TUNS amalgamation had been institutionalized. To what extent had it been internalized? Members of the Faculty of Computer Science suggested during interviews that many of their colleagues had internalized the merger of the former units. Asked whether his colleagues had transferred their identities to the new faculty (i.e., now saw themselves as members of the Faculty of Computer Science rather than as members of their former units), one computer scientist observed: 'There are a few people sitting on the fence, but for all intents and purposes, I'd say that the vast majority of the faculty see themselves as part of the Faculty of Computer Science at Dalhousie.' The merger in Computer Science was thus well advanced. Nevertheless, not everyone had embraced the change. A second computer scientist observed: 'There are a few people who have long histories at either of the institutions for whom the weight of that history is more important than the present. They are unlikely ever to be – or to admit to being – pleased with the process. And the best one can do is provide them with an environment in which they can do things they like and let them get on with those without saying, 'You have to be happy!' A third said:

[The amalgamation] was a very traumatic event for many computer scientists and engineers ... Some of them still really haven't recovered. They aren't working or functioning nearly as well as before the merger ... Some [of the computer scientists at TUNS] found the change no problem at all. A couple found it initially traumatic, but got over it quite quickly. But there are a few who are still finding it very difficult to handle. I think it's affected the health of a couple of people quite badly.

Observation   *Those who are unable to relinquish their former identities and identify with the new unit or institution may suffer. Their outlook, their work, and their health may be affected.*

Suggestion   *Managers should recognize that mergers can be difficult for faculty and staff whose objective situations appear relatively unchanged, as well as for those who experience job loss or change or other dislocations. They should be alert for signs of psychological damage and offer assistance to the afflicted.*

Although some of its members had been left behind, as of early 1999 the Faculty of Computer Science was considerably ahead of the Faculty of Engineering in internalizing change. Why did the extent to which amalgamation had been accepted and internalized vary so much from faculty to faculty?

Three explanations suggest themselves. One, alluded to earlier, is that satisfaction with the outcome of merger is inversely related to the breadth of the gap between premerger expectations and reality. In other words, because engineering professors were generally more sanguine about the prospect of amalgamation than were TUNS's computer scientists, they were less satisfied with the outcome. A second explanation focuses on the relative centrality of the three disciplines that comprised TUNS. As noted earlier, from the point of view of Architecture and Computer Science, Engineering dominated TUNS. In the words of·one computer scientist: 'TUNS was mostly Engineering. Engineering held the reins of power financially and politically. Engineers dominated the committees ... We were continually sent documents and asked to do things as if we were a unit of Engineering ... It did mean that we felt happy to ignore quite a bit of this. But it left one feeling very much on the outside of things.'

Observation   *Those who were at the centre of the old order and who identified most strongly with it tend to be the most reluctant to embrace the new institutional identity and agenda.*

Suggestion   *When enlisting individuals in building the new unit or institution, transition managers should bear in mind that individuals who were not at the centre of the old order may have most enthusiasm for the task.*

A third explanation is simply that amalgamation bestowed many more benefits on TUNS's computer scientists than it did on its engineers. Thanks to the priority given to Computer Science by the provincial government and the university administration and to the entrepreneurialism of its dean, the Faculty of Computer Science secured additional funding, made many new appointments and secured a custom-designed new building. The good match between the pre-existing units, the energy of their faculty and staff, and the vision of the dean generated a host of initiatives that had not till then been possible. There was a sense of new potential. This combination of greater resources and enhanced opportunities made it relatively easy to buy in.

To many engineers, the balance sheet looked different. The *ad hoc* committee of the Faculty of Engineering stated in its May 1999 report on the merger's impact:

> At TUNS, the Faculty of Engineering was the largest fish in a small pond. Now it is a medium-size fish in a much larger pond. Consequently, the clout of engineering has diminished significantly in real terms ... The best interests of engineering is no longer the primary focus of the university ...
>
> During the merger and afterwards, the Faculty of Engineering was not given the same importance as that was given to Computer Science. The purpose of the merger never was ... to enhance the strengths of the Faculty of Engineering. The purpose was just to add engineering on the 'list' of faculties at Dalhousie ... In turn, the Faculty of Engineering did not promote or make use of its strengths in IT, and other areas, but surrendered to the notion that IT is the sole property of Computer Science. As a result, the Faculty of Engineering failed to aggressively compete for resources whereas Computer Science did.
>
> TUNS had direct access to the Government and funding agencies, and since engineering was the largest and most important faculty in the university, engineering had direct representation in these circles. Being part of Dalhousie, engineering has lost this direct access and opportunity to influence government policy. Also, now engineering has to compete with other faculties for budget funding within the Dalhousie system, rather than as a separate entity within the university system. (Fenton et al., 1999, 16)

From the point of view of many in the Faculty of Engineering, the losses from amalgamation have outweighed the gains.

Observation   *The greater the benefits associated with a merger or acquisition, the easier it is for members of a unit or institution to accept and internalize the change.*

Interpersonal Dynamics and Space Planning

One reason why it was easier to integrate the old units and cultures in the case of the Faculty of Computer Science than in that of OISE/UT is that the former was so small that its members were able – indeed, were bound – to work together, meet together, and talk together. In contrast, OISE and FEUT were so large, and were structured so differently, that there was much less day-to-day contact between the two merging faculties in the weeks and months following merger.

Interaction between members of pre-existing groups is not enough to achieve integration. Indeed, such interaction can sometimes work against integration. Nevertheless, talking is a prerequisite for appreciating and eventually overcoming cultural differences. People are unlikely to understand others, and to begin to develop shared understandings, until they talk to them.

Observation   *Other things being equal, interaction between individual members of pre-existing groups facilitates integration.*

Suggestion   *To the extent that integration (rather than co-existence) is sought, design administrative structures and organize processes whereby people choose or are assigned to departments, in such a way as to increase the likelihood of day-to-day interaction between members of the groups that are merging.*

The members of the Dal/TUNS Joint Transition Committee on Computer Science recognized that if the members of the pre-existing units were going to come together as a faculty, they would have to be in one location as soon as possible. The administrations had initially envisaged that the two units would continue to function in their pre-existing locations until the arrival of a new dean; the Joint Transition Committee countered – and the administrations eventually agreed – that additional space must be secured for Computer Science on the DalTech campus so that the two groups could be together in the summer of 1997.

In planning the move of the computer scientists at Dalhousie to DalTech, the interim dean was careful to ensure that the former Dalhousie professors did not end up in one block of offices and their new colleagues in another. Space was renovated and allocated so that members of the pre-existing units worked in offices side by side. As intended, this reinforced emerging collegiality.

The new student labs were not planned as carefully. As one member of the faculty explained: 'We put the UNIX labs, which Dal had always used, on the fifteenth floor, so the Dal students naturally migrated down there. The PC labs and the Mac labs – which had been the TUNS platform – stayed on the sixteenth floor, so the TUNS students stayed there. It was not good. It really contributed to the split [between the two groups of students]. This year, we moved all the labs onto one floor. It's a little crowded, but relations have improved.'

Observation   *The design and allocation of space has a profound influence on social interaction and, hence, integration.*

The Importance of Communication

Good communication about organizational restructuring is rare. For Wyatt's 1993 *Survey of Corporate Restructuring in Canada* 148 senior Canadian corporate executives were asked to describe one major change they would make to the way their organizations deal with restructuring. The most frequent response: 'Improve communications to employees' (The Wyatt Company, 1993). The choice of preposition is telling: good communication takes place *with* people; it is not done *to* them. It is part of a relationship.

Obviously, university officials have many important relationships – with faculty, staff, students, alumni, governments, donors, employers, professional and accreditation bodies, and so on. Merger complicates already complex patterns of communication because sources of official communication – and some of their 'audiences' – change with changes in institutional structures.

During the negotiation phase, communication follows pre-existing channels (although communication about negotiations *per se* may be constrained by mutual agreement). Thus, for example, the presidents of Dalhousie and TUNS each continued to communicate to their boards, senates and faculty, staff, and student and alumni groups about the status of the process until agreement to amalgamate was reached. In keeping with the informal nature of the negotiations, they coordinated their communications informally.

In the OISE/U of T case, coordination was lacking at first. As described in Chapter 4, the communication by the two institutions of different conceptions of integration led to a rocky start to the process. The waters were smoothed, and at the first meeting of the negotiating teams it was agreed that neither party would communicate publicly about the negotiations without the other's consent.

The people from FEUT whom we interviewed told us that in practice, their dean was their principal source of general information about the status of discussions with OISE. At OISE, which operated under a form of 'co-management,' communication from 'management' seems to have been a relatively less important source of information. Our interviewees suggested that faculty and staff got most of their information about the negotiations from their unions.

In the interval between the signing of a merger agreement and the merger itself, the character of communications changes. It changed differently at Dalhousie and TUNS than at OISE and U of T.

On the day the Dal/TUNS amalgamation agreement was signed, faculty, staff, and students at both universities received a joint memo from their presidents stating that 'we are very pleased to announce that we, the Premier and the Minister of Education have signed the Agreement to amalgamate Dalhousie and TUNS. Copies of the Agreement, signed this morning, will be made available on both campuses within the next few days. Planning for the joining of our two universities is now formally under way.' This memo, constituting *Amalgamation Bulletin* #1, went on to remind people of the objectives of amalgamation, to describe the transition planning and management structure, and to say: 'We know that many of you are very eager to know what the amalgamation will mean for you and your units. We don't have all the answers yet and we won't for some time, but we will address as many questions as we can in a further bulletin next week. If there are specific questions or issues you would like us to address, please contact the Executive Coordinator through either of our offices or by e-mail at julia.eastman@dal.ca or eastman@tuns.ca.' Joint formal communication by the two presidents through amalgamation bulletins and other vehicles continued until after amalgamation had taken place.

In the case of OISE and U of T, the signing of the agreement was not accompanied by the initiation of ongoing joint communication. Whereas the finalization of the Dal/TUNS agreement had been expected on the two campuses for months, the conclusion of the agreement between OISE and U of T came as a surprise. Even if the executive director of OISE had not resigned shortly afterwards, it is unlikely that the initiation of joint formal communication to OISE and FEUT immediately after the agreement was signed would have been effective, because for many at OISE, that most fundamental of questions – 'Why are we doing this?' – had not yet been addressed. This is not a question that the two institutions could have addressed jointly. As recounted in Chapter 4, Angela Hildyard, the last director of OISE and former leader of OISE's negotiating team, responded to this question on behalf of the negotiating team in an article, 'The Path to Merger,' that appeared in the January/February 1995 edition of *OISE News*. It explained that the negotiating team was 'convinced that we had struck the best possible deal under the circumstances' – one that 'provides the potential for the creation of a new faculty which could – and should – become the pre-eminent education faculty in all of Canada, if not North America.' The article concluded by noting that 'the two Task Forces charged with developing plans for academic and administrative integration' would begin work soon and by encouraging members of the OISE community 'to take full and positive advantage of this opportunity for change.'

At Dalhousie and TUNS, the presidents of the merging institutions continued to lead the amalgamation process during the transition period. In contrast, at OISE/UT the Academic and Administrative Integration Task Forces were at the centre of the planning process. The people we interviewed suggested that aside from one or two symbolic joint statements, there continued to be separate flows of information to members of the two institutions until the transition process was well advanced and the dean-elect and other university officials began communicating with members of OISE as well as FEUT.

What can we learn from the Dal/TUNS and OISE/U of T cases about the elements of good merger-related communication?

Dalhousie and TUNS placed relatively more emphasis on communication as part of transition management than did OISE and U of T. For example, Dalhousie's Director of Public Relations and TUNS's Executive Director of Community Relations were members of the Amalgamation Planning Committee; in contrast, communications professionals did not play an ongoing role in integrating OISE and FEUT. Although all the transition planning bodies for OISE and U of T had advisory groups and their members reported back to their constituents, there was less emphasis on planning and coordinating communication from 'management' to members of OISE and FEUT.

Participants in the Dal/TUNS process later told us that the effort of establishing formal communication lines had been worthwhile. Several of those involved in integrating OISE and U of T said that in hindsight, they would have placed more emphasis on communication during the transition process.

Observation   Because human factors loom so large in higher education mergers, effective communication is a vital part of merger management.

From the Dal/TUNS experience, we can learn a number of things about the ingredients of effective communication. Participants in that process found that developments in the amalgamation process were not predictable enough for attempts at detailed communication planning to be productive. At the same time, they found that it was important to identify in advance the constituencies with which they would need to communicate about amalgamation, to create appropriate vehicles for communication, and to dedicate staff time and other resources to amalgamation-related communications. All of this enabled them to communicate to their constituencies in a timely manner as the process unfolded.

Suggestion   Think through how institutional relationships will change as a result of merger, identify constituencies with which you will need to communicate and put in place vehicles and resources that will enable you to do so in a timely manner.

The following analysis of 'Amalgamation Bulletin' – a vehicle for formal communication about amalgamation, distributed on paper and electronically at Dalhousie and TUNS – suggests some ingredients for effective merger-related communication.

The main feature of each bulletin was a joint memo from the Presidents, who were leading the process.

Observation   Communications are most likely to be effective if they come from people in positions of authority and trust.

Suggestion   Merger-related communications should come from institutional and unit leaders. Anonymous merger memos or messages from people who are unknown are less likely to be effective.

Suggestion   Formal communication by institutional leaders should be coupled with the dissemination of information through personal communication up and down the organizational chart.

The first bulletin was issued immediately after the amalgamation agreement was signed. At this point in a merger process, people have myriad questions about how merger will affect them. The questions sent to the executive coordinator of the Dal/TUNS amalgamation in the days following the signing of the amalgamation agreement ranged from 'Will there be layoffs in my department?' to 'Can I use Dalplex [an athletic facility]?' to 'Will my child, who is studying at [the other institution], qualify for a dependent tuition waiver next year?' to 'What will be on the parchments issued to TUNS students next year?' The difficulty is, of course, that the answers to many of these questions are not immediately known. One hesitates to say anything for fear of saying the wrong thing. It is easier to say nothing at all!

The problem with saying nothing is that faculty members, students, and staff interpret silence to mean (a) that university officials don't know what they're doing, or (b) – which may be worse – that they don't care. The longer the silence lasts, the more skepticism and disaffection build up and the harder it becomes to begin to communicate. As one member of the Administrative Integration Task Force observed: 'Communication wasn't all that it could be. We were afraid of making mistakes.' Communication in a climate of uncertainty does entail risk.

Suggestion   Begin communicating immediately and keep communicating regularly.

To minimize the risk that the wording of bulletins would imply unintended commitments by Dalhousie and/or TUNS, draft bulletins were reviewed by legal counsel.

Suggestion   Formal merger-related communications (especially written communications from people in positions of authority) should be reviewed by legal counsel.

What about all the unknowns? The approach taken by Dalhousie and TUNS was to communicate what *was* known, to be frank and open about what was not yet known, and to describe the processes by which answers would be arrived at.

Suggestion   When answers to people's questions and concerns are not yet known, explain the processes by which answers will be arrived at, and if possible, provide an approximate time frame.

The amalgamation bulletins were not prepared in a vacuum. Besides reporting on developments, they sought to respond to questions and concerns of faculty members, staff, and students. The nature of these concerns was ascertained by means both formal (e.g., questions submitted to the executive coordinator) and informal.

Suggestion   Ensure that you have mechanisms – formal (e.g., question lines, surveys, focus groups, communications monitoring teams) – and/ or informal (e.g., chatting with those in the know) – for eliciting people's questions and concerns.

The amalgamation bulletins were timely. They got word about major developments in the process (e.g., departmental reorganizations, the introduction of legislation, the universities' application to the Labour Relations Board) out to the campuses without delay. People heard about things first directly from the leaders of their universities.

Suggestion   If at all possible, faculty, staff and students – and, if possible, alumni and friends – should learn about important developments in merger negotiations from the leaders of their institutions.

This is also crucial during the negotiation phase. In the Dal/TUNS case, the president of TUNS had to scramble to ensure that people at his university did not learn about the possibility of a Dal/TUNS merger from the media. OISE officials understood this equally well, and spent an anxious thirty hours awaiting the government's approval to announce that a tentative agreement had been reached for integrating OISE into U of T.

Finally, the amalgamation bulletins were effective because on most issues they did not obfuscate. They did not minimize the possibility of layoffs. They recognized the extent of the uncertainty, anxiety and difficulties to which amalgamation had given rise.

Suggestion   Use language with power and meaning. Don't obfuscate, sanitize, or minimize.

The greatest failing of formal amalgamation communications at Dal/ TUNS was that they allowed – even encouraged – significant numbers of people at TUNS to believe that TUNS would carry on much as before after it became part of Dalhousie. When the reality proved otherwise, these people naturally felt betrayed.

Observation   *There is a price to be paid for communications that mislead people inadvertently or deliberately about what merger will entail.*

It is very possible that the more the communication of a particular expectation elicits support for merger, the more damage there will be to trust, morale, and productivity if the expectation is not met.

EIGHT

On Dollars and Data

As important as the human side of higher education merger is the financial side, for finances drive mergers and constrain what they can achieve. In his pioneering study of mergers in the United States, John Millett wrote:

> If the ten case studies of this inquiry provide a representative sample of the merger experience of higher education institutions over the past two or three decades, it is apparent that mergers result from various circumstances and conditions: geographical proximity, complementary programs, a history of cooperative relationships, the drive to coeducation, the desire to strengthen the quality of higher educational service and complexities of higher education financing ... Of all these forces, finances are the final and determining influence. (1976, 31).

More recent studies have confirmed Millett's finding that finances drive many higher education mergers (Goedegebuure, 1992). Even when financial issues do not motivate merger, they may be important ingredients in its success or failure.

Although the financial motivations for merger vary from case to case, clear patterns are discernable. The two case studies are in several respects typical of the financial dynamics of merger; as such, they provide useful lessons for public universities and colleges contemplating merger. In this chapter, we explain those dynamics and discuss the financial and administrative dimensions of merger.

The Dynamics of Size and Specialization

Several studies have made the observation that in mergers between institutions of different size, the smaller institution is usually under financial duress (Millett, 1976; Chambers, 1983; Goedegebuure, 1992). There is a certain logic to this: in higher education, economies of scale favour larger institutions (Sears, 1983; Brinkman and Leslie, 1986). Both in theory and in practice, there is an upper limit to the inverse correlation between institutional size and unit costs; however, the available evidence indicates that this upper limit is very high (Schumacher, 1983). There is no history of mergers between very large institutions.

A second reason why the smaller institution in a merger is likely to be in financial duress relates to revenues instead of expenses. Especially in North America, public colleges and universities are very often funded under formulas that are sensitive to enrolment. Formulas by their nature are linear; they inherently fund average institutions or average programs. Institutions or programs that are on the statistical fringes of such formulas (i.e., that are significantly unlike the average) usually end up being inadequately funded. This is a particular problem for institutions that are much smaller than the average, or are more specialized (in terms of their arrays of programs) than the average. Specialization usually results in lopsided cost structures that enrolment-sensitive funding formulas fail to recognize.

Size and specialization are often synonymous, but not always. Large institutions, too, may have some programs that are so specialized that they fail to achieve the critical masses that funding formulas assume. Regarding these specific programs, the larger institution may be as far out on the fringes of the funding formula's algorithms as the smaller institution. The key difference, then, between the smaller institution and the larger one is that the larger institution has more flexibility and opportunity to cross-subsidize programs (Massy, 1996).

Given the financial dynamics of size and specialization, it is not surprising that smaller and more specialized institutions, as participants in a merger, have different motivations and perceptions than their larger, more comprehensive partners. Studies suggest that smaller colleges and universities typically seek to merge for these reasons:

• To secure net new resources for their programs and services. More often than not, the net gain is due to reduced unit costs rather than to additional revenue. Thus the 'new' revenue is only notional; the real source of financial gain is reallocated saving.
• To generate truly new revenue from new programs made possible through merger.
• To benefit financially from government incentives to merge with larger institutions.
• In cases where the larger institution is prepared to direct additional

resources to the smaller institution, to take advantage of its willingness to do so. The resources in question usually take the form of budgetary allocations, but in some cases they involve access to better facilities and services than the smaller institution could have afforded itself.

- To migrate toward a more favourable location in a funding formula, in cases of 'tiered' jurisdictions.
- To become less 'lopsided' in terms of program costs.
- To achieve critical mass in small areas of specialization.
- To have the smaller institution's accumulated debt assumed by its partner in merger or by the government.

Intuition suggests that the larger partner in a merger will be motivated less than the smaller partner by financial considerations. In many but not all cases, this intuition coincides with reality.

First, 'large' and 'small' are relative terms. A college with 2,000 students may seem small beside a university with 5,000 students, but this size difference may not be significant enough to alter their unit costs of instruction if they decide to merge. There is some evidence that significant economies of scale do not begin until enrolment reaches about 20,000 (Layard, 1974).

More to the point, the college with 2,000 students may have five different faculties, while the university with 5,000 students may have only two. In that case, the smaller institution is the more complex. Complexity may drive costs more than absolute size (National Commission on the Cost of Higher Education, 1998), as it often does in for-profit firms (Lawler and Mohrman, 1996).

Second, economies of scale are not infinite. There is a point at which size no longer confers financial advantage, and beyond which size can be a financial liability (Blau, 1994; Patterson, 1999).

Larger institutions in mergers share some objectives with their smaller partners:

- They may wish to benefit from government incentives that encourage merger. Some government merger schemes offer more to larger 'host' institutions.
- They may have small, highly specialized programs that on their own are as uneconomic as those in smaller institutions.
- They may gain additional revenue from new programs that merger either makes possible or makes possible at a lower marginal cost than the larger institution could realize on its own.

There are, however, objectives that are more characteristic of larger institutions in mergers:

- Larger institutions tend toward diversity and comprehensiveness. As they do, they become concerned about balance and filling programmatic voids. Merger is a means of filling a void at lower cost – especially capital cost. This explains why a larger institution may be willing to assume the debt of a smaller institution. In practical terms, the larger institution would be buying additional programs for the cost of their debt. In certain cases, that could be a bargain.
- Because of the presumption of economies of scale, larger institutions assume that they can offer the programs of the smaller institution at lower cost, thus producing savings for reallocation.
- They may gain access to highly specialized facilities, some of which may be underutilized.

Formally and legally, mergers are between institutions. However, in the case of mergers of publicly funded colleges and universities, government almost always plays a role. Often governments want the same things as the institutions, be they large or small:

- Governments want new programs, and want them at a relatively low marginal cost instead of at an average cost. Here governments are victims of their own funding formulas, which inherently fund at the average. Merger can make the marginal costs of new programs lower.
- Merger can especially reduce the capital costs of new programs, since the sunk costs of previous investments can be more efficiently utilized.
- Governments are driven toward economies of scale just as individual institutions are – perhaps even more so.

There are some objectives, however, that are of greater interest to government than to public colleges and universities. These objectives are not necessarily antithetical to the interests of the institutions, but they may be of less value to them:

- Especially in older jurisdictions, systems of higher education may or may not be rational or efficient in terms of public policy because, in the first instance, there may not have been any public policy when some of the institutions that make up the system were founded. Or public policy may have changed; an example is the shift toward mass higher education with very high rates of participation.

- Demand may have shifted to the extent that certain institutions – typically in underpopulated areas – that were viable under conventional funding formulas have ceased to be viable. In these cases, merger may be a more attractive alternative than receivership or anomalous funding.
- While affordability is a concern both for institutions and for governments, the government perspective is different. In most jurisdictions, governments fund colleges and universities by block transfer grants; with a few exceptions, they do not specify how an institution should spend the public funding that is made available to it. As a result, governments that are faced with affordability problems tend to think in terms of simple unit costs such as funding per student. Their own funding formulas draw them to such a perspective, and draw them to thinking of merger as a way of moving all institutions to an average unit cost.
- On self-reflection, some governments recognize that they may not have sufficient time or sapience to make sound decisions about all of the public colleges and universities for which they are responsible, particularly smaller and more specialized institutions. In this context, one might consider James March's observations about 'limited rationality' (March, 1994), and Burton Clark's descriptions of 'demand overload' (Clark, 1998). From this perspective, merger is an organizational device for delegating or narrowing some responsibility to a lower level – specifically, to larger institutions, which become hosts through merger to smaller, more specialized institutions (Van Ravens, 1995; Ontario Ministry of Agriculture, Food and Rural Affairs, 1996).

Prior to merger, OISE and TUNS were characteristic of smaller institutions in several respects:

- Both were in very serious financial difficulty. Their accumulated deficits were roughly 10 per cent of their annual operating revenue – a very high ratio, at least five times greater than other universities would regard as prudent.
- Both had received signals from government that no additional funds beyond those normally allocated to universities in their provinces would be made available to solve their chronic financial problems.

- Both were funded mainly according to formulas that did not differentiate among institutions on the basis of size or specialization.
- Both knew beforehand that their respective governments would support bids for merger.

OISE and TUNS were motivated toward merger mainly by financial exigency. Neither could reasonably hope for better financial times. In the case of OISE, there were reasons to believe that its financial situation would become worse: the government had given notice that a $1.6 million annual supplementary grant for research would be discontinued. Moreover, and potentially even worse, the arithmetic nature of the Ontario operating grants formula, combined with the fact that tuition fees were closely regulated, meant that province-wide reductions in operating grants would have a greater impact on OISE than on virtually any other institution in the province.

When it came to balancing their budgets, the only practical choice available to either OISE or TUNS was to compromise quality. As the chair of the TUNS board said: 'It wasn't a question of survival. It was a question of quality.' When it came time to negotiate merger, both would seek guarantees that at the very least, the quality of their academic programs would not deteriorate further.

Dalhousie and U of T shared some of the reasons that larger institutions often cite for seeking merger:

- Both wanted to acquire certain programs to complete and further their institutional missions.
- Both found it less costly to acquire existing programs than to start new ones.
- Both believed that they could realize savings through merger. In the case of the OISE/U of T merger, that belief was borne out rather quickly in certain areas: physical plant costs were reduced by about 40 per cent and financial services costs by about 50 per cent.

The objectives of the Nova Scotia and Ontario governments were, however, quite different. In Nova Scotia there was a strong desire to expand and improve higher education in applied science and technology – especially in Computer Science. The Nova Scotia government was mainly concerned about improving quality and adding programs at the lowest reasonable marginal cost. Cost-cutting and deficit reduction were not predominant concerns. Significantly, the government of Nova Scotia, in the formal merger agreement, sought no funding cutbacks and made a number of commitments to provide additional funding.

The Ontario government had different objectives. It had no particular concerns about programs in the field of Education at either the graduate or the undergraduate level. It was, however, concerned about costs. Without specifically referring to merger, the minister responsible for colleges and universities had been publicly urging universities and colleges to find ways to reduce costs through cooperation.

The financial crisis at OISE confronted the government with a public institution on the verge of bankruptcy. Through a merger, U of T would assume OISE's accumulated deficit, and savings would be realized through economies of scale. Moreover, the government fully expected that some of the resulting savings would accrue to the province.

The formal merger agreement in Ontario called for two significant reductions in funding to the merged institutions. First, the government sought an 8.6 per cent reduction in the formula grants formerly available to OISE. That amount – 8.6 per cent, which at the time was the equivalent of about $2.5 million – was derived from specific assumptions about the extent to which economies of scale could be realized. Table 8.1 explains how the figure was determined. The government assumed that certain non-academic costs at OISE could be reduced to their respective provincial averages.

The second reduction was, from a certain perspective, an addition. The merger agreement reduced the special $1.6 million supplementary grant to OISE for research by 50 per cent. The reduction was phased out over five years. This was the funding that, prior to discussion of merger, the government had indicated would be totally discontinued.

Because the government was seeking significant savings from the merger of OISE and U of T, the formal agreement made a specific provision for transition costs. While the government, through the agreement, did not specify how the required savings would be realized, it did recognize that savings on such a large scale would require major changes in staffing and organization. Therefore, the integration agreement provided a 'transitional fund' of $10 million. This was not new spending on the part of the government. Rather, the government was delaying the extraction of half of the 8.6 per cent reduction of the operating grant. In other words, 8.6 per cent of the previous base funding was removed permanently, and one-half was returned and earmarked temporarily for specified purposes relating to transition. Because the transitional fund could not be used for operating

TABLE 8.1
Estimation of savings through OISE–U of T merger (percentage)

	OISE prior to merger	Ontario system average	Required integration savings
Administration	9.9	4.1	5.8
Library operations	5.6	3.0	2.6
Administrative computing	1.5	1.3	0.2
Total	17.0	8.4	8.6

*expense as a percentage of total institutional expense

purposes, the full amount of the 8.6 reduction had to be removed immediately from the combined operating budgets of OISE and FEUT. The transitional fund thus created was in the government's budget, not the institution's, and was to be allocated piecemeal as the university incurred transitional expenses that were recognized by the integration agreement. It was theoretically possible that the transitional fund might never be spent if the costs of merger were less than anticipated, or if the costs were in areas not recognized by the integration agreement. In practice, the entire fund was spent within three years of full integration, and the financial dimensions of the merger insofar as the government was concerned were completed.

In sum, the financial dimensions of the Dal/TUNS and OISE/UofT mergers were in many respects typical. Each smaller institution was in financial duress and was merging for the sake of securing a more adequate and stable financial future. The larger institutions were motivated less by financial considerations than by a desire to expand the range of their programs. As is typical with mergers of publicly funded institutions, government played a major role, but in this aspect there were key differences. The Nova Scotia government was seeking improved quality in return for limited additional funding; its Ontario counterpart was interested mainly in securing economies and savings. These differences were reflected in the financial commitments and requirements associated with the mergers.

Economies of Scale

The most obvious benefit expected in virtually all mergers and other cooperative schemes is economies of scale. These economies are of all sorts: purchasing, faculty complement, enrolment, instructional facilities, libraries, laboratories, and information technology. The list could be longer.

While economies of scale are an easily understood concept, its application to mergers in higher education is complex and requires a very careful appreciation of cost structures and production cycles, many of which are unique to the sector. Martin and Samels, as the title of their study of mergers in the United States suggests, equate the benefits of merger with the benefits of growth (Martin and Samels, 1994). On the presumption that some colleges and universities do not wish to grow in size – or, more likely, are unable to do so on their own – merger may be seen as a means either of growing in overall size or of expanding curricular offerings.

This concept of growth implicitly assumes that cost functions in colleges and universities are linear. Each additional student, or faculty member, or square meter of assignable space, leads to additional cost, and those costs are average instead of marginal. Government funding formulas almost always operate on this assumption of linearity. So, as a college or university grows through merger, its average costs decline.

This, however, may be too simple as a paradigm for the relationships between scale and cost. Costs in post-secondary education often proceed as a complex series of step functions. Here are some examples:

- Almost all of the costs of developing an information system are at the front end. Once a student record system has been built to issue a transcript, or a payroll system has been built to issue a paycheque, the system can issue an infinite number of transcripts or cheques at virtually zero marginal cost. But if the college or university decides to introduce a new academic program and to issue transcripts for that program, the additional marginal cost will be high.
- While there is and probably will always be debate about optimal class size, there are institutions, programs, and courses that can accommodate additional enrolment without adding to academic complement or classroom space inventories. Again, marginal cost approaches zero. But if an institution is seeking to expand by adding new programs and courses, marginal costs may be high – and in fact may exceed respective marginal revenue.
- Academic libraries are usually designed and built to have considerable excess capacity at the time they open and for several years afterwards. Capacity is measured in terms of linear shelf space. Thus, for a considerable period of time the library's collections can expand without

posing any additional demands on the space inventory. But at some point, one additional volume will theoretically be very expensive to house.

What these examples reveal about growth as a reason for merger is that growth does not necessarily lead to economies of scale. Depending on the match (or mismatch) of institutions in terms of where they are in their various cost step functions, merger could just as easily lead to diseconomies of scale as to economies of scale. A further lesson is that the *measure* of growth makes a difference. An increase in enrolment in an existing program is not the same as an increase in enrolment in a new program. Here, the number of academic programs is the controlling factor, not the number of students. Some jurisdictions – Sweden, for example – operate on the assumption that the number of faculty drives costs more than the number of students or the number of programs, and they therefore very carefully control academic appointments.

Observation The common assumption that economies of scale can be realized through merger is often incorrect.

Suggestion It is advisable for institutions contemplating merger to assess where they each are in their various cost step functions – and where merger would take them – in order to determine whether and to what extent economies of scale are achievable.

Due Diligence

Ultimately, any decision to merge is the responsibility of the directors (or trustees, governors, overseers, or visitors) and officers of the respective colleges and universities. This responsibility cannot be delegated – it is fiduciary. The word fiduciary comes from the Latin noun *fiducia*, which means trust, and more to the point, from the adjective *fiduciarius*, which means having to do with trust. Colleges and universities are entrusted to their boards of directors or trustees. Under the law in most Western countries, those boards have certain duties and obligations, both at common law and under specific statutes (often the enabling legislation that established or chartered the institution, whether public or private). Those duties and obligations fall into two categories: fiduciary, and 'the duty of care, diligence, and skill' (*Directors' Liability in Canada*, 1998).

As it relates to public and not-for-profit entities, fiduciary duty is normally to the institution, the public, certain benefactors, and mutually to fellow directors or trustees. There are no shareholders, as there are with for-profit entities. Even so, there are some parallels: directors (or trustees) of any stripe will have to provide financial statements, auditors' reports, and other financial reports as required by the applicable legislation.

'The duty of care, diligence, and skill' – often called simply 'due diligence' – is the standard of care and expertise that directors or trustees must meet in performing their duties and responsibilities as board members. Directors or trustees are liable if they fail to meet that standard or fail to disclose conflicts of interest. The rule of thumb applied by many courts in determining such liability is whether the directors or trustees acted in the 'best interests' of the institution. In applying the standard of care and determining liability, courts also usually take into account the backgrounds and professional skills of individual directors or trustees. Hence, a member of a college's board of trustees who was a student could be held to a different standard than a member who was the president of a for-profit corporation.

For a college's or university's trustees, it is difficult to imagine a decision more serious than merger. No decision tests more rigorously their fiduciary and due diligence responsibilities. Prior to merger, trustees must pay particular attention to what might be best described as *reverse* due diligence, in the sense that each board of trustees must examine the financial statements, audit reports, and other financial information about its institution's prospective partner. This is far more complex than it may at first appear. Even audited financial statements may not be amenable to 'apples to apples' comparisons. Here are three examples:

- Sometimes ancillary operations are included in consolidated financial statements; other times they are not. In the merger of U of T and OISE, the university's external auditors included such ancillaries in the consolidated financial statements, whereas the institute's auditors did not. The institute had a wholly owned and controlled ancillary operation with an accumulated deficit of roughly $500,000 that did not appear in its financial statements and was not discovered until after an integration agreement was signed.
- Often, for legitimate reasons, pension plans are managed under different actuarial assumptions. Typically, those assumptions do not appear in financial statements or audit reports. Thus, a pension fund that seems to be fully funded under the terms of one institution may not be fully funded under the terms of another, or may have higher annual service costs.

- Depreciation is a problem in not-for-profit institutions, many of which do not depreciate their capital assets at all – at least not in a form that would be apparent from an auditor's report or a financial statement (Berne, 1989; Garner, 1991). On the one hand, this is understandable, because not-for-profit institutions do not have the tax incentives that for-profit institutions do to write down depreciation expenses and create capital reserves. On the other hand, in failing to account for capital depreciation, the institution may be disguising major financial liabilities that will be just as pressing after merger as before.

Ascertaining a prospective partner's assets and liabilities involves far more than reviewing financial statements. All other outstanding issues, such as accreditation problems, legal actions, and health and safety concerns, should also be taken into account.

Suggestion   Institutions contemplating merger should recognize that ascertaining the actual financial condition of a potential partner may be a very complex endeavour, owing to differences in accounting and other practices.

Suggestion   Institutions are well advised to adopt a broad definition of that to which due diligence must be applied – one encompassing academic health, regulatory compliance, and so on, as well as financial condition.

Clearly, trustees have a due diligence responsibility for ascertaining the financial and other condition of the partner prior to merger. But they also have another, and particularly difficult responsibility for exercising the same diligence when they forecast what the newly merged institution will be like, especially in financial terms. Here are three examples from the OISE/U of T and Dal/TUNS mergers:

- The integration agreement between U of T and OISE (and the Ontario Government) was very specific about the funding that would be available to OISE/UT for ten years after merger, and included a provision that on an annual basis, a third-party monitor would review and report on the flow of funding to OISE/UT.
- Had due diligence been exercised more carefully in the merger of Dalhousie and TUNS, two after-the-fact problems arising from the merger agreement might have been avoided or lessened. *First,* the agreement was unclear about a $3 million funding commitment on the

part of the government. Dalhousie was concerned that the commitment seemed temporary and 'year to year'; to TUNS, and later to DalTech, it appeared firm and permanent.

• *Second*, the status of DalTech as a college within Dalhousie might have been clearly understood and defined in other universities that had a tradition of collegiate federation. In the case of Dalhousie, there was no such tradition. Each board of trustees therefore had a quite different image of what DalTech (aka TUNS) would look like after merger.

None of these examples is meant to imply that the respective boards of U of T, OISE, Dalhousie, and TUNS performed poorly or well in reaching the decisions they did about merger. The point is that in cases of merger, due diligence entails more extensive and more onerous duties than it usually does.

Suggestion   Governors of institutions should ensure that due diligence is not only done a priori, but also projected to an ex post facto state – that is, they should ensure that the terms of the merger agreement are clear and that their implementation is feasible.

There is a third dimension of due diligence that applies in the case of mergers. It involves the extent to which the trustees of a not-for-profit institution are required to inform themselves about the various factors that constitute due diligence as applied to merger. This requirement applies to all trustees equally, regardless of their individual expertise or ability. The examples from OISE and U of T, and Dalhousie and TUNS, are again illustrative. Some trustees on the Dalhousie and TUNS boards might have sought a more definitive agreement had they had greater knowledge of accounting procedures and financial controls. In the case of U of T and OISE, the institute's trustees might have moved more quickly toward merger had they sought or otherwise gained more information about the financial condition of the debt-burdened ancillary. Likewise, the university's trustees might have been more wary of merger had the institute's full liabilities been apparent to them.

There is an important issue behind these considerations. How responsible is a corporation (i.e., the officers of the college or university) for educating its trustees sufficiently for them to carry out their fiduciary and due diligence responsibilities? Courts have not been clear about this. The trend, however, is to require trustees to exercise more than a 'trusting reliance' on the officers and managers of the institutions for which they are responsible (Guthrie, 1983). In Canada there is a further requirement: the business of boards of trustees must be conducted at meetings of the boards, and only trustees present at those meetings may vote. These considerations are especially important when trustees are considering merger. If, for whatever reason, trustees believe that the information available to them is not sufficient for them to discharge their fiduciary and due diligence responsibilities, it is their legal duty to demand further information, and the duty of management to provide it.

Transition Costs

Mergers usually and perhaps inevitably are predicated on organizational restructuring, typically to reduce costs but sometimes to pursue specific academic strategies (Rowley, 1997). Sometimes the reduction is expected to be absolute – that is, the combined costs of the participating institutions will be lower after merger. Other times, merger may result in new programs that have new costs, in which case the reduction is in the marginal additional cost of the new programs. In either case, the saving cannot occur in the absence of restructuring and reorganization. In practical terms, merger involves a transition from two or more sets of structural costs to one set – the merged set. This transition itself has a cost, albeit temporary.

Most transitional costs can be anticipated. The costs usually fall into several categories.

Human Resource Costs

Mergers whose principal aim is to reduce existing operating costs almost always involve eliminating and reassigning administrative and academic staff. This means that plans for merger must make financial provision for early retirement, voluntary and involuntary severance, relocation, retraining, and bridging.

In some cases determining transition costs has a strong legal component, in the sense that the terms of severance and early retirement must be in accordance either with collective agreements or with applicable labour relations legislation. Also, early retirement may involve considering the actuarial condition of pension funds, because the costs of such retirement are normally assigned to these funds. In the latter case, the cost of early retirement may be notional in the sense that it is determined more by the actuarially available funding than by the extent to which early retirement can be usefully deployed to realize merger.

A special word should be said about bridging. A key step in planning a merger involves carefully examining the age/salary profiles of the participating institutions, and carefully projecting the complement requirements of the programs and services that will be integrated under merger. Given that the costs of early retirement and severance – voluntary or involuntary – are high and human, they should be incurred only when clearly necessary. A position that may seem expendable in the short term may be necessary in the long term. The reverse may also be true: planning may identify a position that in the post-merger future will become expendable but in the short term cannot be vacated voluntarily. Bridging – that is, financing positions temporarily until they can be vacated by normal retirement provisions – can be an important means of capturing the long-term advantages, including savings, of merger.

In some cases, the cost of bridging can be neutral. Consider a situation where the premium that would be paid to induce early retirement or other voluntary severance is equal to the cost of bridging. Even if the costs are not equal, bridging may be the better course of action in terms of opportunity costs, in the sense that bridge funding purchases a service while also securing a future permanent saving in an appropriate area.

Suggestion   The human resource transition attendant on merger should be planned in light of careful:
- *projection of the future complement requirements of the units to be merged;*
- *examination of faculty and staff age/salary profiles; and*
- *comparison of the relative costs and benefits of early retirement, severance, relocation, retraining, and bridging.*

The greatest transitional costs in any merger involving significant reorganization tend to be for reducing and redeploying academic and/or administrative staff. These costs are among the first to be incurred as merger is implemented.

In the case of OISE and U of T, about 70 per cent of the transition costs were attributable to various adjustments in the deployment of human resources. The combined academic complement of OISE and FEUT was reduced by about 6.5 per cent. The comparable figure for administrative and support positions was about 25 per cent. The total cost was $7.2 million, less than 5 per cent of which was spent on relocation and retraining.

Information Systems

Merger poses many problems for information systems. Some of the problems are unavoidable because of legal audit requirements. In some jurisdictions, for example, organizations, whether for-profit or not-for-profit, are not allowed to use two different financial reporting systems. In such cases, information systems must be fully integrated regardless of the objectives of the merger.

In other areas there may be no legal requirement to integrate information systems but there may be equally powerful practical imperatives. Here are some obvious examples: consolidated transcripts, 'unionized' library catalogues, common course codes for registration and grading. In some jurisdictions, public funding is based on student enrolment, which means that institutions that merge must usually integrate their student information systems. They have no choice, if they are to produce the consolidated enrolment reports on which their funding depends.

A less obvious but nevertheless important aspect of modifying information systems in mergers involves telephone communication. *First,* negotiating a new, single-user contract with a communications provider will reduce costs, but only if the contract is for a single system. *Second,* relocating all telephones to a single exchange with internal extensions and voice-mail addresses can be expensive. In the case of OISE and U of T, the cost estimates of a single telephone exchange ranged as high as $800,000.

The transitional costs of harmonizing information systems are large and easily under-estimated. In the OISE/U of T merger, total transitional costs for information systems were about $400,000, not including the cost of a single, consolidated telephone exchange.

Legal Services, Auditing, and Consulting

At its bare bones, a merger is a legal transaction, and a very complicated one at that. With public institutions – and all four institutions discussed in this book were public – the legal dimensions of merger may extend all the way to formal acts of legislative assemblies, in situations where enabling legislation must be amended or replaced. Also, merger agreements are themselves legal documents; they are a special sort of contract and transfer of property rights.

As part of their fiduciary responsibilities, the boards of the merging institutions must fully disclose all assets and liabilities through external audit.

With most mergers, when consultants are brought in, it is usually to address questions about human resources, so the resulting fees could just as easily be regarded as a cost of that aspect of merger. But consultants may also be engaged to provide neutral advice about how to re-engineer basic processes so as to achieve 'best practice.'

In the merger of OISE and U of T, the overall transitional expense for legal, auditing, and consulting services was about $300,000. Most of this was for legal services.

Space and Facilities

In both cases in this book, a major transitional cost was for altering and renovating space. The need for some of this expense was obvious and would apply to any merger: as departments and services were reorganized, staff had to be relocated and space modified to accommodate them.

To a considerable degree, the transitional costs for space and facilities are elastic. They depend on plans for organizational change. In this sense, they are controllable second-order or residual costs of merger. This, of course, does not mean they are minor costs; they may in fact be very large. Moreover, how space allocation problems are resolved can greatly influence how quickly the programmatic dimensions of a merger move ahead.

Some costs associated with space and facilities in a merger are not truly transitional. For example, if the merging institutions have different standards for maintaining space, the space of one institution will have to be brought to the standard of the other. Another example, which often is very expensive, arises when one of the partners has failed to make provision for the depreciation of its capital assets. If a merger partner has not sufficiently funded the depreciation of its plant, it will bring to the merger a hidden deficit in the form of deferred maintenance. Due diligence should pay special attention to this area.

In the merger of OISE and U of T, about one-quarter of the transitional costs, amounting to about $2.5 million, were for space. A further $2 million was spent on projects that could have as reasonably been classified as renovations. In the merger of TUNS and Dalhousie, the government committed funding for a new building for computer science, a field of study that was offered prior to merger by both institutions.

In summary, in a merger similar to that of OISE and U of T, the greatest transitional costs are for human resources (65 to 70 per cent). The next

TABLE 8.2
Increase and decrease of expense through OISE/U of T merger

Organizational area of expense	Per cent change
Deans's offices	−36
Other administrative offices	−51
Press and publications	−65
Academic support services	+12
Library and information technology	−18
Learning consortia and laboratory schools	+4
Physical plant operations	−40

largest amount (20 to 25 per cent) is for the alteration and/or renovation of space. Smaller amounts (5 to 10 per cent each) are for information and communications systems, legal and consulting services, and auditing.

Whether or not mergers result in reductions in costs and/or increases in income, they entail transitional costs. Most such costs can be anticipated and planned for. Although the costs of transition are often recoverable from the savings generated by merger, such costs are 'up front' and must be bridge financed in some way until the savings are fully realized.

Returns on Investments in Transition

Some transitional costs – information system integration, for example – have to be incurred whether or not the purpose of merger is to realize savings. Other transitional costs are closely related to the extent to which the objectives of merger include cost reduction. In these cases there is a cost/benefit dimension to the determination of transitional expense.

U of T spent at least $10 million merging OISE and FEUT. That expenditure produced permanent annual savings of approximately $3.6 million. In other words, the transitional investment was recouped in about two-and-a-half fiscal years.

The savings were not realized uniformly. Measured in terms of complement, they ranged from a reduction of 65 per cent to an addition of 12 per cent (see Table 8.2),

Is this typical of other mergers? Other studies have also found that the costs of transition in mergers are principally for human resources, space alteration, information systems, and legal expenses (Fielden, 1991). Areas of saving appear to vary with the size of the merging institutions (Patterson, 1999). For example, administrative savings are greater when large institutions merge (Lloyd, Morgan, and Williams, 1993).

Observation   Some transitional costs are necessary as a condition of merger per se, and vary little with the form and objectives of merger. Other types of costs may produce savings, albeit sometimes only after several years have passed. The amount of return on investment in the transitional costs of merger varies with merger objectives and institutional size.

Information and Information Systems

Information and information systems are critical to merger in several ways. On the one hand, reliable and comprehensive information is needed to decide whether or not to merge, and with which partner. On the other hand, once merger has been chosen as the course of action, the integration of information systems is in itself a major and virtually unavoidable expense.

A useful observation is that information systems are sometimes themselves an objective of formalized interinstitutional cooperation. For example, consortia have been formed to build and maintain information systems that serve several institutions (Jonas et al., 1996). There are some lessons that merging institutions can learn from such consortia.

First, the responsibilities for managing the integration of information systems must be extremely clear. Diplomacy and compromise may be important attributes for the overall success of a merger, but in the case of information systems specifically, lines of organizational responsibility must be demarcated as clearly as possible.

Second, the merging of information systems can have both legal and financial consequences. In terms of the law, the partners in a merger may each have had different statutory or regulatory obligations to report and retain data. For example, in the merger of OISE and U of T, the institutions operated in some respects under different sets of government regulations. Those sets of regulations had different reporting requirements. Another example from the same merger: the two institutions had different retention schedules for certain data – differences that resulted in some archival records being lost.

It is expensive to integrate information systems. Sometimes it is cheaper to build new systems to support merged institutions than to adapt one of the earlier systems.

Prior to merger, differences in information systems can cause another sort of problem. The form of financial reporting often determines the form of financial statements. Prospective partners rely on financial statements in determining whether merger would result in a good match, and in determining which assets and liabilities each institution would bring to the merger. Understandably, each partner tends to view and assess the other's financial statements from the point of view of its own information systems. In the world of espionage, this is often called 'mirror imaging' – in other words, viewing the data as if one's enemy viewed the data the same way that you did, when in fact the opposition view might be quite different.

The third lesson is that a plan for integrating or replacing information systems must be set very early in the merger process, and that there must be a firm and clear agreement about that plan. This lesson is partly a matter of common sense: the functionality of information systems cannot be held in abeyance while other aspects of merger are resolved. It is also a matter of timing and cost. If the partners to a merger each had contracts with different software vendors, or had purchased hardware under different capital lease agreements, those contracts and agreements may have to be renegotiated or bought out. If the costs of renegotiation or buyout are high, the merging institutions may choose to operate two systems for a period of time in order to avoid those costs. It is possible to operate parallel systems for a short period of time (Jonas et al., 1996). That period might be set to coincide with the end of the budget or fiscal year, or with a regulatory cycle. In certain cases, the merging institutions may have no choice; in some jurisdictions non-profit institutions are not allowed to end a fiscal year with a financial information system that is different from the system with which they began that year.

Regardless of how and when information systems are integrated in a merger, information systems are important from the very start of the merger process. Here is an example: not long before U of T decided to seek a merger with OISE, the university considered forming a joint program in nursing with Ryerson Polytechnic University, which like OISE was located nearby in Toronto. Thorough analyses of costs were centrally important to the consideration of a joint program. It became apparent early in those analyses that the two universities had quite different information systems. It was not a matter of one set of systems being better or worse; they were simply different. As would be the case in the analyses leading to a merger, the two institutions were looking for comparative advantages and for productive matches of relative strengths and weaknesses. One hope, for example, was that only one university would offer the clinical component of the undergraduate nursing program, while the other would concentrate on the theoretical component. On the basis of initial analyses, it seemed that a specialized division of academic labour would be advantageous for both universities. But once the differences in information systems became known, further analyses produced a quite different result: the cost structures of both programs were in fact quite similar. Having come to that realization, the two universities abandoned consideration of a joint program.

Analyses like the one conducted by U of T and Ryerson with respect to nursing are even more critical to when merger is being considered, because mergers are far more inclusive and are virtually impossible to reverse. Institutions considering merger must secure reliable information about cost structures. This information is not always to be found in financial information systems. For example, age/salary profiles of academic staff – especially staff with tenure – are critical in projecting how a merger would work. That information is more likely to be found in a human resources information system than in a financial information system. Another example is student:staff ratios, which are created by combining data from a student record system with data from a human resources system.

Taking either of these examples, one quickly recognizes the complexity of the analyses: there are two data sets from two institutions. Thus, even after the data have been made accessible, there is a further issue involving information: how to define key data elements. For example, there are many ways to count student enrolment. Another especially complex example arises when institutions do not have the same fiscal year, or have collective bargaining schedules that do not align with the fiscal year. Resolving these differences in definition is an unavoidable first step in planning a merger.

Finally, institutions planning to merge need to know something about their respective information systems beyond their capability to inform a decision about merger. Merger is often the most opportune time to consider three options with regard to information systems: buy a new system, build a new system 'in house,' or adapt one of the existing systems. Given that financial exigency is a common motivation to merge, the initial inclination often is to adapt one of the existing systems on the reasoning that 'two can live as cheaply as one.' That choice is often sound. But it isn't always. If both institutions have old or unstable systems, neither may be sufficient to support the complexity of a merger. The cost structures of information systems usually are not linear. For example, the addition of a new degree program will impose more development costs on a student record system than the addition of students will. Thus, a merger that involves a larger rather than a smaller number of programs might be just as well supported by the construction of a new in-house system that adopts some of the basic modules of both pre-existing systems.

Whatever steps are taken toward the development of information systems under a merger, trustees of not-for-profit colleges and universities are ultimately and expressly responsible for the systems. Under law in most western jurisdictions, trustees are required to inform themselves about the adequacy of management systems. Thus, the failure of information systems under a merger is their responsibility (Guthrie, 1983).

Information systems are vital in the major steps in merger – in deciding whether to merge, in planning merger, and in the process of merger itself. Whether the merging institutions opt to use one of their existing systems or to adopt a new one, the choice and the resulting action should be taken as soon as possible.

Libraries

Usually, libraries are not greatly affected by merger. Given the cost structure of academic libraries, the key to economy and efficiency through merger or other forms of interinstitutional combination (e.g., the many library consortia now in existence) is the removal of duplication among collections – both monographs and serials. Unless the merging institutions are very similar, the opportunity to cull overlapping collections is limited. Other library services will be in the same demand after merger as before. Because library administrations are relatively flat organizationally to begin with, the savings engendered by merger are relatively small. Even in the absence of merger or other forms of interinstitutional combination, the unit costs of acquiring monographs and serials do not vary significantly according to institutional size. This indicates that the principle of economies of scale does not apply to library acquisitions. Where merger could produce economies of scale and other savings is in various library technologies, especially electronic subscriptions and site licensing. Merger is probably the only form of interinstitutional combination that can reduce the costs of electronic subscriptions and site licences. For all other forms of combination, the vendor of site licences and electronic subscriptions would continue to view the participating institutions as separate sites requiring separate licences and subscriptions.

Libraries are an essential component of colleges and universities and constitute major cost centres, but economies of scale do not apply to them as they do to other programs and services. Planning for merger of libraries should recognize that they have a number of unique features.

NINE

The Steps to Merger

So what exactly is involved in making a higher education merger happen? There were many profound differences in how OISE and U of T and Dalhousie and TUNS approached merger. Even so, we have been able to identify two sets of steps common to both. Each step was accomplished in each case, albeit with varying effectiveness. The generic nature of the steps and their applicability to higher education mergers in general was confirmed by the consultants we interviewed.

The first set of steps we have identified consists of process steps by which prospective partners reach agreement to merge and then transform themselves into one organization. They are as shown in Table 9.1. The second set of steps consists of substantive steps by which the particular features of the merged institution are determined. They are as shown in Table 9.2.

Before turning to what each of these steps involves, it may be worthwhile to note that they are a valid approach to take only if merger is a sound strategy even to consider. Mergers and acquisitions are not ends in themselves, but means to achieve other things. A successful higher education merger is one that helps the universities or other institutions involved succeed in their educational and research missions; it must not divert them from those missions.

What, then, do each of the steps in higher education merger entail?

The Process Steps

Getting to Know the Other Party

This first step involves gathering by informal means information that will help the university or other institution decide whether to enter into formal

TABLE 9.1
The process steps in mergers

1 Getting to know the other party
2 Deciding to pursue the option of merger
3 Setting objectives for merger
4 Preparing the organization for merger
5 Entering discussion of merger
6 Performing due diligence
7 Agreeing to merge
8 Securing government sanction (if necessary) and continuity of funding
9 Putting in place transition planning and management mechanisms and resources
10 Giving legal effect to the merger
11 Putting the old order to rest
12 Implementing the new organization

TABLE 9.2
The substantive steps in mergers

1 Articulating the vision (What is it for?)
2 Naming
       The successor institution
       The new unit(s)
3 Governance
4 Administrative structure
5 Finance
6 Budget framework and process
7 New administrative leadership
8 Developing plans for merged units
9 Setting and reallocating budgets
10 Putting personnel in place
       Labour relations issues
       Personnel policies
       Pensions
       Benefits
       Redeployment and severance
11 Policy and procedural transition
12 Academic planning

merger discussions. Typically, private discussions of an exploratory nature are held with the potential partner. There may be a preliminary, informal round of due diligence in which information is gathered from available sources to address questions such as these: What programs does the other institution offer? In what directions has its programming evolved in recent years? How robust are its enrolments? What is the accreditation status of its programs (if applicable)? How much duplication of academic and administrative activity is there between us? How do their governance systems, management/administrative culture, labour relations, and so on compare to ours? How well or poorly disposed are the board members, faculty, students and staff to merger?

This preliminary sounding out of a potential partner is worthwhile whether or not it leads to a decision to seek merger discussions. If it leads a university to rule out a potential partner before large amounts of time and money have been invested in formal negotiations, so much the better. If, on the other hand, it leads to a positive decision, the information thus acquired will inform the university's position in negotiations and its negotiating strategy.

Of course, potential merger partners often already know each other – or think they do. Both Dalhousie and TUNS and OISE and U of T had longstanding relationships. But familiarity can breed contempt. Also, perceptions may be inaccurate or out of date. Getting to know the other party is arguably as important for potential partners with long histories as for those with blanker – and cleaner – slates.

Deciding to Pursue the Option of Merger (one or both parties)

To make an informed decision about whether or not to seek merger, one must not only get to know one's potential partner, but also determine – as accurately as possible based on the information available – whether the proposed merger is a better means of realizing one's own mission and strategic goals than the alternatives. For example, a university contemplating extending its programming by acquiring another institution will want to make sure that this is more effective and cost-efficient than building internal capacity. U of T's president was convinced that integrating OISE into FEUT was the only means available to achieve his institution's goal of creating a world-class Faculty of Education. Similarly, Dalhousie's president was certain that the cost of building full-fledged Faculties of Engineering and Computer Science at Dalhousie would be much greater than the cost of acquiring TUNS – and that the likelihood of succeeding in this endeavour in competition with TUNS was small to nil, given the dynamics of the university system.

Sound assessment of the merits of merger or acquisition relative to the alternatives requires not only that an institution 'get to know the other party' but also that it know itself. Self-knowledge is not a given. For example, an institution may lack information about its own cost structure, or prevailing perceptions of the academic vitality of a unit may be outdated.

Besides all this, institutions should ask themselves some hard-nosed questions about the academic, financial, and organizational rationale for merger. Although the objectives of each merger are unique, the following questions are relevant to many:

With respect to academic rationale:

- Is there evidence to suggest that over the medium to long term, the proposed merger will produce improvements in the quality and attractiveness of educational offerings, research, and related professional services?
- Is there reason to believe that in the short term, it will be possible to bring the people and programs of the two institutions together without loss of enrolment, accreditation, and key faculty and staff, and without disruption of research?

With respect to financial impact:

- Is there evidence to suggest that the proposed merger will result in improved financial health or cut losses over the medium to longer term?
- In the short term, can the institution finance the deal and the costs of the transition without draining resources away from other opportunities and aspects of its activities?

With respect to organizational and cultural compatibility:

- Is there reason to believe that the merging institutions will be able to agree on governance, structural, procedural, and personnel arrangements, and implement them in such a way that the new entity will function well over the medium to long term?
- Is there reason for confidence in the potential to bring the two institutions together with minimal short-term disruption and damage to morale, teaching and research output, and student/client satisfaction?

If the answer to one or more of the above questions is 'no,' a university contemplating a potential merger would be well advised to rethink its intentions. The existence of a strong academic rationale is especially important. This appears to be the *sine qua non* of the successful HE merger or acquisition (Rowley, 1992).

Setting Objectives for Merger

In order to emerge from the merger process with an outcome that advances one's institutional mission and goals, it is important to go into negotiations with clear objectives. This means identifying in quite specific terms what one wants from merger. Is the outcome to be a consolidation? A transformative acquisition? A pure acquisition? A subsidiary? Or is it to be another of the models described in Chapter 5?

The leaders of a relatively small institution should bear in mind that a merger with a substantially larger partner is almost always an acquisition (i.e., a take-over), rather than a consolidation. Other things being equal, an acquired institution will change to conform to its acquirer's systems and values. Especially if the successor to the acquired institution is to be a unique type of unit within the larger university, its prospects for retaining its identity and culture are uncertain. This need not be the case if institutional leaders negotiate a form of acquisition (e.g., a semiautonomous or subsidiary arrangement) that enables their organization to preserve some autonomy. It is also possible to seek a transformative acquisition – one that will transform the acquiring partner as well as the acquired one. Insofar as the latter type of acquisition involves change for both parties, those parties require – besides a good merger agreement – strong leadership, as well as the commitment of political, managerial, and financial resources on the part of the acquiring institution.

The leaders of a large institution should recognize that if they want to preserve features of the smaller institution they are acquiring, they will have to take deliberate steps to do so. They should ask themselves how much post-merger autonomy will be necessary in order to preserve what they value. As Joseph McCann and Roderick Gilkey have suggested with respect to corporate mergers: 'The greater the size difference between firms, the lighter the touch needed by the larger firm. It is all too easy to smother and squash the very thing you sought' (1988, 60).

Extending some of the features of an acquired institution to one's own organization entails substantial change for both. This is why transformative acquisitions involve greater political, managerial, and financial challenges than pure acquisitions.

Having established which merger model is most consistent with one's institutional position and goals, it is advisable to carry the analysis one step further: to identify how the desired model would be reflected in each of the substantive areas listed in Figure 9.2. By this means, one can define the outcomes one wishes to bring about with respect to programs and services, finance, governance, administrative structure, labour relations, policies and procedures, and so on.

How realistic these objectives are should be tested to the extent possible, given the availability of information. For example, what do recent trends in enrolments at both institutions and in demographics suggest about the likelihood of given enrolment (and related revenue) objectives being achieved? The feasibility of attaining particular objectives is tested more fully in the due diligence stage.

Prospective merger partners should ensure that their objectives are consistent, and recognize which objectives are interdependent. For example, U of T wanted to avoid an increase in unionization – particularly, faculty unionization – as a result of integrating OISE, an institution that, as one interviewee put it, was 'not only unionized, but unionist.' Given Ontario labour legislation and practice, the university believed that this would be eminently possible since its objective was to integrate the combined OISE and FEUT into U of T as a faculty. Had the university strayed from this objective in the course of negotiations and conceded to federated or subsidiary status for the combined institution, it would have greatly reduced the likelihood of attaining its labour relations objective.

Institutions may consider and set objectives for process as well as substance. How soon after the merger or acquisition is negotiated will they seek to bring it about? How much integration will they seek to achieve on 'day 1' (i.e., the day the merged organization comes into being)? This will inform the merger date, as well as the planning and management of the transition.

Some institutions develop formal statements of the objectives they are trying to achieve through merger; others do not. Both OISE and U of T articulated their objectives for merger before they entered into negotiations. Neither Dalhousie nor TUNS did so. The cases suggest that formal public statements of objectives have both advantages and disadvantages. The advantages of formal statements of objectives include these:

• They make it clear to all involved what the institution's purpose is. They also guide negotiations and planning, and provide a basis for evaluating success.
• They guide and protect those negotiating the deal. This is especially important for the leaders of an institution that is considering becoming part of a larger one. A voluntary acquisition places immense strain on the leaders of the institution that is being acquired. Typically, its members are loathe to give up their independent institutional identity, even

when they recognize the necessity. They may vent their anger on those responsible for the deal. In each of the cases in this book, the people who led the negotiations on behalf of the smaller institution were accused by some of betraying their institution. Leaders of small institutions contemplating merger (or, more accurately, being acquired) are better able to respond to and cope with these sorts of sentiments if they have negotiated within the framework of an approved statement of institutional objectives.

• They make it possible to assess the desirability of merger in light of the institution's mission statement.

The disadvantages of formal statements of objectives include these:

• They can make it more difficult to change one's position and hence to get agreement.
• They can offend the other party by making apparent the differences in the parties' objectives. This can sour the climate and lead to adversarial negotiations.

Preparing One's Institution for Merger

Mergers and acquisitions involve change for both partners, even when they differ in size as greatly as OISE and U of T. Because higher education institutions are so highly decentralized, their members can be effective either in resisting change or in supporting it and making it work. Preparing the groundwork for merger is therefore an important step. Since merger negotiations in higher education rarely proceed in secret for long, it is wise to begin this groundwork early, so that the negotiations, once publicized, are perceived as appropriate and legitimate and so that a positive foundation for eventual integration is laid.

For the leaders of the smaller partner in a prospective merger/acquisition, and for those of both prospective partners in a genuine merger/ consolidation, this means articulating what may be gained through merger and cultivating support for merger. However, the benefits must not be exaggerated. Unrealistic expectations – whether about funding, job security, or the extent of change (e.g., 'things will continue much as they are now') – should not be encouraged. If widespread, feelings of frustration and betrayal will quickly arise once a different reality begins to unfold.

For the leaders of an acquiring university, preparing one's institution for merger involves addressing pockets of opposition and anxiety and creating a positive climate for the negotiations and for the eventual integration of the acquired party. In the case of U of T, it involved overcoming widespread opposition to the acquisition of OISE within the administration and in some faculties other than FEUT. This is crucial, because internal resistance may jeopardize not only ratification of an agreement but also a merger's success. In the delicate and important days and weeks after merger, the members of an acquired organization should be welcomed into, and treated with respect by, the larger organization of which they have become part. Creating this climate may require concerted awareness-raising beginning early on. Some demythologizing may be called for.

Another commonsensical preparation is to establish a policy of filling vacancies and new positions only as absolutely necessary. By preserving vacancies or making only limited term appointments, institutions can acquire greater flexibility and maximize opportunities for internal redeployment.

Entering into Merger Discussions

The form the negotiations take (which includes who the actual negotiators are) appears to be a function of the cultures of the institutions and the differences in their positions. As we suggested in Chapter 6, if the institutions' positions are reasonably compatible, they should begin negotiations in a collaborative spirit, especially if the continued allegiance of the faculty, staff, students, alumni, and friends of the smaller institution is important for the future success of the merged institution. The parties should keep things relatively informal, and begin by exploring what they hope to achieve through merger. The goal here is to define shared goals and identify means of realizing them. By beginning with an exchange of formal positions, they would be highlighting their differences.

Who should conduct the negotiations? Our cases offer two very different models: negotiations by presidents, and negotiations by teams. McCann and Gilkey, writing about corporate mergers, suggest that chief executive officers should not negotiate in isolation from other members of their firms unless they have extensive merger experience. In most cases they should function as part of a merger team consisting of selected executives, corporate staff, and functional managers; also, decisions should emerge from discussion and consensus (McCann and Gilkey, 1988).

The consultants we interviewed were divided in their views about whether negotiations should be conducted by CEOs or by teams (of which CEOs might be part). Those whose experience of mergers was mainly in the private sector tended to take the view that it is up to the president or CEO to negotiate the deal; those with relatively more public sector experience tended to favour a team approach. This may reflect the greater authority and legitimacy of presidents or CEOs in the corporate sector, relative to professional bureaucracies such as universities and hospitals. In the latter, the existence of 'professional expertise and authority at the shop-floor level,' coupled with relatively loose structures, produces a 'more marginal position of the institutional management' (Goegedebuure, 1992, 76).

One of the consultants characterized negotiation of merger agreements by presidents as the 'trust me' approach. He described a good merger agreement as one that is a minimally acceptable compromise between the two institutions on all the key issues at stake. He contended that representatives of major institutional interests should be involved in forging that compromise so that their fundamental interests are articulated and addressed. When presidents negotiate an agreement on their own and 'sell' it to their respective institutions, its acceptance is as much a function of the esteem in which they are held and of their powers of persuasion as of the extent to which the contents of the agreement reflect institutional interests.

In our view, when a small institution is considering becoming part of a larger one, it is particularly risky for the president to negotiate alone. Relinquishing autonomy is a wrenching process. If the president conducts the negotiations himself or herself, the almost inevitable subsequent unhappiness on the part of other members of the institution may imperil the merger process, or result in the repudiation of his or her leadership, or both.

If merger discussions begin in a context in which the parties' interests are substantially different, adversarial bargaining is probably inevitable, but efforts should be made to ensure that relations between the parties do not deteriorate into distrust and conflict. In adversarial bargaining, the institutions elucidate their positions, establish negotiating teams, and enter into formal negotiations. In general, it is inadvisable for presidents – and especially for presidents who may end up heading the merged institution, should negotiations succeed – to participate directly in the negotiations unless possible agreement is in sight. If negotiations deteriorate into conflict, attempts can be made to re-establish communication by injecting a trusted third party into the process as a mediator, as was done by OISE and U of T.

In deciding how to approach negotiations, potential merger partners should also take into account their relative positions – in particular, the sources and extent of their power. Small institutions can safeguard their interests by taking a relatively formal approach to negotiations and by insisting on clear, comprehensive agreements. For their part, large institutions should be aware of the sensitivities of much smaller partners, and of the hurdles involved in negotiating with them. To cite but one example: any perceived slight or threat emanating from the larger, more powerful institution will be magnified many times in the eyes of a smaller, more vulnerable partner. Overreaction may be the direct result, with friendly negotiations being transformed abruptly into hostile ones. With respect to substance, large negotiating partners should recognize that ambiguity, while it can make agreements easier to reach and provide latitude in the implementation of the merger, may entail real costs in trust, morale, and productivity.

Performing Due Diligence

Formal due diligence generally begins early in the process, with the searching out and analysis of information about the prospective merger partner. The nature of the investigation changes when both parties recognize that a merger agreement is nigh. At this point, it is usual for the parties to agree to make their records available to each other. Given that the principal purpose of due diligence is to inform the board's decision on a proposed merger, the process normally concludes before the tentative agreement is made public (if possible) or before it is signed (if not).

Officials of the institution that is the target for acquisition may be very sensitive to scrutiny by the acquiring partner. The latter's requests for previously confidential information may make them feel vulnerable and exposed. Tact on the part of the acquiring institution is crucial. Difficulties can be minimized if both parties understand from the outset that due diligence is a necessary and legitimate part of the process.

Agreeing to Merge

Once the parties reach an agreement to merge, that agreement must be encapsulated in a written document, explained, and approved by the bodies with the necessary authority.

Just as there is no one path to merger, no single model agreement fits all. That being said, sound agreements share these basic attributes:

- They are clear about the nature of the new organization (i.e., not susceptible to multiple interpretations).

226 Reflections on Experience

- They address the vital interests of the major constituencies of the partner institutions in ways that are, on balance, acceptable to them.
- They are legally binding.
- They are implementable.
- They provide just sufficient time before the merger takes effect to accomplish the degree of integration sought.

The absence of any of these qualities increases the likelihood of problems in the transition or implementation phases, or both.

When there is no legally binding merger agreement, transition planning and preparation tends to be undermined by doubt and second-guessing. According to those we interviewed, once the integration agreement was signed between OISE and U of T, there was no doubt in the minds of people at those institutions that the merger was going to happen. In contrast, those close to the Dal/TUNS amalgamation process had reason in the early fall of 1996 to doubt that the two institutions would be able to translate their statement of intent into reality. Had it not been for the exceptional powers of negotiation and persuasion of Dalhousie president Tom Traves, and for the conviction of TUNS president Ted Rhodes that amalgamation was necessary, the Dal/TUNS merger might well have come to naught. Even though they were able to find sufficient common ground to keep the process moving forward, some of the time and energy that should have been devoted to transition planning was taken up with what were in essence additional negotiations. Non-binding agreements risk resulting in non-mergers; they also permit – indeed, invite – issues to be revisited. In contrast, a binding agreement settles the question of whether merger will occur, so that attention during the transition phase focuses on the 'how.'

With respect to the date of merger: The transition period should provide just enough time to achieve the degree and the nature of the integration sought on day 1. In her study of British higher education merger (1992), Gillian Rowley found that eighteen months was typical. The nine-month transition period provided for in the Dal/TUNS amalgamation agreement was exceptionally short for the higher education sector. The period between the passage of the legislation (which made the merger a certainty) and the merger was even shorter – a mere three-and-a-half months. In that time, the re-engineering of administrative services called for by the amalgamation agreement was simply not possible. Had both institutions actually sought to accomplish re-engineering – rather than the extension of Dalhousie's administrative services to TUNS – a longer transition period would have been called for. Conversely, a longer than necessary transition period keeps people in limbo and permits the process to bog down.

Another practical consideration in deciding the merger date is that a great deal of legal and accounting work can be avoided if the merger date coincides with the beginning of a new fiscal year. This is why April 1 was selected as the date on which Dalhousie and TUNS would merge. Both universities operated on a 1 April to 31 March fiscal year, so TUNS's books were closed on 31 March 1997 and DalTech was on Dalhousie's books as of the following day. Things are obviously not as simple if the merger partners use different fiscal years.

In order to maximize flexibility and opportunities for redeployment of personnel, it is usual for merging institutions to agree not to make new continuing appointments without prior consultation and agreement.

Securing Government Sanction (As Necessary) and Continuity of Funding

The importance and character of this step obviously depend on the nature of the government's authority and responsibility for higher education – for example, on whether and to what extent it funds the institutions involved, and on whether merger requires government legislation.

In both cases, although the merger agreements were tripartite, the institutions drafted the agreements themselves and entered into negotiations with government only once they themselves were in agreement. The virtue of this strategy (of involving government late in the process) is that it does not invite government interference in internal university affairs. Its success obviously requires that the institutions understand the government's position sufficiently well that they can draft a realistic agreement – realistic in the sense that it will provide an effective basis for negotiation with government.

Above and beyond sanction for a particular merger agreement, the institutions may seek a reduction in the risk that the merger will fail by attempting to secure continuity in the 'rules of the game.' Changes in these rules can be devastating. For example, a university acquiring a professional school on the assumption that there will continue to be limited competition in its jurisdiction may seek assurance that the government will not grant new competitors degree-granting status.

An important step in considering and planning merger is the construction of a model that can project the implications of merger for funding under the applicable funding formula. Institutions considering merger

228 Reflections on Experience

tend to regard funding too simplistically – to assume that public funding after merger will be the sum of the public funding that was available to the two institutions prior to merger. Except under the most elementary funding formulas, it usually does not work that way. The merger of OISE and U of T provides an example of this: when the two institutions merged, the provincial ministry reduced the level of formula funding on the rationale that greater economies of scale could be realized.

A related issue involves the status of pre-existing programs. Under some systems for regulating and funding colleges and universities a merger amounts, first, to the closure of previously existing programs, and second, to the creation of new ones. The funding eligibility and status that programs had prior to merger may not automatically carry forward to the new institution. In a competitive environment, other institutions may take advantage of the vacuum to promote and protect their own interests. It is essential that institutions considering merger come to a clear understanding with the government about the status of their programs after merger.

A government is most likely to provide funding commitments and assurances of regulatory continuity if it perceives the proposed merger as important to – or at a minimum, consistent with – its public policy objectives. Such understanding is necessarily cultivated over an extended period of time.

Establishing Transition Planning and Management Mechanisms and Resources

This step involves developing and putting into effect a plan, structure, staff, and budget:

- for resolving those substantive issues to be addressed prior to the merger;
- for communicating to internal and external constituencies; *and*
- for managing and monitoring the transition process.

The transition planning schedule and structure reflects (a) how much integration is sought (i) by merger day and (ii) over the longer term; (b) what issues must be resolved to achieve that degree of integration; (c) when each issue must be resolved; and (d) who must participate in resolving each issue, by virtue of authority, expertise, influence, ideas, and political weight. Time, quality, and legitimacy are lost if the individuals who should participate in decision making are not identified carefully.

Given the immense demands placed on managers and staff by the transition planning and management process, it is advisable to appoint or second some personnel to work full-time on the merger.

A common approach to transition planning is to establish joint teams, representative of both institutions, for each major function or unit. The Dal/TUNS Joint Transition Committee for Computer Science was an example of this. Although neither Dalhousie and TUNS nor OISE and U of T struck joint teams to plan the merger of administrative functions such as human resource services and financial services, the consultants we interviewed expressed the view that such teams would be equally well suited for that purpose.

If, as we advocated in Chapter 6, those who will head merged units are appointed early, they can assume the chair of the planning team for the function for which they will be responsible.

However transition-planning bodies are structured, they need the following:

- clear terms of reference
- clear deadlines
- good, thoughtful leadership
- a clearinghouse function

Giving Legal Effect to the Merger

What is required to give legal effect to a merger of course depends on the legal status of the merging institutions. Canadian universities are established by acts of provincial legislatures, so legislation was required to bring about the Dal/TUNS and OISE/U of T mergers. The institutions' approaches to securing legislation were very similar. They consulted with government officials and with experienced legal counsel. They prepared proposals for legislation. (At Dalhousie and TUNS these proposals were circulated internally for comment.) They sought the minimum necessary legislation so as to avoid any legislative inroads on their autonomy and to obviate political complications when the bills reached the floor of the respective legislatures. They briefed both government and opposition party officials on the need for the legislation, and sought their support.

Putting the Old Order to Rest

As William Bridges and other students of organizational change have explained, members of an organization that is disappearing must recognize and come to terms with the passing of the old order before they can identify with and participate fully in the new regime. Most eventually do so on their own, but it expedites and facilitates the process if there is some form of official recognition of the change, and some expression of respect for that which is ending. How this is done depends very much on the particular circumstances of the merger, but some symbolic recognition of the change is common, as is some opportunity for those affected to mourn their loss. For example, FEUT held an end-of-FEUT party prior to its integration with OISE. In the same vein, the last TUNS convocation was an occasion to mark the end of TUNS as an independent institution.

Implementing the New Organization

This last step in the merger process involves bringing the merged institution to life in all its aspects. It entails marking the change; adopting new identities; overcoming cultural differences; launching new governance bodies; building the new management team; integrating functional units, both academic and support; providing orientation, training, and development; integrating policies, processes, and systems; and sustaining and building external relationships.

The Substantive Steps

While carrying out the process of merger (in other words, the twelve steps above), merger partners resolve the substantive issues identified in Table 9.2. In Table 9.3, the substantive steps in merger are elaborated.

Putting It All Together

If there is one lesson we can draw from how the resolution of substantive issues was integrated with process steps in our two cases, it is that there are many paths to merger. Many ways of integrating the substantive steps with the process steps are possible. No formula dictates that particular issues must be resolved at particular stages in the process.

For example, the units produced by the OISE/U of T and Dal/TUNS mergers were named at very different stages of the two processes. The name OISE/UT was specified in the OISE/U of T merger agreement; the name of the successor to TUNS was not decided until several months after that merger had taken place. Similarly, in the Dal/TUNS case, the structure of the post-merger bargaining units was established before the merger took place; OISE/UT came into existence with two separate bargaining unit structures. Faculty and staff from the former OISE continued to

TABLE 9.3
The substantive steps elaborated

1. The vision	What the merger will achieve. What the merged institution will be.
2. The name	Of the successor institution, and of new units within it.
3. Governance	How the new institution will be governed, and what the terms of reference and membership of the governing bodies will be.
4. Administrative structure	How the merged institution will be organized and administered, and what the terms of reference of senior managers will be.
5. Finance	What revenues will flow to and within the merged institution.
6. Budget framework and process	What form the budget will take and how it will be developed.
7. New administrative leaders	Who the heads of the new or merged units will be.
8. Plans for merged units	What the operational plan (output, organization, staffing, facilities) for each unit will be.
9. Budgets	What the units' budgets will be.
10. Personnel	Who will occupy positions in the merged institution.
Labour relations	What the bargaining unit will be and who the bargaining agent will be.
Personnel policy	What personnel policies will apply.
Pension	Whether and how plans will be integrated.
Benefits	Renegotiation of benefit package.
Redeployment and severance	Who will be redeployed within the institution and how, and who will leave and on what terms.
11. Policy and procedural transition	What policies and procedures will apply in the merged institution.
12. Academic planning	How the educational and research programs of the merged units will develop in the future.

belong to their pre-existing bargaining units and to be covered by their collective agreements; the faculty and staff from FEUT were not unionized and were governed by the personnel policies of the university. The bargaining unit structure of OISE/UT was established in the months – indeed, years – after merger as the university negotiated extinguishment of the bargaining rights of members of some former OISE unions.

The sequence in which substantive issues can be tackled most effectively will depend on the circumstances of the particular merger or acquisition.

A Path to Merger

There are many possible ways of integrating substantive with process steps. That being said, there is a logical sequence for resolving issues (see Figure 9.1).

Other things being equal, this sequence represents a commonsense approach to establishing the organizational character of the merged institution. The institution's framework, and its people, systems, facilities, and plans, are put in place sequentially, with each step paving the way for the next. For example, the appointment of administrative leaders permits the development of unit-level operating plans and budgets under the leadership of those who will be responsible for implementing them. Approval of these plans, coupled with the establishment of the bargaining unit structure, makes it possible to redeploy employees prior to merger, so that the new organization comes into being with its units appropriately staffed.

The circumstances of particular mergers may well necessitate or make advisable departures from this path. For example, officials at U of T hoped to receive the approval of the Ontario Labour Relations Board to terminate the bargaining rights of some OISE employee groups prior to merger, so as to be able to restaff OISE/UT; however, they received legal advice that the OLRB would want to see evidence of intermingling before granting such approval. They therefore waited until after the merger to apply to that board. This reduced the risk of a delayed or adverse ruling, but it certainly entailed costs. U of T anticipated this, but decided that these costs were outweighed by the risk of a premature application to the OLRB.

The fact that departures from the suggested path are often appropriate, confirms that in strategic terms, mergers in higher education reflect broader principles of organizational planning behaviour. Henry Mintzberg (1998) speaks of *deliberate* strategies, *unrealized* strategies, and *emergent* strategies, all of which lead ultimately to *realized* strategy. Good planning allows for and accommodates all three. This is an especially apt and important lesson for mergers.

Combining Substance with Process

Not only must parties to merger decide – in light of their particular circumstances – whether to follow the path suggested above or to address substantive issues in a different sequence, but they must also decide which issues to resolve in the merger agreement, which to resolve in the transition phase, and which to leave until after the merger.

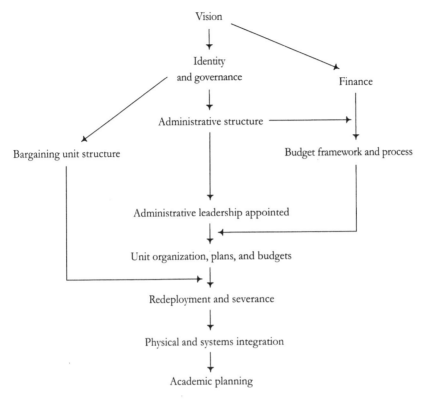

Figure 9.1 A path to merger

Merger agreements normally address, at a minimum, the issues of governance, identity, administrative structure, and finance and budget framework. All the details need not be spelled out. Thus, for example, the OISE/ U of T agreement specified that there would be one faculty of education, bringing together OISE and FEUT, and that its departmental structure would be determined during the transition phase. Similarly, the Dal/ TUNS agreement specified that the college succeeding TUNS would have an academic council, the terms of reference of which would be determined during the transition period.

The minimum requirement for a merger to take effect appears to be the existence of a governance mechanism, an administrative structure, administrative leadership, and a budget. However, mergers usually become effective later in the sequence of substantive steps (e.g., after plans have been approved for new units and policies and personnel are in place).

What all this means is that merging institutions need not – probably should not – aspire to have everything integrated on day 1. As long as determinations have been made about how and by whom decisions will be made, what policies and procedures will apply (at least temporarily), who will be in charge, and what resources will be at their disposal, the organization can begin to function as a merged one – and to integrate structures, people, systems, and facilities over time.

That said, if significant job loss is anticipated as a result of the merger, it is advantageous to get through the severance process before the merger, for both legal reasons and those relating to organizational psychology.

How quickly the path to the desired degree of integration should be completed will depend on a host of factors, and may vary from one functional area to another. For example, it may be necessary to maintain two separate student information systems for a period of time, delaying the date at which registrarial operations can be completely integrated. Similarly, the integration of academic units may have to await the renovation, rental, or acquisition of appropriate space.

One step that should probably be deferred until after merger is the review and planning of academic programs. Dalhousie and TUNS did not intend for any review or planning of their programs in Computer Science to take place prior to merger. In fact, because of the history of tension between the two groups of computer scientists, it was agreed that academic planning would not take place until the appointment and arrival, post-merger, of a new dean. In contrast, U of T and OISE initially envisioned that an academic plan for OISE/UT would be completed prior to integration. The main task of the Academic Integration Task Force was to produce an academic plan and budget for consideration by the appropriate university authorities. In the event, however, the academic programs and research activities of OISE/UT received little attention from the task force. Its report dealt mainly with the mission, organization, operation, and budget of the new faculty. In retrospect, this seems to have been desirable, if not inevitable.

Changes in academic programs and areas of research emphasis are highly sensitive. To plan such changes prior to merger, at a time when myriad other issues must be dealt with, is to invite controversy and division among the faculty and to raise the level of uncertainty and anxiety experienced by students. Most institutions guarantee their students – as did the four parties in our cases – the opportunity to complete their programs under the degree regulations in place at the time they were admitted, so complete and rapid overhaul of academic offerings is out of the question. Deliberately postponing the review and planning of academic programs and/or research until new faculties or other academic units are in place lowers the anxiety of faculty members and students and enables them to participate in the process through normal channels. The future of their programs and activities remains in their hands, rather than being entrusted to an *ad hoc* body, however representative. A final advantage of postponing academic planning until after merger is that faculty members and students learn about the programs of the other former institution by experience. This facilitates integration. Once academic planning does begin, it benefits from their understanding and knowledge.

Staging and Sequencing of Issues

As should be readily apparent, the issues that must be resolved in the course of a higher education merger are vast in scope. A key to successful planning and management of the process is to be selective: do not attempt to tackle too many issues at once. If you put too many issues on a given agenda at once, people will likely become overwhelmed and the process will bog down.

Focus attention on the key issues that must be resolved to enable the merger process to advance. Once those issues are resolved, one can proceed to tackle the next most vital issues. When issues arise that need not be decided immediately, seek agreement on a process for resolving them, and an associated time line.

It is also important to know when any given issue has been resolved sufficiently that it can be referred to another level or group to work out the details. This passing down process is often referred to as 'staging.'

Finally, beware of backtracking. It is not uncommon for issues that were thought to have been resolved to come 'unstuck.' One consultant remarked on reviewing our 'Path to Merger,' 'Yup, that's it – except that there are no backward arrows!'

Consideration of the finer points of an issue will sometimes bring to light other issues that strongly suggest that an earlier decision should be reconsidered. At the same time, one cannot permit decisions to be revisited lightly. Pressure to do so may arise out of simple resistance to change. If one succumbs to this pressure, and permits issues to be reconsidered every time they are challenged, progress toward integration will undoubtedly bog down.

Transition Scheduling

Less than nine months elapsed between the signing of the (non-binding) Dal/TUNS agreement and amalgamation; only three-and-a-half months passed between the passage of the legislation that made amalgamation a certainty and the merger itself. Relative to the forty-one British cases of merger that Gillian Rowley studied (1997), this was an exceedingly short transition period, so some disarray in the weeks leading up to amalgamation was perhaps unavoidable. People at TUNS and Dalhousie were forewarned that there would be difficulties, and their patience and cooperation were requested.

In contrast, OISE and U of T had more than eighteen months to prepare for integration – seemingly plenty of time! Nevertheless, some parts of the OISE/U of T transition process became badly backlogged. Although the report of the Academic Integration Task Force was submitted more or less on schedule in July 1995, a revised version, containing the administrative structure for OISE/UT, was not approved until the following year. With only months remaining prior to the merger, searches for academic and administrative heads had to be conducted, faculty members had to select and be appointed to departments, the administrative support structure had to be finalized, severances had to be processed, staff had to be redeployed, and so on. The last few months were a blur. New chairs and managers did not have an opportunity to 'find their feet' prior to integration. There wasn't time to put in place the membership of OISE/UT's faculty council or advisory board. Staff departures could not be managed in an orderly manner: many felt 'pushed out the door.'

The lesson? There is never 'enough' time to plan and prepare for merger! Even relatively lengthy transition periods provide little or no slack. One is well advised to prepare a transition plan and schedule for achieving the necessary process and substantive steps identified above – and to do one's best to stick to it.

TEN

Concluding Observations

Having studied the dynamics of the Dal/TUNS and OISE/U of T mergers in some detail, let us step back in time. Prior to the mergers, what does one see?

In each case, one sees a relatively large comprehensive university in close proximity to a smaller, more focused institution. The members of each pair are linked and have been for many years – Dalhousie and TUNS by a longstanding cooperative arrangement, OISE and U of T by a formal affiliation agreement. In each case, there have been prior attempts at more far-reaching integration, all unsuccessful. In the Nova Scotia case, these attempts have been motivated mainly by the need to secure more adequate resources for technical education and research in the province. In the Ontario case, the need for greater resources has been one of several motivating factors.

By the early 1990s, pressure for economy and efficiency in the delivery of mass higher education has intensified. Public funding of universities per student has dropped. The Nova Scotia Council on Higher Education has conducted a multiyear exercise to 'rationalize' the province's institutions of higher education into a system it can afford. The Ontario government is preaching to all public sector institutions the need to 'do more with less.' Though all universities are suffering, the resource constraints on smaller, highly specialized institutions are especially intense. Neither TUNS nor OISE has resources sufficient to maintain its programs at reasonable levels of quality. The stage is set for the adoption by the two sets of institutions of more far-reaching forms of integration – that is, for movement to the right along the continuum of possible linkages.

The smaller institutions would prefer not to move too far along the continuum – that is, they would prefer to sacrifice only limited autonomy in return for more secure resources. Indeed, OISE proposes that it merge

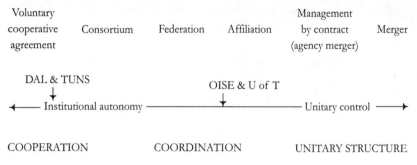

Figure 10.1 The cases on the continuum of higher education linkages

with the Faculty of Education and that the merged OISE/FEUT be federated with the university. TUNS officials also favour federation, along the lines of the École Polytechnique and the Université de Montréal.

In the event, both TUNS and OISE move farther to the right along the continuum than they had intended. They become parties to mergers. Moreover, those mergers are acquisitions. OISE manages to secure some of the trappings of semiautonomy (e.g., retention of its name, responsibility-centre budgeting, a separate bargaining unit for a group of employees whose functions are unique at the university), but TUNS forgoes even these.

These similar outcomes emerged from vastly different processes. Through a process of courtship, Dalhousie and TUNS reached an ambiguous agreement in principle to merge. OISE and U of T reached a detailed, binding merger agreement through mediation following combat. The transition processes were also very different – informal and centralized in the Dal/TUNS case, rational/bureaucratic in that of OISE and U of T. The greatest similarity in these contrasting merger processes was in the roles played by the provincial governments.

What does all this tell us about the factors that determine the outcomes of higher education mergers?

The Role of Government Confirmed

First, it confirms that government plays a crucial role in mergers of publicly funded universities. Though less brutally obvious than in involuntary mergers (i.e., mergers legislated against the will of the institutions involved), the role of government in voluntary mergers is considerable. That role is both direct and indirect. Besides encouraging particular mergers by means such as those identified in Chapter 5, governments often inadvertently create incentives and constraints that shape institutions' motivations. One means by which they do so is the regulatory environment. Although colleges and universities sometimes bristle in reaction to government regulation because it limits institutional autonomy, regulation often protects and supports institutional roles and identities. Sometimes such protection amounts to enforcing institutional monopolies, either in terms of geography or in terms of specialized programs. In either case, competition among institutions is limited and controlled, usually by a 'buffer' agency. Neil Marshall, in his 1990 study of mergers in Australia, observed that the removal of buffer agencies – in the case of Australia, the Commonwealth Tertiary Education Commission (CTEC) – increases the propensity toward merger by removing the protection of institutions that otherwise might be too marginal to stand alone.

A second indirect effect of government policy on voluntary mergers is financial. Although funding formulas are sometimes promoted as being neutral and objective, most in practical fact are instruments of public educational, social, and fiscal policies. Thus formulas play a policy role by providing incentives to institutions that are otherwise outside direct government control (Lang et al., 1989). One such incentive has to do with institutional size. Most funding formulas are based on linear algorithms and average costs. Nominally, those averages represent optimal sizes and the economies of scale that underpin those sizes. Seen in this light, funding formulas do not provide adequate funding for small institutions, especially small, highly specialized institutions with anomalous cost structures. In the absence of funding that recognizes the cost structures of small institutions, interest in merger grows as small institutions come together to realize the economies of scale implicit in the funding formula. Thus, even when a government does not have the authority to force mergers, and otherwise appears agnostic toward them, it may inadvertently or deliberately create a climate that operates as a powerful incentive toward merger. Insofar as the mechanisms by which TUNS and OISE were funded failed to account fully for their cost structures, they provided such incentives.

The Importance of Institutional Characteristics

A second lesson to be drawn from the cases is that the characteristics of merging institutions – in particular, their relative size and power – are important determinants of the outcomes of merger. Consolidation – that is, the emergence of a new entity – seems to be possible only if the merging institutions are comparable in size and strength. Otherwise, a form of acquisition is the probable outcome. The likelihood that one party will be entirely absorbed by the other (i.e., instead of retaining some of its characteristics) seems to increase with the difference between the institutions as to size and power. In other words, the merger of a large, comprehensive, financially healthy institution with a small, specialized, financially troubled one is all but preordained to be an acquisition. At the same time, institutions that are substantial in size and power relative to larger partners may succeed in securing outcomes that preserve some of their characteristics, or that extend those characteristics to the larger institution.

The cases suggest that this relationship between relative size and merger outcome holds in mergers of faculties or units as well as in institutional mergers. The possibility that the outcome of a given merger – whether at the institutional, faculty or unit level – will be a consolidation seems to be greatest if the parties are of approximately equal size and power. A transformative or semiautonomous acquisition is most probable if the smaller party is substantial in scale relative to its partner. Finally, if the smaller party is dwarfed by the other, it is very likely to be acquired and absorbed.

Although this study of two institutional-level and three faculty-level mergers is grounded in existing literature and theory and reflects the experience of a number of professional consultants, it is nonetheless a study of cases. Case studies have limitations but can be built upon through further investigation. To this end, it would be fruitful to investigate further the nature of the relationship between the characteristics of merging parties and merger outcomes. Specifically, recent higher education mergers might be categorized according to the relative size and power of the merging institutions and units, on one hand, and the outcomes of the mergers, on the other, so as to ascertain the nature and strength of the relationship. It would also be most interesting to identify the reasons for outcomes other than those expected. In an instance in which an acquired institution or unit preserved more autonomy than its relative size would have led one to expect, was that attributable to strategy on the part of the acquiring institution or unit (in other words, to recognition on its part of the desirability of giving its former partner 'a free hand')? Or to inability on the part of the acquiring institution/unit to achieve the degree of integration sought? Or to the process by which the institutions or units merged? Or to leadership, perhaps? For if relative size and power determine merger outcomes, what does that say about the importance of process and leadership?

Do Process and Leadership Matter?

Many early students of corporate management tended to ascribe organizational success or failure principally to leadership (Pfeffer, 1987). This tendency is still readily apparent in the business press. In articles on mergers, process is also commonly deemed to be an important ingredient of success. The failure of corporate mergers to produce desired results is often attributed to poor implementation. For example, *The Economist* argues: 'What seems to link most mergers that fail is the acquirer's obsession with the deal itself, coupled with too little attention to what happens next – particularly the complex business of blending all the systems, informal processes and cultures that make the merging firms tick' ('Why too many mergers ...', 4 January 1997).

This argument is also made in recent management literature. According to McCann and Gilkey (1998), mergers often 'fail because the merger-acquisition process itself is inherently flawed, particularly in the last and extremely important transition and integration stages ... The cornerstone of effective merger-acquisition implementation is sound transition management.'

Karen Hult (1987), who studied mergers of public agencies in the United States, also found that management and leadership were important factors:

The selection of management strategies – and thus indirectly the people in high-level positions – appears crucial. Even with favorable external conditions and a carefully designed merger, individuals seize upon or miss chances to promote change or channel behavior in certain directions ... The evident importance of management skill highlights Philip Selznick's notion that leadership becomes particularly significant at 'critical junctures' in an organization's history.

In contrast, a recent study of two major Canadian teaching hospital mergers questioned the importance of leadership and process. Denis, Lamothe, and Langley studied two sets of merging hospitals that shared many characteristics. They found that the outcomes of the mergers were very similar, notwithstanding very different management strategies and processes:

Despite a smoother pre-merger process, more harmonious and collaborative leadership, and a more open strategic frame, the hospitals of Merger 2 were not *merging* (in the sense of building integrated operations) any faster or more successfully than those of Merger 1 ... A natural deduction ... could be that if the contexts for the two mergers are similar but the processes of merging are different, the fact that results are similar is essentially a reflection of the context. In other words, context matters a great deal – so much so that it dominates the effect of differing processes. We believe there is a strong element of truth to this (Denis, Lamothe & Langley, 1999, 305).

The cases detailed here are similar to those of the hospitals in that mergers of similar sets of institutions produced similar outcomes in spite of different processes. Should one conclude that process is of little consequence?

That would be rash. Leadership and process did appear to shape outcomes, though not as powerfully as government action and institutional characteristics such as relative size and power. In particular one can argue that leadership was in part responsible for the fact that the two mergers occurred at all. For example, had the leadership of TUNS opposed merger with Dalhousie, it is by no means a foregone conclusion that the Nova Scotia government would have imposed it. The government might well have backed off from its declared intention to rationalize the province's universities unilaterally if they did not rationalize themselves voluntarily. Or it might have imposed a quite different conclusion on the rationalization process. Similarly, had the president of U of T not been a strong proponent of merger with OISE, it is doubtful that his administrative colleagues' resistance to it would have been overcome. In these and other respects, leadership *did* matter. That said, the cases suggest that leadership may affect outcomes differently than other factors – that, as Selznick and Hult suggest, it may become relevant at 'critical junctures' and may therefore be more important in determining whether a particular merger takes place at all than what the actual outcome is. It can likewise be argued – especially on the basis of the OISE/U of T case – that the impact of leadership varies by level of organization. In that case, it appeared that presidential leadership had relatively more influence on the merger's occurrence and timing and that decanal leadership had relatively more impact on its outcome. The impact of leadership at various levels on whether potential mergers take place, on their timing, and on what they produce appears to be a very interesting topic for further research.

Reflection on the cases also leads to the conclusion that process has an impact. For example, it appears that the confrontational nature of the negotiations between OISE and U of T enabled the former to secure more continuing identity and autonomy than it otherwise would have, given its relative size. It may be that another factor that contributed to this outcome was that U of T had, prior to the merger, introduced (1) a process of multiyear planning and budgeting that helped it finance and manage the transition of merger, and (2) responsibility-centred budgeting. Both processes provided the pragmatic basis for OISE's continuing measure of autonomy. That basis did not exist at Dalhousie, which made it more difficult for both it and TUNS to perceive the mechanisms from whence real post-merger autonomy could flow.

Leadership and process thus do appear to be among the factors that determine whether mergers succeed and what they produce – albeit not the most important of those factors.

A Contingency Theory of Higher Education Merger Management

To the extent that the process of merger in higher education matters, what can one learn from the cases about how it should be planned and managed?

The processes by which the two sets of institutions merged differed greatly, but also had much in common. It seems that merger consists of two sets of generic steps, one for completing the process of merger, and the other for resolving substantive issues. In Chapter 9 we presented one possible path for institutions contemplating merger to follow. Also, our comparative analysis of the cases generated observations and suggestions, presented in Chapters 6 to 9, about how particular steps on that path might be approached. The utility of these observations and suggestions will no doubt be tested through further study and experience.

While suggesting some general lessons, the cases made it abundantly clear that there is no single best approach to merger. How the steps involved should be tackled, and the best sequence in which to tackle them, depends very much on the context. Thus, for example, the most effective approach to merger negotiations depends on the relative size of the parties, the compatibility of their positions, and other factors. Similarly, the appropriate balance between rational planning and incrementalism depends on the particular context.

Balancing Planning and Incrementalism

André Mayer, writing on strategic planning for college mergers, observed that though each merger raises unique issues, 'one point remains constant: the merger plan is not the merger. It is rather an outline and guide to be used in shaping the development of the new institution' (1994, 112). He advised managers 'to approach planning carefully, always aware that a merger ... requires reasoned improvisation.' This is a crucial point. The literature on organizational behaviour suggests that the more complex and turbulent the organizational environment, the more desirable it is for decision makers to sense out, experiment with, and test the appropriateness of particular courses of action.

Universities are extremely complex organizations, and mergers unleash powerful forces. Much is unpredictable. It is therefore vital to manage the implementation of the plan actively – to stay in touch with major constituencies, to be alert to the emergence of unanticipated issues, to seize unforseen opportunities, and to be open to the adoption of courses of action superior to those initially planned – in other words, to be prepared to improvise.

Of the two cases we studied, the Dal/TUNS merger was much more unorthodox and improvisational than that of OISE and U of T. The latter merger conformed much more closely to the descriptions provided by the consultants we interviewed of 'how it should be done.' U of T and OISE approached merger 'by the book.' In contrast, Dalhousie and TUNS broke many of the rules. For example, they agreed to a government announcement of the merger before there was a signed written agreement – something that would be unthinkable to most institutions. The two presidents drafted the amalgamation agreement themselves – a practice frowned upon by most of the consultants we interviewed. Unlike most merger agreements, the Dal/TUNS agreement was a statement of intent rather than binding and legal. There was no one clear decision point in the process: the institutions moved toward amalgamation in stages. Only after legislation was passed was there no turning back.

Even after legislation was passed, issues were dealt with as it became possible to do so. Instead of forcing decisions on contentious issues, the universities allowed more time for consideration of them, while moving very rapidly to decide issues that could be resolved. For example, when it became apparent in the fall of 1996 that the future relationships of the TUNS library and graduate studies office to their Dalhousie counterparts would be more difficult to resolve than other issues of administrative structure, the presidents provided more time for considering the former, while making announcements about the latter. They thus avoided forcing decisions that would be contentious, on one hand, and holding up decisions that could be made, on the other.

In sum, Dalhousie and TUNS approached merger by something akin to what Karl Weick (1984) once described as a strategy of 'small wins.' He advocated this strategy for dealing with social problems such as hunger and crime – problems so big as to defy solution. When people are confronted with problems of this magnitude, the quality of their thought and action declines as psychological processes such as frustration, arousal, and helplessness set in. They become overwhelmed. Weick suggested that such problems be broken down into smaller problems that do not exceed people's capacity to grasp or resolve. Success in overcoming a problem of the latter kind represents a 'small win' – a 'concrete, complete, implemented outcome of moderate importance':

> By itself, one small win may seem unimportant. A series of wins at small but significant tasks, however, reveals a pattern that may attract allies, deter opponents, and lower resistance to subsequent proposals ... Small wins [also] provide information that facilitates learning and adaptation. Small wins are like miniature experiments that test implicit theories about resistance and opportunity and uncover both resources and barriers that were invisible before the situation was stirred up. (1984, 43)

The bitter historic rivalries between Nova Scotia's universities – intensified in the early 1990s by the Council on Higher Education's efforts to 'rationalize' them – made the prospect of merger with Dalhousie a daunting and anxiety-provoking prospect for TUNS. In other words, it evoked some of the same types of reactions as a daunting social problem. It can be argued that the universities' approach to merger – to take it one step at a time, tackling the possible first, and building confidence in the outcome and momentum along the way – was more appropriate in the circumstances than attempting to make one big decision would have been.

Incrementalism undoubtedly entailed costs. The Faculty of Engineering's *ad hoc* committee on the impact of merger reported (p. 30):

> Although the trials and tribulations of the merger process itself is water under the bridge, there are those who feel that these should be recorded at least to allow us to learn from our mistakes ... The most fundamental mistake was to carry out the entire merger process without a clear and detailed business plan that addressed all pertinent issues. Instead, almost every issue was treated as 'a detail that can be ironed out later.' Consequently, there have been many disagreements and misunderstandings between the two institutions that soured the well for a long time to come. We definitely would have benefited from a clear and detailed business plan drafted, agreed upon by both institutions, and written down, well in advance of the merger.

For TUNS to have secured a clear, detailed business plan would have required not only more planning but also, and above all, more negotiation. One plans for something. Planning, in other words, requires shared goals and objectives. In retrospect, it is clear that Dalhousie and TUNS had very different conceptions of what amalgamation should mean.

Had TUNS insisted on knowing the details of how the merged institution would work before agreeing to merge, it would have been consistent with the advice offered to small institutions in Chapter 6 (i.e., seek to achieve a clear, comprehensive agreement through formal negotiation). Would it have resulted in merger? It is impossible to know, but a number of those we interviewed were doubtful. Their comments suggested that amalgamation could not have been done 'by the book' – that the demand characteristics of the situation were such that incrementalism may have been the only possible route to Dal/TUNS merger (other than legislation against the institutions' wishes).

Would we recommend such radical incrementalism to other institutions? As with the choice of negotiating strategies, it depends on the context. For the great majority of mergers, such an extreme approach is unlikely to be necessary or appropriate. Furthermore, not every institutional leader is capable of applying it: intuition, experience, political acumen and willingness to take risks are required. Organizational improvisation entails capitalizing on developments to further one's desired end – in other words, opportunism.

But on a more limited scale, incrementalism is effective and, indeed, necessary in most mergers. Quinn and Voyer (1996) described the benefits of logical incrementalism in large-scale reorganization:

> Large-scale organizational moves may have negative effects on organizational politics and social structure. Logical incrementalism makes it easier to avoid those negative effects. As the organization proceeds incrementally, it can assess the new roles, capabilities and individual reactions of those involved in the restructuring. It allows ... organizational actors to modify the idea behind the reorganization as more is learned. It also gives executives the luxury of making final commitments as late as possible ... Logical incrementalism works well in large-scale reorganization because it allows for testing, flexibility and feedback. (1996, 97)

The location of the Computer Science faculty formed by the Dal/TUNS merger illustrates how incrementalism makes it possible to test the functionality and acceptability of potential outcomes before commitments are made. The amalgamation agreement presumed that the three DalTech faculties would continue to be bundled in one location. But the decision about where a new Computer Science building would be located was not made until months after the merger. In the interim, the merged faculty was based on the former TUNS campus. Through experience, the faculty came to realize that being distant from other faculties that were teaching first- and second-year students posed significant practical and educational disadvantages. Its subsequent recommendation that the new building be located on the former Dalhousie campus was eventually accepted, much to the chagrin of others at DalTech, who regarded the change as a betrayal of the college concept. Notwithstanding the upset arising from the decision, the outcome of incrementalism was in this instance a functionally superior location.

Though the OISE/U of T merger was much less *ad hoc*, it too featured some improvisation. For example, when it became apparent several months into the transition period that some institutional issues were not receiving adequate attention because they fell within the purview of neither integration task force, a 'third task force' came into being to deal with them. In this instance, improvisation enabled the merging institutions to respond effectively to issues that would otherwise not have been addressed.

In sum, the degree of incrementalism evident in the Dal/TUNS merger was extraordinary. That said, many of the elements involved in that merger – staging; sensing; experimenting; testing; eschewing rigidity and detail; allowing structures and positions to emerge – are very valuable complements to rational/linear planning techniques in any merger situation. The appropriate *balance* between rational planning and incrementalism in a given merger seems to depend on the extent of the uncertainty confronting the institutions, and also on the level of sophistication of their existing approaches to planning and budgeting.

Thus, the balance that should be struck between planning and incrementalism depends on the particular context. So does the approach to negotiations that will be most effective, and so does the optimum sequence for undertaking the steps involved in merger. All of this is consistent with the paradigms depicted in Chapter 2, which emphasize the role of environmental factors in higher education merger.

The Paradigms Revisited

Implicit in the concept of the continuum of interinstitutional linkages is the view that universities and colleges elect voluntarily to combine their structures in order to achieve gains in economy and efficiency, when pressures on resources intensify. This view is regarded by many contemporary students of organizational behaviour as rather outmoded and naïve, implying as it does that organizational decision-makers are rational, altruistic actors. After all, this view 'pays very little attention, if at all, to concepts like coercion, force, bargaining, conflict of interests, and dissension among members of the system ... These are perceived as being but temporary imbalances in an otherwise well-balanced, mutually beneficial and altogether happy state of affairs' (Goegedebuure, 1992, 82). Conflict of interest, dissension, bargaining, and other expressions of power and politics were certainly evident in the two cases. But at the same time, the key participants did make rational decisions for the greater good at crucial points in the process. For example, the president and board chairman of TUNS chose to pursue a merger with Dalhousie, notwithstanding the costs, because they had concluded that TUNS would have to sacrifice its independent identity and autonomy in order to secure the resources necessary to maintain the quality of its programs. Similarly, the members of OISE's negotiating team compared OISE's probable future as an independent institution with its future as part of U of T and concluded, notwithstanding their predisposition against merger, that the latter would be more attractive. Self-interest certainly plays a role in the lives of academic institutions, but the cases suggest that members of universities are capable of acting for the greater good, rationally perceived, difficult as the consequences may be for them as individuals.

Besides confirming that the assumptions about behaviour underlying the continuum are within the realm of human possibility, the cases lend support to that continuum's broader implications. It was suggested in Chapter 2 that, faced with a widening gap between public expectations and resources, universities and other institutions of higher education will move progressively to the right along the continuum. In the cases of Dalhousie and TUNS, and OISE and U of T, that is precisely what occurred. This confirms the existence of the continuum and validates the hypothesis that merger is an ultimate step in an interorganizational quest for economy and efficiency.

The paradigm of resource dependence also provides important insights into the two cases. Most obviously, it explains why TUNS and OISE agreed to merger: they had to in order to secure a continuing flow of critical resources. It also explains why large, comprehensive universities pursue acquisitions. For one thing, it reduces uncertainty. Just as corporations may be motivated to acquire firms that supply critical resources to them, universities may acquire smaller institutions that supply students for their programs or the actions of which affect their programs in other ways. The fact that the existence of a School of Computer Science at TUNS constrained Dalhousie in what it could do in that field may have been one of the factors that predisposed Dalhousie toward merger.

According to resource dependence theory, universities also acquire in order to expand their 'domain claims' (i.e., the fields in which they have authority to operate), thereby maximizing their independence and future capacity to attract students, funds, and other resources (Goegedebuure, 1992). Thus, by acquiring OISE, U of T gained authority and responsibility for graduate education and research in a field of great social and economic importance. Similarly, by absorbing TUNS and its roles in technical education and research, Dalhousie became a comprehensive university – *de facto*, Nova Scotia's provincial university – and was able to claim an academic domain perceived as a key driver in the province's economic development strategy.

Besides illuminating the parties' motivations, the resource dependence paradigm sheds light on why the mergers happened when they did – why they succeeded in 1996 and 1997, respectively, when previous attempts had failed. The paradigm conceives of power as a relational concept. Specifically, it defines the power of organization A over organization B as the former's capacity to supply the latter with critical resources (Goegedebuure, 1992). The more difficult it is for organization B to obtain those resources elsewhere, the greater is organization A's power. In light of this, one perceives that the two mergers occurred when they did, rather than at the times of previous attempts, in part because the larger universities had acquired more power relative to their partners during the intervening years. Between the mid-1980s and the mid-1990s, OISE became financially weaker and more isolated; in the same period, U of T carried out a successful multiyear financial plan and its Faculty of Education began a program of revitalization. Similarly, Dalhousie reduced its accumulated deficit and debt dramatically in the years leading up to amalgamation, while TUNS's financial condition and prospects worsened. The fact that the large institutions' power (i.e., their ability to secure resources) was increasing while that of the smaller institutions was decreasing had two implications. *First*, the larger institutions were better able to make commitments. Since they had rebalanced their budgets, their governing bodies were willing to enter into merger agreements they might previously have deemed too risky. *Second*, the value of what they were offering their smaller partners had increased in the latters' eyes: relatively weaker and with fewer alternatives, OISE and TUNS could not easily dismiss offers they might previously have spurned.

Finally, the resource dependence paradigm accounts for the outcomes of the two mergers. Very simply, because U of T and Dalhousie were powerful relative to their partners, they were able to secure outcomes closer to what they wanted than to what their partners sought at the outset of negotiations.

Other paradigms also shed light on the cases. For example, the paradigm of natural selection describes very aptly the behaviour of the Faculty of Computer Science produced by the Dal/TUNS merger. As that paradigm would suggest, that faculty very quickly evolved into a brand new entity with characteristics different from its predecessors and began to seek out new niches. The experts engaged separately by OISE and U of T to advise on the structure of an integrated institution described its advantages in terms of natural selection. Both observed that the context for teaching and research in the field of Education had changed greatly since the creation of OISE and FEUT, and that combining the two would produce a genuinely new entity, capable of greater effectiveness and success in the contemporary environment.

In sum, paradigms are not mutually exclusive. Different paradigms shed light on different aspects of case experience. A paradigm's validity for explaining a particular merger – or a particular aspect of a merger – seems to depend on the extent to which the merger's context resembles the environment the paradigm postulates. Given that the cases detailed here involved publicly funded institutions, it is not surprising that the resource dependence paradigm illuminates them more clearly than do paradigms that assume the existence of markets and/or dispersed funding sources.

The Future of Mergers in Higher Education

Even in the corporate sector, it is difficult to define and measure success in merger. Various measures of post-merger performance are employed, and agreement is lacking on the crucial question of when a merger should be deemed complete (Bengtsson, 1992). It is even more difficult to measure the success of mergers in the higher education sector, in which agreement on basic goals is lacking and the very concept of institutional performance measurement remains controversial. In this context, outcomes may be interpreted in very different ways. For example, an increase in an institution's student/faculty ratio in the wake of a merger may be interpreted in some quarters as evidence that desired improvement in efficiency has been achieved, and in other quarters as evidence that instructional quality has declined. Similarly, a post-merger increase in enrolments from outside a university's local area may be perceived either as a reflection of enhanced academic quality and reputation, or as a retreat from that university's commitment to its local or regional base of support.

There is no right or wrong here. The point is that higher education mergers are undertaken for a variety of reasons and therefore raise expectations of a variety of outcomes. Even more so than in the private sector, the success of a merger in higher education is in the eye of the beholder.

There are indications that most higher education mergers do meet the expectations of the leaders of the merged institutions. For example, 90 per cent of the leaders of the British institutions that Rowley surveyed (1997) declared that the mergers they were involved in had been successful. In stark contrast, only 50 per cent of corporate mergers are deemed to be successful by the firms' leaders. What accounts for this difference is not clear. Part of the difference may be attributable to relative lack of consensus on institutional objectives in the higher education sector. Or higher education leaders may simply be less hard-nosed. But these factors are insufficient to explain the difference in reported success rates.

Contrary to common belief, it seems that some of the characteristics of universities may actually lend themselves to success in merger. Because professors are inclined to identify with their fields rather than with their institutions, it may be easier for them to come together quickly with disciplinary colleagues. The 'loose coupling' characteristic for which universities are notorious can provide greater flexibility – and limit the spread of problems more effectively – than is possible in the corporate world. The benefits to be reaped by bringing faculty members, students, and staff together in new constellations may often be greater than in the corporate sector.

Whatever the explanation, the balance sheet on higher education mergers appears to be positive. On the basis of a review of the literature, Goegedebuure concluded: 'An assessment of outcomes appears to be tilted toward the positive. Agreed, merger processes seldom if ever have a smooth and easy run, and are interspersed with major and minor problems and battles, but they appear to have surprising results considering their largely involuntary nature. Educational offerings appear to have expanded, there are indicators that suggest an increase in quality, and community links have been strengthened' (1992, 74).

Given this positive record, can more mergers in higher education be expected?

The answer depends on the paradigm. If mergers result from a drive for economy and efficiency – and if the gap between the resources that society invests in the higher education sector and its expectations continues to widen – the answer is probably yes. That said, there is a point at which the gains in economy and efficiency will begin to diminish as institutional scale reaches optimal levels. This suggests, first, that the prospect of merger will remain significant for smaller and more specialized institutions, and second, that such institutions will tend to seek large, relatively comprehensive institutions as partners rather than institutions like themselves. The reverse is also likely to be true: in the future, large universities are likely to be more interested in gaining curricular variety than in realizing economies of scale. More mergers like the cases in this book are therefore likely to unfold.

Of course, the scope for achieving additional economies through merger varies from jurisdiction to jurisdiction. In some systems, the waves of mergers that occurred in the last decade of the twentieth century may have exhausted the potential for mergers. The institutions that those systems have come to comprise may be so similar in size or role or quality that few realistic candidates for merger remain. There are, however, still jurisdictions in which merger, whether voluntary or involuntary, may still have considerable potential to improve efficiency. For example, some former Soviet republics in eastern Europe have large numbers of small, specialized institutions that could realize economic gains through merger. The same is true in the People's Republic of China.

This prediction assumes that pressure will continue for greater and greater efficiency in the delivery of mass higher education. But perhaps, in some jurisdictions, that pressure will abate. Mergers lead to more standardization and less diversity in the delivery of higher education. At some point the drive for increased scale, breadth, and distribution diminishes quality. With renewed recognition of the link between higher education, health, and prosperity, quality and diversity may be qualities that societies want – and that some can afford. If that is the case, and if it results in increased resources flowing to universities and colleges in some systems, the incidence of merger and other forms of combination may decrease, and there may be movement back toward the left – movement toward autonomy – on the continuum of interinstitutional linkages.

But what if the mechanisms by which universities and colleges are funded change even as resources are reinvested? Any significant change is bound to threaten the supply of resources to some types of institutions. The resource dependence paradigm suggests that this will trigger mergers as institutions seek to establish more secure supplies of critical resources in the new context. To the extent that higher education systems continue to become more like markets, the paradigm of competition may predict institutional behaviour: universities and colleges may be expected to merge in order to achieve competitive advantage, whether through limitation of competition, complementary marketing, realization of economies of scale or critical mass, diversification of risk, or other means. Insofar as environments for higher education become more like markets, universities and colleges are likely to become more businesslike in their approach to merger and to rely increasingly on planning, scanning, and analytical tools such as those in use in the private sector. There are indications that this is taking place. Rowley, for instance, found that the incidence and sophistication of merger due diligence rose steeply in England in the late 1980s and early 1990s. Whether, and the extent to which, higher education mergers have come to resemble corporate mergers is a fascinating question for further research.

Though the shift from a state-dominated to a market context is certainly significant, the environment for higher education seems to be changing in even more profound ways. For example, the rate at which knowledge and practice are advancing at the interstices between disciplines is tremendous. It is conceivable that this will disadvantage small, specialized institutions just as a long-term change in the physical environment can weaken or cause the disappearance of certain organisms. Similarly, it can be argued that the ongoing revolution in information technology will be akin to a cataclysmic physical event in its impact on the higher education environment. To the extent that new modes of teaching and learning, spearheaded by non-traditional providers of higher education, replace the old, universities and colleges will have to change to survive. This suggests the potential for transformative mergers similar to the corporate mergers that are shaking up many industries as the twenty-first century begins.

One thing that unites the paradigms for merger is the conviction that merger is a response to developments in the external environment. The environments in which higher education is offered today are changing rapidly and profoundly. To the extent that universities and other institutions can anticipate those changes, merger is likely to be among the strategies by which they respond. As mergers are studied more, understanding of the precise roles they can play in institutional evolution will be advanced. In the meantime, it is hoped that the lessons elucidated here will enable universities and other institutions to employ merger as a strategy with greater confidence.

Agreement between The Province of Nova Scotia, Technical University of Nova Scotia, Dalhousie University

(1) The parties to this agreement agree that the public benefits of advanced technical education and research, as well as provincial economic renewal, can be advanced by an amalgamation of Technical University of Nova Scotia (hereafter "TUNS") and Dalhousie University (hereafter "Dalhousie").

(2) Her Majesty the Queen, in right of The Province of Nova Scotia (hereafter "the Province") considers that, as a matter of strategic public policy, the strengthening of computer science, information technology, engineering, advanced technical education and research and a strong college/institute of applied science and technology are fundamental cornerstones of the economy and the future of Nova Scotia.

(3) TUNS, Dalhousie and the Province agree that the college/institute of applied science and technology is TUNS suitably renamed and amalgamated with Dalhousie.

(4) The amalgamation of Dalhousie and TUNS will be known as Dalhousie University. All the assets and liabilities of Dalhousie and TUNS will become the property of the amalgamated institution.

(5) The college/institute of applied science and technology, a new constituent part of Dalhousie, will be known as TUNS until a suitable name can be mutually agreed upon.

(6) TUNS will have at least three closely located professionally-accredited Faculties with strengths appropriate for an internationally renowned research-based university such as Dalhousie. These faculties will initially be Architecture, Computer Science and Engineering.

(7) TUNS will have a new mission statement extending the current statement of TUNS ("to contribute to the highest possible quality

education, research and community/industry collaboration in Architecture, Computer Science and Engineering") to include wording appropriate to the new Dalhousie/TUNS relationship. The mission statement will recognize the new opportunities for interdisciplinary teaching and research.

(8) Dalhousie and TUNS will reorganize their current academic and administrative structures to amalgamate TUNS with Dalhousie.

(9) All the administrative, budgetary and academic powers enjoyed by the Faculties of Dalhousie will, through the administration of TUNS, be extended to TUNS and its Faculties.

(10) The period between the execution of this Agreement and the date of completion of the amalgamation is to be called the "transition period".

(11) TUNS will be administered by a President reporting in the transition period of this agreement to the Board of TUNS. After the amalgamation, the title of President of TUNS will be changed to Principal who will then report to the President of Dalhousie. The new terms of reference of the Principal will be developed by a joint committee of the Dalhousie and TUNS Boards during the transition period. The TUNS President will give best efforts in working with the President of Dalhousie and vice versa. The President/Principal of TUNS will have the status of Vice-President, on the Dalhousie Board.

(12) The amalgamation of TUNS and Dalhousie will occur on March 31, 1997.

(13) In order to ensure the realization of the public policy of the Province (#2 above) and the desires of all parties, the following financial commitments will be made.

(13.1) Beginning on September 1, 1996 the Province will transfer the $1 million per year it currently pays (prorated against monies already expended on the lease) on behalf of TUNS for leased property directly to TUNS, on an ongoing basis, for the provision of space and academic programs.

(13.2) Over the next three fiscal years (1996/97–1998/99) the Province will provide additional grants that enable the development of TUNS programs to international standards in all its faculties in the following stages:

(A) on April 1, 1996 a grant of $100,000.

(B) on April 1, 1997 an additional grant of $900,000.
(C) on April 1, 1998 an additional grant of $2,000,000.
(D) any future funding arrangements will recognize this priority investment and be considered an integral part of the Province's higher education commitment.

(13.3) The Province will complete its current plan to contract with TUNS to undertake industrial cooperative research. This will be funded on a 50/50 basis between industry and the Province in accordance with the proposal currently being considered by InNOVAcorp. It is understood that an agreement in principle has already been signed.

(13.4) The Province will provide the necessary matching funds for the technology transfer and licensing organization to be called UTECH Inc. ($130,000 per year for three years). Federal funding for this has already been granted to the two universities as well as the Nova Scotia Agricultural College and University College of Cape Breton.

(13.5) In each of the fiscal years 1996/97 and 1997/98 the Province will make available $50,000 to support the legal, financial and other consulting and administrative costs associated with planning and implementing the amalgamation.

(14) In the event the Province provides programs to cover transition costs and severance/early retirement costs to the Metro Halifax Universities Consortium such programs will be extended, as appropriate, to similar costs associated with the TUNS/Dalhousie amalgamation.

(15) The Province will, as appropriate, enable TUNS employees who are members of the Province of Nova Scotia Public Service Superannuation Plan at the time of amalgamation to continue to be members of the plan and take advantage of early retirement available to members of the plan. If the existing employees choose not to continue to participate in this plan, appropriate financial arrangements will have to be made with the Province to cover outstanding early retirement costs for employees who have already retired under the program.

(16) The Parties will abide by the provisions of all their applicable collective agreements.

(17) During the transition period the Board of Governors of Dalhousie

and TUNS will continue to govern their respective institutions. The President of TUNS will be appointed a member of the Dalhousie Board and the President of Dalhousie will be appointed a member of the TUNS Board.

(18) At the time of amalgamation the Board of Governors of TUNS will name five members to the Dalhousie Board. After amalgamation, there will be a board of TUNS which will then nominate and name governors to replace the five members referred to, when they are needed. This TUNS Board will be a subcommittee of the Dalhousie Board, comprised of eleven members, five of whom will be nominated by the Dalhousie Board. The method of appointment of the remaining 6 members will be agreed upon by Dalhousie and TUNS. Both Dalhousie and TUNS will make all reasonable efforts to ensure appropriate representation on the Dalhousie Board of the communities served by TUNS.

(19) During the transition period, the terms of reference of the Board of TUNS, referred to in paragraph 18, will be developed and agreed upon by Dalhousie and TUNS. The terms of reference will include, but not be limited to the following:

(a) to provide the necessary degree of autonomy to TUNS to sustain, protect and advocate the integrity of the TUNS professional programs;

(b) within the constraints of allocated budgets, to approve and recommend on academic and administrative appointments at TUNS;

(c) while there are collective agreements at TUNS, to be the custodian of those agreements;

(d) to strive to sustain, protect and advocate for the necessary physical facilities and resources needed by TUNS.

(20) All students currently enrolled at the two institutions will be entitled to complete the programs of study under the requirements applying at the time of their admission.

(21) After completion of the amalgamation, the academic and administrative support staffs currently in the departments of Engineering and Computer Science at both institutions will be reassigned to the new faculties of Engineering and Computer Science at TUNS.

(22) After completion of the amalgamation all students at TUNS will study and be governed by regulations adopted by Dalhousie Univer-

sity. Recommendations for such regulations will normally be made to the Senate by the faculties of TUNS through a TUNS Academic Council.

(23) TUNS and Dalhousie are committed to establishing four year (eight term) Engineering and Computer Science undergraduate programs with opportunities for up to four terms of cooperative, industrial experience. Students enrolled in Engineering and Computer Science at the Associated Universities having received the necessary course credits will be accommodated into the TUNS/Dal program, so that they may obtain their degrees under the terms of the revised four-year program, as coordinated with the programs of the Associated Universities.

(24) TUNS and Dalhousie are committed to strengthening their amalgamated Computer Science program and working closely with allied disciplines interested in Computer Science to ensure the highest standards of undergraduate and graduate education, as well as research. Dalhousie and TUNS are also committed to a strong industrial outreach program with interested private sector partners.

(25) TUNS will have a representative Academic Council chaired by the TUNS President/Principal. The TUNS representatives on the Dalhousie Senate will be members ex officio of the TUNS Academic Council. During the transition period, the terms of reference of the Academic Council will be agreed upon by a TUNS and Dalhousie joint committee of Senates and shall include, but not be limited to, provision for inquiry into all academic matters that might enhance the usefulness of TUNS for the purpose of making recommendations in respect thereof to the TUNS Board and directly to Dalhousie Senate.

(26) The representative Senate of Dalhousie will be expanded to include the requisite representation of faculty members and others from TUNS. The TUNS Senate will cease to exist.

(27) To continuously seek improvement of operational efficiency, during the transition period, both institutions may request studies and, by mutual agreement, implement re-engineering of administrative and academic organization infrastructures with a particular focus on maximizing resources for academic/research activities and minimizing administrative costs.

(28) To the extent that amalgamation of the two institutions leads to fewer administrative and staff jobs, the employees of the two institutions

will be entitled to compete for available positions on a fair, open and equal basis consistent with applicable collective agreements.

(29) Dalhousie and TUNS agree that until the end of the budget year 1998/99, the budget allocated to TUNS will be in a state of transition. The target budgets for TUNS and its three Faculties will be the existing budgets of the combined academic units and their associated administrative staffs plus the funds itemized in 13.1 and 13.2 above. After three years Dalhousie will treat the attained budget as the normal base budgets of TUNS, and Dalhousie will then continue to manage them in its normal manner. Current administrative budgets of TUNS and Dalhousie will in the most part be automatically merged as administrative service groups are merged.

(30) TUNS will maintain best efforts to deliver world-class revitalized Faculties of learning and research.

(31) Immediately after the announcement of this agreement TUNS will be invited to join the current capital campaign of Dalhousie with some strategic incremental fundraising goals.

(32) TUNS and Dalhousie agree to provide full information to each other in the transition period on all matters involved in the administration of the university including, but not limited to such items as financial data, physical plant data and personnel records in order to facilitate their individual and joint obligations for due diligence concerning outstanding or possible future liabilities of the amalgamated institution.

All information provided shall be held in confidence and shall not be disclosed without the consent of Dalhousie and TUNS.

(33) The Province will provide a letter to Dal/TUNS setting out the Province's intentions respecting the future use of the infirmary lands by Dal/TUNS.

(34) There will be a joint communications strategy among all the participants of this agreement.

(35) Dalhousie/TUNS will provide an annual report on the amalgamation process, including but not limited to, reduced administrative costs and the development of enhanced computer science and engineering programs.

(36) Best efforts and goodwill will be given by all parties to ensure the implementation of this agreement.

(37) It is understood and agreed that this agreement should be regarded as a statement of intent to amalgamate TUNS and Dalhousie substan-

tially in accordance with this Agreement. It is recognized by all parties that the amalgamation may require legislation.

(38) This Agreement may be amended with the mutual written consent of the parties.

(39) Time is of the essence.

SIGNED ON THE 11TH DAY OF JULY 1996

Her Majesty the Queen in right of the Province of Nova Scotia

---

HONOURABLE JOHN SAVAGE
Premier

HONOURABLE ROBERT S. HARRISON
Minister of Education and Culture

SIGNED ON THE 10TH DAY OF JULY 1996

For Technical University of Nova Scotia

For Dalhousie University

DR. EDWARD RHODES
President, Technical University of Nova Scotia

DR. TOM TRAVES
President, Dalhousie University

University of Toronto/Ontario Institute for Studies in Education Integration Agreement

11/18/94

Agreement dated this day of December 16, 1994
BETWEEN:

THE ONTARIO INSTITUTE FOR STUDIES IN EDUCATION

– and –

THE UNIVERSITY OF TORONTO

**A Proposal for Integrating OISE and FEUT
within the University of Toronto**

The representatives of the University of Toronto and OISE agree subject to ratification by Governing Council and the Board of Governors respectively that OISE be integrated into the University of Toronto on the following terms:

1. OISE and FEUT, including the ICS Laboratory School and UTS, will be integrated effective July 1, 1996 into a new professional Faculty of Education under the Governing Council of the University of Toronto. (UTS and ICS would be integrated on the basis of their currently planned full cost-recovery operations).

2. The name of this new Faculty will be the Ontario Institute for Studies in Education of the University of Toronto (hereinafter OISE/UT). Enjoying full status as a major organizational unit of the University,

OISE/UT will have all the rights and responsibilities pursuant to which individual University Faculties undertake to develop their academic initiatives and to allocate their budgetary and human resources.

3. The mandate of OISE found in Section 3 of the OISE Act will be continued in its current language. Both parties agree to petition the Government to enact legislation to achieve this result which will take effect on July 1, 1996.

4. The mission of OISE/UT will be as follows:

a) The Ontario Institute for Studies in Education of the University of Toronto (hereafter OISE/UT) will be established as a Faculty dedicated to national pre-eminence and international distinction in graduate studies, research and field development in education, and preservice and inservice teacher education, providing exemplary leadership within and outside the province, building on the reputations and accomplishments of the current OISE and FEUT, and consistent with OISE's current province-wide mandate and national and international reputation, and the University's current provincial, national and international role.

b) Each aspect of the mission should reinforce the others, and faculty members should be encouraged, so far as possible, to contribute to all aspects.

c) OISE/UT is committed to the study and pursuit of education in the context of broad social issues in which learning is necessarily a life-long activity. This vision emphasizes issues of equity and access, involves working partnerships with others in a collaborative effort to solve a wide array of problems, draws upon the insights of academic disciplines and a variety of professional perspectives, and aspires to the highest standards of scholarly and professional excellence.

d) In pursuit of its mission, OISE/UT may, subject to developing an academic and budget plan (see paragraphs 13 and 17 *infra*) undertake activities including: OCGS-approved graduate programs, internal centres for research in key areas, field centres, field services and community support, distance education to off-campus sites throughout the province, preservice and inservice teacher education, the work of UTS and ICS, relevant contractual partnerships with business and other agencies and francophone education in each of these areas.

5. All qualified faculty, staff and students will be afforded a reasonable opportunity to participate in preservice and inservice teaching, research and field development, and, subject to paragraph 7, graduate supervision and teaching.

6. OISE/UT will be headed by a Dean appointed in accordance with the University of Toronto's rules governing decanal appointments and reporting to the Provost. The Search for the Dean will be initiated immediately following the approval of this agreement by the respective parties. The appointment of the first Dean will be subject to approval by the OISE Board and will take effect on July 1, 1996. Prior to July 1, 1996 the Dean-designate may, on an *ex officio* basis, participate in planning for integration.

7. The Graduate Department of Education (which already includes faculty members from both OISE and FEUT) will continue within the School of Graduate Studies of the University of Toronto. As well, the existing criteria and processes governing membership in the faculty of the School of Graduate Studies will continue to apply to faculty members in the OISE/UT. Faculty members from OISE and FEUT who already have membership in the Graduate Department will maintain it. Those who do not and all new faculty appointments may be nominated for membership under the rules of general application.

8. The governing body of the OISE/UT will be a Faculty Council established in accordance with the University of Toronto Act and will have membership from faculty, staff, students and others. The structure and jurisdiction of the Faculty Council will be similar to the arrangements in place for other faculties at the University of Toronto.

9. OISE/UT will have an Advisory Board. The members of the Advisory Board will, except in the case of the initial Advisory Board, be appointed by the Governing Council on the advice of the President. The membership of the Advisory Board will include but not be limited to, representatives of: Ontario Teachers' Federations, Ontario School Trustee Organizations, Ontario Directors and Superintendents of Education, Presidents of CAAT's, Ministry of Education and Training, Ontario Association of Deans of Education, professional, business and labour communities, OISE alumni and the faculty, staff and students of OISE/UT. In addition the Dean will serve ex-officio on the Advisory Board. The appointments to the Advisory Board will respect the principles of diversity as stated by the Minister's memorandum on appointments to university governing boards. The Advisory Board's responsibilities will include: serving as trustees of OISE/UT's mission;

providing advice to OISE/UT on realization of its mandate and mission; receiving reports from the Monitor referred to in paragraph 16 *infra*; reporting on matters within its authority and responsibilities; and otherwise advancing and advocating the interests of OISE/UT. Any report from the Advisory Board will be placed on the agenda of Governing Council (or its appropriate board or committee) if requested to do so by a majority of the Advisory Board. Members of the initial Advisory Board will be agreed upon by the University and OISE. A majority of the members will have an initial term of office of three years and no member shall have an initial term of more than three years.

10. *Beginning in 1996–97*, the financial resources available for the OISE/UT will be the sum of a) and b):

a) the funding available to OISE in 1995–96 from all sources, including:

    i. actual tuition fee revenue

    ii. reserve for equipment replacement, qualified only by the terms under which the reserve was established

    iii. restricted funds, qualified only by the terms of the respective gifts, or bequests

    iv. all direct revenue from research grants and contracts. Effective July 1, 1996, such revenue will be governed by policies and regulations of the University.

    v. effective July 1, 1996, 55 per cent of all overhead revenue from research grants and contracts according to University policy

    vi. the new base funding established and adjusted pursuant to 11(b)

    vii. a proportional allocation from the University's share of the differential tuition fee remission program, calculated annually and used in accordance with the terms of the program, which terms shall also be the basis of the proportional allocation

    viii. an allocation equal to the amount that OISE received in 1995–96 from the designated grant program for research infrastructure. The amount will be indexed by the University to the value of the new base determined under 11(b). The indexation will be guaranteed by the University for the same period as the new base.

    ix. an allocation equal to all grants received for francophone education, to be used in accordance with the terms of such grants

x. the transitional fund established under 11(d) less any repayments required under 11(e), to be used in accordance with the terms of the fund

xi. the NewTransfer Grant established under 11(k), to be used in accordance with the terms of the grant

b) the funding available to FEUT, including specifically:

i. the Faculty of Education base budget, including UTS and ICS Laboratory School, as of May 1, 1996 *less* the average budget reductions – base and 'one-time-only deficit control' – already assigned under the *Long-range Guidelines for Planning and Budgeting* and *Budget Report* for 1994–95, *plus* any negotiated increases in compensation. The UTS and ICS Laboratory School budgets will be those established under current plans for cost-recovery operation

ii. revenue from faculty-specific ancillary fees which the new faculty may set under University of Toronto policy

iii. all tuition and ancillary fee revenue and restricted fund revenue from UTS, and the ICS Laboratory School

iv. all direct revenue from research grants and contracts in accordance with policies and regulations governing the expenditure of such funds

v. 55 per cent of all overhead revenue from research grants and contracts according to University policy

vi. restricted funds which are currently committed to the Faculty of Education, qualified only by the terms of the respective gifts, or bequests

c) The University of Toronto will guarantee and protect the component of the new faculty's budget previously attributable to FEUT, as established, for ten years from and including 1995–96 through 2004–2005 from any budget reductions – base or one-time-only – which would otherwise exceed the average reductions assigned to other colleges, faculties, and schools under the *Long-range Guidelines for Planning and Budgeting* or its comparable successor.

d) On July 1, 1996 the University of Toronto will take responsibility – managerial and financial, as well as expense and revenue – for the operation, maintenance, capital improvement, leasing and rental of all space which the new faculty occupies, leases, or books, pending the outcome of discussions with the Government about ownership of the building and land at 252 Bloor Street West.

e) The University's guarantee shall be conditional on OISE/UT's maintaining the current FEUT and OISE enrolments, expressed as an undifferentiated sum of BIUs. Within that sum, OISE/UT may set differential enrolment targets, provided that the tuition revenues generated by current FEUT enrolment, indexed to increases in the University's Tuition Fee Schedule, is maintained. If, without the prior approval of the Vice-President and Provost, OISE/UT fails to maintain its enrolment, any consequent loss of revenue to the University shall be a first claim against OISE/UT's budget in the following year.

f) With the exception of the reserve for equipment replacement, the University shall assume the assets and liabilities of OISE.

11. The University and OISE will obtain the agreement of the Ministry of Education and Training to guarantee its components of the following:

a) The initial base amount will be all amounts committed by the Ministry of Education and Training to OISE in 1995–96 pursuant to 11(h) from the basic grants envelope and the transition to new corridors envelope, plus an amount equal to one-half the current Transfer Grant of $1,571,200.

b) A new base amount will be established which shall be 91.4 percent of the initial base amount defined in 11(a).The new base thus determined shall be guaranteed and fully funded by the Ministry of Education and Training for ten years from and including 1996–97, and, using 1995–96 as the base year, will vary only in direct proportion to changes – increases or decreases – in overall funding for general operating purposes for the Ontario university system or with changes in the value of the BIU as described in Schedule B. The new and unique BIU OISE/UT graduate program weights and their effective value which will result as an arithmetic corollary of establishing the new base shall be guaranteed for the same ten year period regardless of any and all changes that may occur in other BIU weights for other programs throughout the university system.

c) In addition to the new base determined pursuant to 11(b), the Ministry of Education and Training will guarantee an amount equal to 91.4 per cent of the amount which OISE receives in 1994–95 for francophone studies. The guarantee will apply after OISE/UT has applied for and received funds from any other Government of Ontario program which provides funding for francophone education, and for which OISE/UT is eligible. The purpose of the guarantee will be to compensate for any shortfalls between 91.4 per cent of the amount which OISE receives in 1994–95 for francophone studies and the amounts actually received from other Government programs. Nothing in this provision shall preclude OISE/UT from applying for and receiving amounts greater than the amount currently provided for francophone studies.

The guarantee will be provided as follows:

  i) Amounts received by OISE/UT from other Government sources for francophone education will be deducted on a slip-year basis beginning in 1995–96.

  ii) In each following year, the University will report separately and annually to document and account for the expenditure of any amounts needed to meet the guarantee.

  iii) For each year in which a guarantee is provided, the Ministry and the University will agree jointly on the programs and services to be supported by funds provided for the guarantee.

  iv) Any funds provided for the guarantee which are not expended for purposes agreed on under 11.c.iii will be deducted from future guarantees

  v) Nothing in the provision of the guarantee should be construed as designating the University of Toronto as a bilingual institution.

d) In addition to the new base determined and guaranteed pursuant to 11(b), a transitional fund will be created by the Ministry of Education and Training, and made available to the University of Toronto for OISE/UT through a series of Special Purpose Grants over the same period for which the new base is guaranteed by 11(b). The amount of the transitional fund shall be capped at but not less than an amount equal to the product of one half of the difference between the new base 11(b) and the previous base 11(a) times the number of years (ten) of the period guaranteed by 11(b). The transitional fund thus created shall be available in any year and, if necessary, in differential amounts. The differential amounts will in no year exceed 20 per cent of the total fund. Subject to the conditions of 11(e) and 11(f), the University may expend an amount greater than 15 per cent using its own funds as a loan, the principal and interest of which will be repaid from the transitional fund in a subsequent year.The interest rate will be an amount equal to that which the University would have realized had it invested a sum equal to the loan for the same period of time, as indicated by the University's annual Budget Report which will be provided to the Ministry.

e)   i) No allocations from the transitional fund shall be made for purposes other than those specified in 11(f) without the prior approval of the Ministry of Education and Training.

   ii) The University shall submit two annual reports to the Ministry of Education and Training which account for the expenditure of the transitional fund:

   – To assure the Ministry that the planned allocations are for eligible purposes, the first report shall specify the expenses budgeted and planned to be made from the transitional fund. The first report shall be submitted for the Ministry's review and acceptance two months prior to the beginning of the University's budget year. The Ministry's acceptance shall not be unreasonably withheld, and shall be based on the report's consistency with the purposes specified in 11(f). The first report shall indicate how the expenses relate directly and demonstrably to the restructuring of programs, services, and facilities.

   – The second report shall contain actual expenditures as of year-end. Except for 1995–96, the second report shall be submitted two months after the close of the University's budget year.

   iii) Eligible expenses (as specified in the first report) which have not been actually expended (as indicated by the second report) may be carried-forward automatically for two budget years, provided that they are accounted for in a subsequent year-end report. Unexpended amounts may not be carried forward for

more than two budget years without the approval of the
Ministry of Education and Training.

iv) Any actual expenditures made for purposes other than those
specified shall be repayed by the University to the Ministry of
Education and Training. *Any such repayments may be made
by deductions from future grants to the University for OISE/
UT.* Any transitional funds remaining at the end of the guaranteed period shall be returned to the Ministry of Education
and Training.

f) Eligible expenditures from the transitional fund shall include:
  - Human resources: early retirement, severance payments, bridging, retraining, relocation, redeployment
  - Informations systems and automation: integration and reorganization of information and communications systems, library automation
  - Space and facilities: alterations, renovations, reorganization of space and furnishing, buy-outs of sub-leases
  - Miscellaneous: consulting and professional fees, alignment with University policies (other than compensation policies), other expenses related directly and demonstrably to the restructuring of programs, services, and facilities.
  Other expenditures may be allowed with the approval of the Ministry of Education and Training.

g) Beginning with 1995–96, nothing in this agreement will prejudice OISE's and, after 1995–96, the University of Toronto's access to any designated funding envelopes not covered by the guarantee in 11(b), existing or new, including increases or decreases that arise from changes in the sizes or distributive mechanisms of the envelopes. After 1995–96 the University's access to these funds *which are not covered by the guarantee in 11(b)* will be determined and calculated to include all factors, except institutional floors, previously attributable to OISE.

h) Notwithstanding 11(b), for 1995–96 OISE will receive from the Ministry of Education and Training:
  - the sum of all the grants that OISE would have otherwise received were this agreement not in place
  - an amount equal to one half of the current Transfer Grant of

$1,571,200 [This amount will be in addition to the New Transfer Grant specified in 11.(k).]
– an amount equal to the 1994–95 grant for francophone studies

These amounts will not be charged against the transitional fund established in 11(d).

i) During 1995–96 OISE and the University jointly and by agreement may, subject to the reporting and eligibility requirements of 11(e) and 11(f), have access to an advance commitment of the transitional fund for the purpose of facilitating the integration process prior to July 1, 1996. The University and OISE may initially use their own funds against this commitment and recover them plus the cost of debt service as a first claim against the total transitional fund stated in 11(d). The cost of debt service shall be determined as specified in 11(d). The first report required by 11(e) may be submitted at anytime during 1995–96 and will be responded to by the Ministry within one month of its receipt.

j) The Ministry of Education and Training's guarantee, pursuant to 11(b), shall be conditional on the University's maintaining an un-differentiated sum of eligible graduate and undergraduate BIUs not less than the 1995–96 level of eligible OISE enrolments, expressed as BIUs, as adjusted pursuant to 11(b), within the range of institutional discretion allowed by the current Operating Grant Distribution Manual. Nothing in this condition shall exempt the University of Toronto from any system-wide changes which the Ministry of Education and Training may mandate for undergraduate teacher education.

k) The New Transfer Grant
The Ministry of Education and Training will guarantee the New Transfer Grant for expenditure by OISE and subsequently OISE/UT for the years 1995–96 through 2004–2005. The amount of the New Transfer Grant in 1995–96 will be $785,000. Over the subsequent nine years, the New Transfer Grant will be reduced in a linear fashion until it reaches $78,500 in 2004–2005 at which time the grant will expire and may be reviewed and renewed. The University will report separately and annually to the Ministry of Education and Training about the expenditure of the New Transfer Grant. The Ministry and the University will consult and agree annually on the

research objectives for expenditure of the New Transfer Grant on an annual basis except in 1995–96 where the consultation and agreement will be between the Ministry of Education and Training and OISE.

12. Nothing in this agreement will prejudice OISE's or subsequently the University of Toronto's access to funding for pay equity, municipal taxes, and facilities renewal. Such access will be on the basis of standard formulas where applicable or other terms which are the same as those applied to other universities system-wide.In calculating facilities renewal allocations after 1995–96, the Ministry of Education and Training will include in the University's allocation all of the factors, except an institutional floor, previously attributable to OISE.

13. The budget of OISE/UT including the transitional fund in 11(d) and the New Transfer Grant in 11(k) must meet all the direct costs of the Faculty, its programs, and its students. It must also provide for eliminating any deficit at OISE at June 30, 1996. The OISE/UT budget must also meet the transitional costs of integration. As in the case of all faculties at the University of Toronto, OISE/UT will be responsible for keeping its expenditures within the established budget. Following existing policy and practice, any overspending, as well as any repayments required under 11(e), will become a first charge on the Faculty's next year's budget and any underspending may be carried forward by the Faculty for spending in the subsequent year. The budget for OISE/UT must be reviewed and recommended for approval by the Planning and Budget Committee and approved by the Academic Board of the Governing Council on the advice of the Provost. The University of Toronto on behalf of FEUT agrees to make best efforts to ensure that there will be no deficit as of May 1, 1996.

14. The budget of the OISE/UT will draw upon the pooled resources stated in 10.(a) and 10.(b). While the contributions to the base and transitional amounts of the pooled resources coming from FEUT and OISE are different, no implications shall be drawn from this difference with respect to where or how the efficiencies from integration will be identified and achieved. The budget for OISE/UT will be drawn up to achieve the fullest possible realization of the mandate and mission of OISE/UT consistent with the total available resources.

15. OISE/UT faculty will qualify as applicants for the University of Toronto's annual Connaught Fund programs. At present the Connaught Fund distributes approximately $3.1 million annually in income from its endowment fund for research, fellowships and

scholarships. In addition, FEUT and OISE scholarship and bursary funds will continue to be applied for the sole benefit of OISE/UT students.

16. A Monitor will be appointed to report annually during the ten year period from 1995–96 to 2005–2006 on the University's compliance with the financial provisions of this proposal for integration. The Monitor will report to the Advisory Board, Faculty Council, the Dean, the Governing Council (through the President), and the Ministry of Education and Training. The Monitor must be mutually agreed upon by the Governing Council, and the Advisory Board and, failing agreement, will be appointed by the President of the Canadian Institute of Chartered Accountants. For the term of the funding guarantees made by the Ministry of Education and Training under 11, the Ministry will provide to the University for the use of the Monitor a report specifying the payments made and the calculations on which they were based. The Ministry's report shall be provided within 90 days of the end of the Government's fiscal year. Any costs associated with the appointment of the Monitor will not be charged against the transitional fund.

17. **Academic Integration**
Immediately after ratification of this agreement, a Task Force, co-chaired by the Dean of FEUT and the Director of OISE, or their designates, and which includes equal representation from OISE and FEUT will be established: (a) to review the academic programs, research and field development activities of OISE and FEUT with a view toward establishing closer linkages between pre-service, in-service and graduate programs, research and field development; (b) to explore possible linkages between OISE and other Departments and Faculties of the University; and (c) to determine an appropriate departmental structure for OISE/UT; (d) to make recommendations on the appropriate constitution for the Faculty Council for OISE/UT. This Task Force may also consider revision of programs including strengthening existing programs, opening new programs involving faculty, staff and students from both institutions and reducing or closing current programs. In undertaking its work the Task Force will be guided by the OISE/UT mission as stated in paragraph 4 *supra*. In discharging its responsibilities, the Task Force will consult widely throughout OISE, FEUT and the University. These consultations will include, but will not be limited to, OISE and FEUT faculty, qualified staff and students.

The report of the Task Force will be completed within six months of its establishment, and when approved by the Provost, the report will constitute a complete academic and budget plan for OISE/UT. As in the case of all other academic plans for Faculties, the academic and budget plan will include appropriate provisions and indicators for annual accountability and assessment of progress.

18. **Administrative Integration**
Immediately after ratification of this agreement a Task Force consisting of two management representatives from the University of Toronto/FEUT, and two management representatives from OISE will be established to develop a plan and an implementation schedule for integrating administrative support services as appropriate. In discharging its responsibilities the Task Force will consult widely throughout OISE, FEUT and the University. These consultations will include, but not be limited to, a representative designated by each of the bargaining units and associations representing faculty and staff of OISE and FEUT. The report of the Task Force will be completed within six months of its establishment. The financial implications of this report will be reflected in the budget approved pursuant to paragraph 13 supra and in the academic and budget plan described in paragraph 16 supra.

19. Severance packages (which may be enhanced beyond those contained in existing OISE collective agreements and policies and the University of Toronto's policies for administrative staff in order to facilitate and accelerate integration) will be available to non-academic staff whose positions are eliminated as a direct result of the merger in cases where reasonable comparable employment and compensation is not offered elsewhere in OISE/UT or the University of Toronto. The acceptance of a severance package will be conditional upon waiving internal status and recall rights under any applicable collective agreement. The cost of such severance packages will be charged against the transitional fund described in paragraph. 11(d) *supra*. Prior to July 1, 1996, no employee of FEUT or OISE will be provided a severance payment greater than that provided by policy or by the applicable collective agreement without prior consultation between OISE and FEUT.

20. In the event that any collective agreements and bargaining rights are terminated by agreement or by law after July 1, 1996, then:

   a) persons previously represented by a trade union or association will receive the benefits of Schedule 'A' attached hereto.

b) Except for positions in the University of Toronto which must be filled in accordance with the provisions of a collective agreement, any non-academic staff of OISE and FEUT who are not placed in OISE/UT will be considered for other positions within the University of Toronto based on the following factors:

   i) length of service
   ii) skill, competence, efficiency and ability to train for or adapt to changed duties

Where the qualifications in factor (ii) are relatively equal between two or more staff, length of service shall take precedence.

21. If the OISE Faculty Association's collective agreement and bargaining rights are terminated by agreement or by operation of law at any time prior to June 30, 1997, the University of Toronto will, subject to its retirement policy, grant tenure at the rank held at OISE at the University of Toronto to faculty members holding tenured appointments at OISE as of June 30, 1996 and all faculty members will be subject to the terms and conditions of the Memorandum of Agreement between the University of Toronto and the University of Toronto Faculty Association. Faculty in the tenure stream on June 30, 1996 and faculty at present in the tenure stream whose appointments will lead to tenure consideration between the date of ratification and June 30, 1996, will be considered for tenured appointments pursuant to OISE's policy on tenure and the University of Toronto will grant tenure and rank to these individuals on the same basis as individuals holding tenure prior to July 1, 1996 so long as the OISE tenure decisions are taken in good faith and in accordance with the current policies and standards applicable at OISE. No accelerated tenure decisions shall be taken for individuals in the tenure stream prior to July 1, 1996 without the prior agreement of the Provost of the University of Toronto. Upon creation of OISE/UT, or as soon thereafter as possible, appointments, tenure and promotions will be made in accordance with the University's policies and procedures for academic appointments and promotions. Notwithstanding the above, the employment contracts of the nine current OISE faculty who are on extended employment beyond the normal age of retirement and whose contracts do not extend beyond June 30, 1997 will be honoured.

22. Where employees are represented by unions, and where collective

agreements applicable to such employees and the unions' bargaining rights are terminated by agreement or by operation of law at any time prior to June 30, 1997, the University of Toronto policies and procedures will apply and OISE employees will be credited with University of Toronto service equivalent to their OISE service as of July 1, 1996 for purposes of all University of Toronto policies, agreements and benefits (except pensions).

23. OISE and the University of Toronto agree, subject to the restrictions of the Freedom of Information Act, to make full disclosure to each other of all relevant information about employees.

24. In light of the University's agreement to assume the assets and liabilities of OISE as a result of integration, OISE agrees to make full disclosure to the University of any information requested including but not limited to the following: liabilities, claims, potential claims under any statute or contract, indebtedness, properties and encumbrances, contracts, leases, inventories, receivables and payables, equipment, ancillaries, insurance and financial statements and forecasts. The University of Toronto agrees to provide OISE with relevant information related to FEUT at their request.

25. Both OISE and the University of Toronto agree that between the date of reaching this agreement and June 30, 1996, they will each act in a manner fair to the other's interests and will consult in advance with the other prior to taking any decisions that could have a significant adverse effect on the other or result in a material change to OISE or FEUT. With the exception of paragraph 26 infra OISE will not enter significant new agreements that will bind OISE/UT without the prior consent of the University.

26. Between the date of this agreement and July 1, 1996 both OISE and FEUT agree that in pursuit of their shared interest in not creating additional redundancies they will not hire new regular/continuing non-faculty employees without prior consultation of the Director with the Dean or vice-versa. OISE and FEUT further agree that between the date of this agreement and July 1, 1996, not to appoint any new faculty members without the prior consent of the other except in the case of positions already advertised publicly as of the date of this agreement.

27. It is agreed that a Facilitator will be appointed to assist the parties in the resolution of disputes which may arise between the date of ratification and June 30, 1996. It is understood that the fees of the Facilitator

will be borne by the transitional fund. It is further agreed that in the event OISE and the University are unable to agree on the Facilitator, the Facilitator will be appointed by Dr. John O. Stubbs after consultation.

28. Integration of OISE within the University of Toronto and the establishment of OISE/UT shall take effect on July 1, 1996 and until such time OISE and its Board of Governors shall continue in all respects.

29. This agreement is subject to:

a) the approval by the Governing Council of the University of Toronto and the Board of Governors of OISE. OISE and the University agree to place this agreement before their respective governing bodies as soon as practicable for approval;

b) the approval of the Minister of Education and Training confirming the Ministry's agreement to make the commitments required by this agreement. The Minister, by approving this agreement, agrees to use his best efforts to have the Management Board Secretariat on behalf of Her Majesty the Queen in Right of Ontario agree to the conveyance referred to in (c) below;

c) the agreement of the Board of Governors of OISE and the Management Board Secretariat representing Her Majesty the Queen in Right of Ontario:

i) to convey to the Governing Council of the University of Toronto all their respective right, title, and interest, free of encumberances, in all the buildings and lands known as 252 Bloor Street West and registered as Plan No. R-4882 recorded in the Land Registry Office for the Land Titles Division of Metropolitan Toronto, and

ii) that nothing in this agreement will prejudice OISE's and subsequently the University of Toronto's access to funding to which OISE currently has access for lease payments, lease maintenance (including escalation), and currency fluctuation.

Dated at Toronto this ____ day of November, 1994.

for the University of Toronto   for the Ontario Institute for
                                       Studies in Education

The Minister of Education and Training for the Province of Ontario hereby agrees to make the commitments required of the Ministry under this agreement

---

Schedule 'A'

For all non-union employees and, in the event any collective agreement and bargaining rights are terminated by agreement or by law at any time prior to June 30, 1997, the following shall apply:

A) The salary of OISE staff shall be red circled provided the employee remains in a comparable position at OISE/UT or elsewhere in the University as he/she occupied at OISE. Salary shall be red circled until the University of Toronto salary range equals or exceeds the red circled salary.

B) Salaries of OISE faculty and librarians shall not be reduced at the date of merger or when the collective agreement ceases to apply, whichever is later.

C) Unused credit towards study leave earned by faculty members while at OISE shall be applied towards their research leave application eligibility. Such leave to be granted in accordance with the University of Toronto policy.

D) The University of Toronto agrees that in the event of any change to the pension plan provisions affecting future benefits, it will give proper notice to employees in accordance with the Pension Benefits Act of Ontario. Further, prior to implementation, the University and its actuaries will consult with and inform affected employee groups. The University of Toronto actuaries will meet with OISE actuaries upon request to discuss pension matters.

E) Employees covered by Schedule 'A' shall have access to University grievance procedures in the event of alleged non-compliance with parts A, B, and C of Schedule 'A.'

Bibliography

Albo, Wayne P., and A. Randal Henderson. 1987. *Mergers and Acquisitions of Privately-held Businesses*. Canadian Institute of Chartered Accountants.

Association of Commonwealth Universities. 2000. *VC-NET*, no. 7 (June).

Atkin, J. Myron. 1983. 'American Graduate Schools of Education: A View from Abroad.' *Oxford Review of Education* 9, no. 1.

Aucoin, Peter, and Herman Bakvis. 1993. 'Consolidating Cabinet Portfolios: Australian Lessons for Canada.' *Canadian Public Administration* 36, no. 3.

Awender, M.A., and A.E. Harte. 'Teacher Education: What's Wrong with Current Practice.' 1986. *Education Canada*, (Spring).

Bacharach, S.B., and E.J. Lawler. 1981. *Bargaining*. San Francisco: Jossey-Bass.

– 1982. *Power and Politics in Organizations*. San Francisco: Jossey-Bass.

Baker, Max. 'Nova Scotia Technical College 1907–1966: A History of the Tech System.' Halifax: Dalhousie University Archives.

Bakvis, Herman. 1995. 'On "Silos and Stovepipes": The Case of the Department of Human Resources Development.' Ottawa: Canadian Centre for Management Development.

Beer, M. 1980. *Organization Change and Development: A System View*. Santa Monica, CA: Goodyear.

Ben-David, Joseph. 1972. *American Higher Education*. New York: McGraw-Hill.

– 1977. *Centers of Learning*. New York: McGraw-Hill.

Bengtsson, Ann M. 1992. *Managing Mergers and Acquisitions*. Aldershot: Gower.

Berne, R. 1989. 'Accounting for Public Programs.' In *Handbook of Public Administration*, ed. by J.L. Perry. San Francisco: Jossey-Bass.

Birnbaum, Robert. 1983. *Maintaining Diversity in Higher Education*. San Francisco: Jossey-Bass.

Blau, Peter M. 1994. *The Organization of Academic Work*. 2nd ed. New Brunswick, NJ: Transactions.

Boberg, Alice. 1979. 'Mergers in Higher Education: A Comparative Analysis.' Center for the Study of Higher Education, University of Michigan.

Bosworth, Stuart R. 1992. 'Adaptation and Survival in Challenging Conditions: The International Context.' *Journal of Tertiary Educational Administration* 14, no. 2.

Bradley, Denise. 1993. 'Illusion or Reality? Diversity in the Unified National System.' *Journal of Tertiary Educational Administration* 15, no. 2.

Breidenbach, Susan. 2000. 'Managing Mergers.' *Network World* 17, no. 23.

Brinkman, Paul T. (1987) 'Effective Institutional Comparisons.' *New Directions for Institutional Research* 53.

Brinkman, Paul, and Larry Leslie. 1986. 'Economics of Scale in Higher Education: Sixty Years of Research.' *Review of Higher Education* 10, no. 1.

Brinkman, Paul T., and Deborah J. Teeter. 1987. 'Methods for Selecting Comparison Groups.' *New Directions for Institutional Research* 53.

Bryson, John. 1988. *Strategic Planning for Public and Non-Profit Organizations*. San Francisco: Jossey-Bass.

Buono, Anthony, and James Bowditch. 1989. *The Human Side of Mergers and Acquisitions*. San Francisco: Jossey-Bass.

Burkhardt, John. 1994. 'Getting to Yes on a Merger.' *Planning for Higher Education* 22 (Spring).

Cameron, David. 1991. *More Than an Academic Question: Universities, Government and Public Policy in Canada*. Halifax: Institute for Research on Public Policy.

Cameron, Jill, and Lee Cameron. 1959. 'Nova Scotia "Tech": The First 50 Years.' Halifax: Dalhousie University Archives.

Carruthers, James S. 1906. 'Letter to the Editor.' *Halifax Herald*, 4 August.

Chambers, Gail. 1983. 'The Dilemma of College Merger.' *AGB Reports*, no. (November/December).

– 1984. 'Approaching College Merger: A Manual with Case Documents.' ERIC.

– 1986. 'Merger between Private Colleges: An Empirical Analysis.' Doctoral dissertation, University of Rochester.

Christie, Brian D. 1997. 'Higher Education in Nova Scotia: Where Past Is More Than Prologue.' In *Higher Education in Canada: Different Systems, Different Perspectives*, ed. Glen A. Jones. New York: Garland.

Clark, Burton. 1998. *Creating Entrepreneurial Universities*. Oxford: Pergamon.

Cleaver, Grace S. 1981. 'Analysis to Determine a Ranking in Similarity for Institutions in Higher Education.' Lawrence: University of Kansas, Press.

Cochkanoff, Orest. 1998. 'A Possible Model for the DalTech College.' Unpublished memo, 9 January.

Copp, W.P. 1945. Letter to A.E. Kerr, president of Dalhousie, 21 December. Dalhousie University Archives, Halifax.

Council of Ontario Universities Committee on Accountability, Performance Indicators and Outcomes Assessment. 1993. 'Report to the Minister's Task Force on University Accountability.' Toronto.

Dalhousie University. 1995. 'Response to the Report of the Nova Scotia Council on Higher Education's Computer Science Review Committee.' Halifax.

Dalhousie University DalTech Academic Council. 1997–8. *Minutes.*

Dalhousie University Senate Steering Committee. 1998. *Minutes.*

Dalhousie University/Technical University of Nova Scotia. 1996–7. *Amalgamation Bulletin.*

Dal-Tech Negotiating Committee. 1974. 'Proposed Administrative Structure for the Faculty of Engineering.' Halifax: Dalhousie University Archives.

– 1974. 'Report to the Board of Governors, Dalhousie University, the Board of Governors, Nova Scotia Technical College and the Nova Scotia University Grants Committee.' Halifax: Dalhousie University Archives.

Dawkins, John. 1987. 'Higher Education: A Policy Discussion Paper.' Canberra: Australian Government Publishing Service.

– 1988. 'Higher Education: A Policy Statement.' Canberra: Australian Government Publishing Service.

de Jong, H.W. 1976. 'Theory and Evidence Concerning Mergers: An International Comparison.' In *Markets, Corporate Behaviour and the State*, ed. A.P. Jacquemin and H.W. de Jong. The Hague: Nijhoff.

Deetman, Wim. 1983. *Scale-enlargement, task-reallocation and concentration.* Gravenhage: SDU.

Denis, Jean-Louis, Lise Lamothe, and Ann Langley. 1999. 'The Struggle to Implement Teaching-Hospital Mergers.' *Canadian Public Administration* 42, no. 3.

Directors' Liability in Canada. 1998. Toronto: Specialty Technical Publishers.

Fenton, Gordon, et al. 1999. 'Dalhousie-TUNS Merger Impact Report.' Halifax: Dalhousie University Faculty of Engineering.

Fielden, John. 1991. 'Resource Implications of Mergers: Are there any economies?' *Higher Education Quarterly* 45, no. 2.

Fielden, John, and Lucy Markham. 1997. 'Learning Lessons from Mergers in Higher Education.' Commonwealth Higher Education Management Service.

Fleming, W.G. 1972. *Education: Ontario's Preoccupation.* Toronto: University of Toronto Press.

Fogarty, W.P. 1975. 'Dal-Tech Merger Serious Error' (letter). *Chronicle-Herald/Mail-Star*, 20 January.

'From the Mind of Abhi.' 1996. *TUNS News*, September.

Fullan, Michael. 1998. 'Leadership for Change in Faculties of Education.' In

Agents, Provocateurs: Reform-Minded Leaders for Schools of Education, ed.
D. Thiessen and K.R. Howey. Washington, D.C.: American Association of
Colleges of Teacher Education.
– 28 September 1998.
Garner, C. William. 1991. *Accounting and Budgeting in Public and Nonprofit
Organizations*. San Francisco: Jossey-Bass.
Geiger, Roger. 1986. *Private Sectors in Higher Education*. Ann Arbor: Univer-
sity of Michigan.
Goedegebuure, Leo. 1992. *Mergers in Higher Education: A Comparative
Perspective*. Utrecht: Uitgeverij LEMMA BV.
Goedegebuure, Leo, and Vos, Arjan. 1998. 'Mergers and the Restructuring of
Higher Vocational Education in the Netherland.' In *Institutional Amalgama-
tions in Higher Education*, ed. G. Harman and V.L. Meck. Armidale: Univer-
sity of New England Press.
Goodings, Joey. 1999. 'Mergers Failing Without HR factor.' *Canadian HR
Reporter*, 5 April.
Guthrie, H. Donald. 1983. 'Directors of Non-Profit Corporations.' Toronto:
Cassels, Brock and Blackwell.
Guttman, M.A. 1988. 'The Case of the Transfer of the Ontario Institute for
Studies in Education to the University of Toronto.' In *Institutional Amalga-
mations in Higher Education*, ed. Grant Harman and Lynn Meek. University
of New England Press.
'Halifax City Council Opposes Proposed TUNS Move.' 1999. *Chronicle-
Herald/Mail-Star*, December.
Harman, Grant. 1989. 'The Dawkins Reconstruction of Australian Higher
Education.' *Higher Education* 2, no. 2.
– 1991. 'Institutional Amalgamations and Abolition of the Binary System in
Australia under John Dawkins.' *Higher Education Quarterly* 45, no. 2.
Harman, Grant, and V. Lynn Meek. *Institutional Amalgamations in Higher
Education*. University of New England Press, 1988.
Harris, R.S. 1976. *A History of Higher Education in Canada 1663–1960*. To-
ronto: University of Toronto Press.
Henry, Miriam. 1994. *The Restructuring of Higher Education in Australia*. Paris:
International Institute for Educational Planning.
Hildyard, Angela. 1995. 'The Path to Merger.' *OISE News*, January/February.
'How to Make Mergers Work.' 1999. *The Economist*, 9 January.
Hughes, K. Scott, and Daryl Conner. 1989. *Managing Change in Higher Educa-
tion: Preparing for the 21st Century*. Washington: College and University
Personnel Association.
Huisman, Jeroen. 1998. 'Differentiation and Diversity in Higher Education.' *In*

Higher Education: Handbook of Theory and Research, ed. John C. Smart. New York: Agathon.

Huisman, Jeroen, and Christopher Morphew. 1998. 'Centralization and Diversity: Evaluating the Effects of Government Policies in the U.S.A. and Dutch Higher Education.' *Higher Education Policy* 11, no. 1.

Hult, Karen. 1987. *Agency Merger and Bureaucratic Redesign*. Pittsburgh: University of Pittsburgh Press, 1987.

Irvin, George. 1978. *Modern Cost-Benefit Methods*. London: Macmillan, 1978.

Jonas, Stepen et al. 1996. *Campus Financial Systems for the Future*. Washington: NACUBO.

Jones, Glen A. 1996. 'Diversity within a Decentralized Higher Education System: The Case of Canada.' In *The Mockers and the Mocked: Comparative Perspectives on Differentiation, Convergence and Diversity in Higher Education*, ed. V.L. Meek. et al. Oxford: Pergamon/IAU.

– ed. 1997. *Higher Education in Canada: Different Systems, Different Perspectives*. New York: Garland.

Judge, Harry. 1982. 'American Graduate Schools of Education: A View from Abroad.' New York: Ford Foundation.

Kerr, A.E. 27 April 1946. Dalhousie University Archives.

Lang, Daniel. 1975. 'The Consortium in Higher Education.' *Journal of Educational Administration* 13, no. 2.

–1999. 'Responsibility Centre Budgeting and Responsibility Centre Management in Theory and Practice.' *Higher Education Management* 11, no. 3.

Lang, Daniel, with A.L. Darling, M.D. England, R. Lopers-Sweetman. 1989. 'Autonomy and Control: A University Funding Formula as an Instrument of Public Policy.' *Higher Education* 18, no. 5.

Lang, Daniel, and Roseanne Lopers-Sweetman. 1991. 'The Role of Statements of Institutional Purpose.' *Research in Higher Education* 32, no. 6.

Lawler, Edward, and Susan Mohrman. 1996. 'Organizing for Effectiveness: Lessons from Business.' In *Resource Allocation in Higher Education*, ed. William Massy. Ann Arbor: University of Michigan.

Layard, Richard. 1974. 'The Cost-Effectiveness of the New Media in Higher Education.' In *Efficiency in Universities: The La Paz Papers*, ed. Keith Lumsden. Amsterdam: Elsevier.

Learned, William S., and Kennth C.M. Sills. 1922. *Education in the Maritime Provinces of Canada*. New York: Carnegie Foundation for the Advancement of Teaching.

Lebow, R.N. 1996. *The Art of Bargaining*. Baltimore: Johns Hopkins University Press.

Lee, John. 1987. 'The Equity of Higher Education Subsidies.' College Park: University of Maryland National Center for Postsecondary Governance and Finance.

Levin, Malcolm. 1995. 'Thirty Years of OISE 1965–95.' *OISE News*, October.

Lloyd, P., M. Morgan, and R. Williams. 1993. 'Amalgamations of Universities: Are There Economies of Scale or Scope?' *Applied Economics* 25.

Lumsden, Keith, ed. 1974. *Efficiency in Universities: The La Paz Papers*. Amsterdam: Elsevier.

Lysons, Art. 1993. 'The Typology of Organizational Effectiveness in Australian Higher Education.' *Research in Higher Education* 34, no. 4.

MacAskill, C. 13 April 1976. Dalhousie University Archives.

MacTaggart, Terrence. 1996. *Restructuring Higher Education*. San Francisco: Jossey-Bass.

Mahony, David. 1995. 'Academics in an Era of Structural Change: An Australian Experience.' *Higher Education Research and Development* 14, no. 1.

Mahony, David. 1990. 'The Demise of the University in a Nation of Universities: Effects of Current Changes in Higher Education in Australia.' *Higher Education* 19.

March, James. 1994. *A Primer on Decision Making*. New York: Free Press.

Marginson, Simon. 1997. *Markets in Education*. St Leonards, NSW: Allen & Unwin.

Marshall, Neil 1990. 'End of an Era: The Collapse of the "Buffer" Approach to the Governance of Australian Tertiary Education.' *Higher Education* 19.

Martin, James, and James E. Samels. 1994. *Merging Colleges for Mutual Growth*. Baltimore: Johns Hopkins University Press.

Massy, William. 1996. 'Productivity Issues in Higher Education.' In *Resource Allocation in Higher Education*, ed. William Massy. Ann Arbor: University of Michigan.

Massy, William, and David Hopkins. 1996. 'Lessons from Health Care.' In *Resource Allocation in Higher Education*, ed. William Massy. Ann Arbor: University of Michigan.

Mayer, Andre. 1994. 'Strategic Planning for Growth Mergers.' In *Merging Colleges for Mutual Growth*, ed. J. Martin and J. Samels. Baltimore: Johns Hopkins University Press.

McCann, Joseph, and Roderick Gilkey. 1988. *Joining Forces: Creating and Managing Successful Mergers and Acquisitions*. Englewood Cliffs, NJ: Prentice Hall.

McLaughlin, R.R. 1966. 'A Study of Engineering Education in the Province of Nova Scotia.' Halifax.

McLaughlin, Thomas A. 1996. 'Seven Steps to a Successful Nonprofit Merger.' Washington: National Center for Nonprofit Boards.

Meek, Lynn. 'Notes on Higher Educational Mergers in the United Kingdom.' In *Institutional Amalgamations in Higher Education*, ed. Grant Harman and Lynn Meek. University of New England Press, 1988.

Messersmith, J.C. 1965. 'Consortia and Related Inter-Institutional Arrangements.' In *Emerging Patterns in American Higher Education*, ed. W. Wilson. Washington: American Council on Education.

'Meeting of Minds.' 1994. *The Toronto Star*, 7 February.

'Memorandum re. Technical Education for R.M. MacGregor. 1916. Dalhousie University Archives, Halifax.

'Mergers and Acquisitions in Private Higher Education – Threat or Promise? A Report on a National Conference at Wingspread.' 1987. Paper presented at the the Milliken Conference, Wingspread, 19, June.

Middaugh, Michael. 1998–9. 'How Much Do Faculty Really Teach?' *Planning for Higher Education* 27, no. 2.

Millett, John D. 1976. *Mergers in Higher Education: An Analysis of Ten Case Studies*. American Council on Higher Education.

Mims, Sue, and Donald LeLong. 1987. 'The Michigan Peer Institutions Information Study.' *New Directions for Institutional Research* 53.

Mintzberg, Henry. 1998. *Strategy Safari*. New York: Free Press.

Morris, V.C. 1985. 'The Education Professor and the President's People.' *Journal of Educational Thought* 19, no. 1.

NACUBO with Coopers & Lybrand and Barbara Shafer & Associates. 1993. 'Benchmark '92: Final Report.'

National Commission on the Cost of Higher Education. 1998. *Straight Talk about College Costs and Prices*. Washington, Oryx.

Nova Scotia. 1996. *Assembly Debates*.

– 1992. 'Framework for Rationalization of the Nova Scotia Universities: Discussion Paper.' Halifax.

Nova Scotia Council on Higher Education. 1994. 'Draft Report of the Review Committee on Computer Science.' Halifax.

– 1995. 'Shared Responsibilities in Higher Education.' Halifax.

Nova Scotia Department of Education and Culture. 1996. 'Plan for University Renewal Released (news release).' Halifax.

Nova Scotia Technical College Board of Governors. 1997–8, 1974. *Minutes*. Halifax: Dalhousie University Archives.

Nova Scotia Technical College Faculty of Engineering Review Committee. 'Engineering Education in Nova Scotia.' Halifax: Dalhousie University Archives, 1972.

Nova Scotia Technical College Senate. 1996. *Minutes*. Halifax: Dalhousie University Archives.

'NS Higher Education Panel Draws Fire.' 1994. *Globe and Mail*, 11 July.

O'Neill, Joseph P., and Samuel Barnett. 1980. *Colleges and Corporate Change: Merger, Bankruptcy and Closure*. Princeton, NJ: Conference-University Press.

Ontario Institute for Studies in Education. Annual Reports.

– *News & Notes*.

Ontario Institute for Studies in Education Board of Governors. 1995–6. *Minutes*.

Ontario Institute for Studies in Education Strategic Planning Committee. 1994. 'Toward Better Education and Financial Stability.' Toronto.

Ontario Legislative Assembly. 1965. *Official Debates*.

Ontario Legislature. 1967–8, 1971. *Debates and Proceedings*.

Ontario Ministry of Agriculture, Food and Rural Affairs and the University of Guelph. 1996. Memorandum of Agreement.

Patterson, Glenys. 1999. 'Findings on Economies of Scale in Higher Education: Implications for Strategies of Merger and Alliance.' Paper presented at the EAIR 21st Annual Forum, Lund University, Sweden.

Pfeffer, Jeffrey. 1987. 'A Resource Dependence Perspective on Intercorporate Relations.' In *Intercorporate Relations: The Structural Analysis of Business*, ed. M.S. Mizruchi and M. Schwartz. New York: Cambridge University Press, 1987.

Phillips, W.J. 1973. 'Dal-Tech Union Must Be Stopped.' *Halifax Mail-Star*, 16 November.

Pitman, Walter. 1994. 'OISE Still Plays a Vital Role on Frontiers of Education.' *Toronto Star*, 29 March.

'Power to the Students.' 1995. *Chronicle-Herald/Mail-Star*, 22 February.

Provostial Commission on the Design of an Integrated Faculty of Education. 1994. 'Report.' Toronto: University of Toronto.

Pruitt, Dean. 1981. *Negotiation Behavior*. New York: Academic Press.

Quinn, J.B., and J. Voyer. 1996. 'Logical Incrementalism: Managing Strategy Formation.' In *The Strategy Process*, ed. H. Mintzberg and J.B. Quinn. Englewood Cliffs, NJ: Prentice Hall.

Raffel, Jeffrey, and Robert Shishko. 1969. *Systematic Analysis of University Libraries*. Cambridge, MA: MIT Press.

Raiffa, Howard. 1982. *The Art and Science of Negotiation*.

Ramsey, G.A. 1989. 'Report of the Task Force on Amalgamations in Higher Education.' Canberra: Australian Government Publishing Service.

Rawson, Thomas R., Donald P. Hoyt, and Deborah J. Teeter. 1983. 'Identifying "Comparable" Institutions.' *Research in Higher Education* 18, no. 3.

Rekila, Eila. 1995. 'Contracts as a Management Instrument.' *Tertiary Education and Management* 1, no. 1.

Research Associates of Washington. 1989. *State Profiles: Financing Public Higher Education 1978 to 1989*. 12th ed.

Rhodes, Edward. 1996. 'TUNS Bulletin on Rationalization.' Halifax: Technical University of Nova Scotia.

Rowley, Gillian. 1997. 'Mergers and Acquisitions in Higher Education: A Strategic Analysis.' *Higher Education Quarterly* 51, no. 3.

Schumacher, C. 1983. 'The Problem of Scale in Higher Education.' In *Economies of Scale in Higher Education*, ed. S. Goodlad. Guildford, UK: Society for Research in Higher Education.

Sears, K. 1983. 'Economies of Scale in Higher Education.' In *Economies of Scale in Higher Education*, ed. S. Goodlad. Guildford, UK: Society for Research in Higher Education.

Segil, Larraine. 2000. 'More than Mergers.' *Industry Week* 249, no. 11 (12 June).

Sexton, Frederick H. 1929. 'Data re. Nova Scotia Technical College.' Halifax: Dalhousie University Archives.

Simpson, William, and William Sperber. 1998. 'Salary Comparisons: New Methods for Correcting Old Fallacies.' *Research in Higher Education* 28, no. 1.

Skodvin, Ole-Jacob. 1999. 'Mergers in Higher Education – Success or Failure.' *Tertiary Education and Management* 5.

Slaughter, Sheila, and Larry Leslie. 1997. *Academic Capitalism*. Baltimore: Johns Hopkins University Press.

'A Smart Bomb.' 1994. *Daily News*, 13 July.

Steiner, P.O. 1975. *Mergers: Motives, Effects, Policies*. Ann Arbor: University of Michigan Press.

Stewart, B. 1961. 'Cooperation by Independent Colleges: The Associated Colleges of the Midwest.' *Liberal Education* 47, no. 3.

Task Force on University Accountability. 1993. 'University Accountability: A Strengthened Framework.' Toronto: Ontario Ministry of Education and Training.

Taylor, Michael. 1994. *Amalgamation at the University of Sydney, Australia: The Institutional Viewpoint*. Paris: International Institute for Educational Planning.

Technical University of Nova Scotia Senate. 1996–7. *Minutes*.

Teeter, Deborah J., and Melodie E. Christal. 1987. 'Establishing Peer Groups: A Comparison of Methodologies.' *Planning for Higher Education* 15, no. 2.

Terenzini, Patrick, Leif Hartmark, Wendell Lorang, Jr., and Robert Shirley. 1980. 'A Conceptual and Methodological Approach to the Identification of Peer Institutions.' *Research in Higher Education* 12, no. 4.

Thiessen, Dennis, and Kenneth Howey, eds. 1998. *Agents, Provocateurs: Reform-Minded Leaders for Schools of Education*. Washington: American Association of Colleges of Teacher Education.

Thompson, High L. 1985. 'Considering a Merger?' *Planning for Higher Education* 13, no. 3.

Topping, Sharon, et al. 1999. 'Academic Health Centers in Turbulent Times: Strategies for Survival.' *Health Care Management Review* 24, no. 2.

Tuinman, Jaap. 1995. 'Productive Co-operation and Collaboration among Educational Institutions of Perceived Unequal Status.' *Tertiary Education and Management* 1, no. 1.

University of Guelph. 1996. 'Memorandum of Agreement between Ontario Ministry of Agriculture, Food and Rural Affairs and the University of Guelph.' 1996.

University of Toronto. 1994–6. *The Bulletin.*

University of Toronto/Ontario Institute for Studies in Education Academic Integration Task Force. 1995. 'Report.' Toronto.

Van Ravens, Jan. 1995. 'The Franchise Model.' *Tertiary Education and Management* 1, no. 1.

Volkwein, J. Fredericks. 1989. 'Changes in Quality among Public Institutions.' *Journal of Higher Education* 60, no. 2.

Waite, Peter B. 1994. *The Lives of Dalhousie University.* Volume 1. *1818–1925.* Montreal: McGill-Queen's University Press.

– 1998. *The Lives of Dalhousie University.* Volume 2. *1925–1980.* Montreal: McGill-Queen's University Press.

Weick, Karl. 1984. 'Small Wins: Redefining the Scale of Social Problems.' *American Psychologist* 39, no. 1.

Weifang, Min. 1994. *A Case Study of an Institutional Merger in Hubei Province, People's Republic of China.* Paris: International Institute for Educational Planning.

Whiteley, Meredith A., and Frances K. Stage. 1987. 'Institutional Uses of Comparative Data.' *New Directions for Institutional Research* 53.

'Why Too Many Mergers Miss the Mark.' 1997. *The Economist,* 4 January.

Wyatt Company. 1993. 'Best Practices in Corporate Restructuring: Wyatt's 1993 Survey of Corporate Restructuring in Canada.'

Zartman, I. William, and Maureen R. Berman. 1982. *The Practical Negotiator.* New Haven: Yale University Press.

Ziderman, Adrian, and Douglas Albrecht. 1995. *Financing Universities in Developing Countries.* Washington: Falmer.

Index